Corporate Governance and Chairmanship

Corporate Governance and Chairmanship
A Personal View

Adrian Cadbury

OXFORD
UNIVERSITY PRESS

OXFORD
UNIVERSITY PRESS

Great Clarendon Street, Oxford OX2 6DP

Oxford University Press is a department of the University of Oxford.
It furthers the University's objective of excellence in research, scholarship,
and education by publishing worldwide in

Oxford New York

Auckland Cape Town Dar es Salaam Hong Kong Karachi
Kuala Lumpur Madrid Melbourne Mexico City Nairobi
New Delhi Taipei Toronto Shanghai

With offices in

Argentina Austria Brazil Chile Czech Republic France Greece
Guatemala Hungary Italy Japan South Korea Poland Portugal
Singapore Switzerland Thailand Turkey Ukraine Vietnam

Published in the United States
by Oxford University Press Inc., New York

British Library Cataloguing in Publication Data

Data available

Library of Congress Cataloging in Publication Data
Cadbury, Adrian, Sir.
    Corporate governance and chairmanship: a personal view / Adrian
    Cadbury.
        p. cm.
    Includes bibliographical references and index.
    1. Corporate governance. 2. Directors of corporations. 3. Boards of
directors. 4. Corporate governance—Great Britain. 5. Directors of
corporations—Great Britain. 6. Boards of directors—Great Britain. I. Title.
    HD2741 C22 2002   658.4′22—dc21   2002025022

ISBN 0–19–925200–9

10 9 8 7 6

Typeset by Newgen Imaging Systems (P) Ltd., Chennai, India
Printed in Great Britain
on acid-free paper by
Biddles Ltd., King's Lynn, Norfolk

To: Susan

Contents

Foreword

The first time I met Sir Adrian Cadbury was on a two-day course, some years ago, for non-executive directors. Until and after his session, this course was a thorough disappointment. What had I expected? Well, something useful on each of the issues that were even then hotting up: best practice on audit, remuneration, risk management. Perhaps, I thought, for light relief (!) we might role-play a takeover bid. Instead we were subjected to hours of questionnaire-filling, the purpose of which was clearly to aid the 'teachers' with their theses rather than to train us to be better NXDs. By the time Adrian joined us in the evening, I was thoroughly fed up, and treated him to a distinctly uncivil attack on the box-ticking effect of the series of corporate governance inquiries that he had begun.

His answers were a revelation: tough, unrepentant, sensible, flexible, informed. I still believed there was too much box-ticking going on, but I was readier to accept this was the result of imperfect execution rather than poor principles. And now, in this book, Adrian provides the guidance I was longing for in that disappointing course, perfectly tuned to my present need.

I can imagine no better primer for a FTSE-100 Chairman. A much-needed primer, too. As a member of the Class of '02, I have found the literature on corporate governance to fall depressingly easily into two categories: the tautologous and the obscure. Either one is offered blinding glimpses of the obvious, or treatises in that new dialect of legal language, compliancese. (Often these two categories overlap.)

Of course there are some exceptions. The academic world is beginning to fill part of the gap: along with the rent-a-mouth commentators, it contains a number of able specialists, possessed of the ability not merely to think intelligently about the theory of governance but also to articulate their thoughts. Few, however, have real-world experience of what they write.

For excellent practical advice, meanwhile, I can turn to the works of 3i's own Patrick Dunne, which I am delighted to find quoted approvingly in this book. However, Patrick writes about, and for, all sorts and sizes of companies, reflecting the range in which 3i is invested. And chairing an unquoted business, however large, is a very different task.

Adrian has been there, and got the t-shirt, as Chairman of one of Britain's major FTSE companies, before becoming the trail-blazer for governance reform. His focus on the chairmanship of large companies fills a serious gap, and runs through the gamut of issues confronting those taking on the job.

Best of all, for those who might use this book as a starter pack, the author spends time on the techniques of chairmanship: not just the 'what' or the 'why', but also the 'how'.

This book emphasises the patience, skill, and sheer preparation needed to assemble, lead, motivate, monitor, and refresh a fully functioning board. It offers two useful warnings to those who suppose that conducting a good board meeting is easy: reminding us both that a committee is not a natural decision-making machine, and that the chairman's job is to see the board reaches not merely a consensus but a good decision. The best tips? Keep a sense of humour, don't take yourself too seriously, don't talk too much—try to be like a good steersman, sitting quietly at the tiller and moving not at all.

One of Adrian's repeated arguments for the separation of Chief Executive and Chairman is the work needed to run boards properly. He points out a paradox of the modern board: that it is more interesting and useful if it brings together a range of cultures, geographies, and skills, but that this also makes it more difficult to run it effectively. Although open-minded, it is clear that he prefers the unitary model, but stresses its implications: notably, the need to ensure executives enter the boardroom thinking of themselves as full directors, and not just as back-up for the Chief Executive.

He is keen on Chairmen having (within reason) other commitments, believing in the cross-fertilisation of ideas. He is not dogmatic on board size, though notes the tendency for them to contain fewer executives, and expresses doubts about a table ringed by more than 10 members (excluding the Chairman and company secretary). Nor does he neglect the size and shape of the table itself, noting that too many companies seem to conduct board meetings in as much physical discomfort as they can achieve. (My own past experiences, and both of these examples are taken from the FTSE 100, include a windowless room in which the air-conditioning deep-freezes at least one-third of the seats, and a Piccadilly drawing room with no air-conditioning at all.)

Adrian is certainly not alone in emphasizing the relationship between Chairman and Chief Executive as key to the smooth functioning of the board, but is clearer than most as to how this relationship is to be kept in good working order. Many models work, in Adrian's view, but clarity is essential – as is recognition that the relationship will change over time. The sensitive boundary, of course, is strategy. Indisputably, this is a board function, but how is strategy set? Where do strategic discussions end and management responsibilities begin? This book offers a useful mixture of brisk practical advice (against meddlesome chairmanship) and broad principle. A theme that emerges repeatedly is the need to see the board's strategic responsibilities as long-term, aspirational, and qualitative, in contrast to short-term budget-setting or competitive strategies.

Perhaps it is this sense of board responsibility for the 'character' of the company that leads Adrian to place such emphasis on questions of corporate and social responsibility. Or perhaps it is just his interest in the latest reporting fashion, which is adding yet greater bulk to companies' annual accounts. Either way, however, I think he is right to say that companies were slow to see this one coming, and that they need to think sensibly and proactively about the issues, if only because no one else will. This book sets the best framework I have seen, by distinguishing three levels of involvement between companies and the community: moving up from legal requirements, specific to operational locations, to corporate values – or, once more, to the character of the company. All of these are set sensibly within a context of which both lobby groups and politicians need reminding, which is that companies neither can, nor should, take on the government's work for it.

A framework is not a template: there are no easy answers here. Talking recently to the chairman of a major international company that prides itself on leadership in social responsibility, I asked where he drew the line as to the culture of the country in which he would operate. The company would not, he said, operate in countries where bribery was common business practice; but it would operate in countries in which it was effectively debarred from employing, or at least promoting, women. I'm not criticizing. Corporate social responsibility is a large glasshouse in which everyone should be careful of throwing stones; but this seemed to me a good illustration of the issues that confront companies in trying to articulate their policies, and the difficulty of drawing the line between respecting the social culture of the country in which you operate, and diluting your own corporate culture. That, in turn, explains why Adrian is right to believe these questions are going to require increasing attention.

Which leads me to perhaps the only one point where this book caused me a wry smile: where Adrian expresses the wish that all the corporate governance requirements of the past decade could be allowed to bed down before new ones are added. Yes, that would be nice, but for bad reasons as well as good, the governance industry shows no sign of recession. Competition between the governance specialists in large institutions is leading to different, and sometimes even contradictory, shareholder demands. These institutions are coming under different, and again even conflicting, pressures from those whose funds they manage. Companies on the receiving end of these mixed messages have, therefore, to rely as much on their own judgement as ever.

This excellent book should, however, also be a primer for the latest official holders of the governance candle (or short straw): Mr Derek Higgs and his committee examining the role of non-executive directors. As well as encouraging them to think seriously about the role of chairmanship, this book should send them one other important message: Adrian Cadbury is still arguing the need for better training. He's right. And while that is a job for chairmen and boards themselves, the code-writers must also take on some responsibility for improving the quality of training available. If we cannot hope for any slowdown in the pace at which they add to the list of board must-do's, can we hope that they will spend some time thinking about how the regulators might actively help directors to do these things better?

Sarah Hogg
Chairman of 3i Group PLC

Preface

The aim of the book is to be of practical use to chairmen and members of boards. It covers the two interrelated themes of corporate governance and chairmanship. They are inextricably linked, because corporate governance is concerned with the system by which companies are directed and controlled, which is clearly the responsibility of their boards of directors. Equally clearly, it is chairmen who are responsible for the working of their boards. Thus, the way in which corporate governance principles are put into practice is primarily a matter for board chairmen.

Although the book is addressed to company chairmen and directors, many of the issues with which it deals are relevant to chairmen of bodies outside the business sector. The principles of codes of corporate conduct provide guidelines which are being applied, in part and not always appropriately, to the governing bodies of colleges, trusts, and a range of voluntary organizations. Similarly, the need to distinguish between the task of direction and that of management is as central to the governance of most institutions as it is to the governance of companies. A discussion of the responsibilities of chairmen for matters of governance should, therefore, be of interest to those charged with chairing organizations of all kinds.

There is also, and this is a welcome development, a burgeoning academic interest in both corporate governance and in the workings of boards. While the book is written primarily for practitioners, it does provide a background to the theory of governance and its application in the business world. I have not hesitated in the book to give my personal views on the issues under discussion. This is to provoke debate and to bring issues to life, not in order to proselytize.

There is no doubt about the profundity of the changes which have taken place in the corporate scene since the committee, which I chaired, began its work. Corporate governance has developed from a subject of interest to a minority of lawyers and accountants to a mainstream influence on the systems and processes by which businesses are run around the world. The way in which English words and definitions have been used worldwide to describe corporate governance in all its aspects adds an international dimension to a study of its development in Britain.

The book traces the way in which corporate governance has emerged as a dominant factor in the manner in which businesses are structured and run, with consequences for other types of organization as well. The principles underlying the concepts of corporate governance are expressed in codes of best practice and their origins and implications are explained. Since boards of directors are the focus of corporate governance, it follows that the issue for them, and in particular for their chairmen, is how best to implement these governance principles in terms of the constitution and functions of their own boards.

The board scene has been transformed worldwide through the influence of the corporate governance movement. The composition of boards has changed as a result, and so has their structure. The demands made on directors have grown significantly and the issues with which they have to deal have broadened. In a world where, in many cases, power has shifted from the public to the private sector, the expectations which society has in relation to the environmental, social, and ethical responsibilities of companies have risen. The degree to which these expectations have changed is discussed in the book, as are the steps that boards need to consider in order to meet them.

A central issue for boards is the relationship between chairmen and their chief executives, where they are not the same person. Again, similar relationships apply in the majority of other types of organization. The book describes ways in which these two key figures may divide duties between them, as well as considering such issues as their appointment and replacement. One aspect of the division of responsibilities is the role which they share in representing their companies to the outside world.

Against this background of rapid change, a long-awaited reform of company law is being undertaken in Britain. It is the first for forty years, or possibly longer, and the nature and scope of the proposed reforms are outlined and their implications discussed. Although these reforms are a British initiative, they will have their influence on the regulation of companies in other jurisdictions, just as British codes of best practice have done. The direction which company law is expected to take is among a number of governance issues, that are likely to feature on the agendas of chairmen and their boards. One of them is that the governance spotlight may switch, at least to an extent, from boards to institutional investors in the wake of the Myners Report. This opens up a whole new field, whereby pension fund members could begin to exert some influence over the decisions and actions of those who invest on their behalf.

One of the book's themes is the shift in the balance of power over a relatively short period, from weak boards, strong management, and passive investors, to boards strengthening their position in relation to management, and to investors holding boards accountable to a greater degree than before. The question which follows on is, to whom are investors accountable and to whom should they be? Advances in information technology now provide the means, in an increasingly 'wired' world, for individuals to hold to account the institutions which invest on their behalf.

As the climate of governance has changed, boards have had to adapt to these changes. This is where chairmen play a key role. A basic reason for the book's focus on chairmen is that they are the connecting link between governance principles and the turning of those principles into action. It is their responsibility to ensure that their boards match up to the standards today expected of well-run businesses. These standards are increasingly being enforced by institutional investors and by capital markets.

I have written about the role of chairmen as I have, and have drawn on past writings in doing so, because I continue to be convinced that the value of good chairmanship is underestimated. The difference which competent chairmanship can make to any kind of meeting is profound. I remain astonished that so little has been written on the subject. The paucity of useful guidance on chairmanship confirms an apparent lack of appreciation of the importance of the chairman's role. I still rely on Hugh Parker's *Letters to a New Chairman* for advice and on Sir John Harvey-Jones' *Making It Happen* as an account of effective chairmanship in action. To these I would add the recent publication of Henry Bosch's admirable *Conversations Between Chairmen* and *Conversations with a New Director*. I am encouraged that a Chairman's Forum is becoming established in Britain, as a means of enabling chairmen to meet, to discuss issues of common interest, and to learn from each other's experience.

I have used the word 'chairman' throughout, because that is at present a generally accepted title for those who chair boards and committees in much of the world. In doing so, I use it strictly in its dictionary sense: 'The occupier of a chair of authority; the person chosen to preside over a meeting, a company, a corporate body, etc.' (Shorter OED 1975). The word 'chairman', therefore, applies to women and to men, equally. It is, of course, a matter for the individuals who take the chair at a meeting to decide how they wish to be addressed. No one title is specifically correct. It is a question of personal choice.

My own experience of boards and committees has largely been in Britain, but I believe that the central issues of governance and chairmanship know no boundaries and are universally relevant. My hope, therefore, is that this book will be found useful by those who chair, or who are members of, boards and governing bodies of all kinds, both in Britain and abroad. It will have served its purpose if it helps to stimulate interest in the arts of good chairmanship and good governance.

Acknowledgements

I would like to express my grateful thanks to everyone who has contributed to the publication of this book. It began with the willingness of the Oxford University Press to commission me to write about the two aspects of the world of business which interest me most, chairmanship and corporate governance. It has been a pleasure to work with OUP and I have appreciated their unfailing help and encouragement.

That the book has emerged in printable form is due to Joyce Schofield's professional mastery of the complexities of the computer, on which I simply type. She has kept a watchful eye on the book's progress from designing the layout to the final disk, patiently dealing with all the technical problems which arose along the way.

My views on chairmanship are based on the time I have spent on boards, governing bodies and committees of all kinds. I am greatly indebted to my fellow members of these bodies, and particularly to those who chaired them, for enabling me to learn from their example.

In the field of corporate governance, my particular thanks go, first, to all the members of the Committee on the Financial Aspects of Corporate Governance. The report which we published was very much the work of the Committee as a whole with everyone contributing to the final result. I could not wish to have worked with a better or more companionable team. My involvement in the governance field, however, goes further back to my time at The Bank of England and with PRO NED. There I had the good fortune to work with Jonathan Charkham and Sir David Walker, both of whom have had a marked influence on British thinking on the role of boards and the governance of companies.

On the other side of the Atlantic, I owe a considerable debt to Hugh Parker. When I first became chairman of a corporate board, Hugh Parker gave me invaluable advice as a consultant and as a friend. His book, *Letters to a New Chairman*, remains the standard work on board chairmanship and I am grateful to him for allowing me to quote from it in this book.

I have greatly benefited as well from my links with those at the leading edge of research into the ways in which corporate governance is developing—Dr John Roberts at Cambridge, Professor Keith MacMillan and Professor Bernard Taylor at Henley Management College, Dr F.-Friedrich Neubauer at IMD Lausanne, and Dr John Carver in Atlanta. They have all been generous in their counsel and encouragement.

My knowledge of how corporate governance has developed internationally has been primarily due to merging PRO NED into Egon Zehnder. Egon Zehnder have formed a Global Corporate Governance Advisory Board and, largely under their aegis, I have had the opportunity to visit some twenty-seven countries to discuss corporate governance issues. As a result, I have learnt much and made many lasting friendships. My particular thanks go to Dr Egon Zehnder himself and to Julia Budd, Tony Couchman, and Ken Taylor for the personal trouble they have taken to enable me to take advantage of all manner of unexpected opportunities to broaden my understanding of governance practice around the world.

My last corporate governance assignment came as a member of the OECD Business Sector Advisory Group, chaired by Ira Millstein, which published its report to the OECD on corporate governance in April 1998. Ira skilfully draws the twin threads of this book together, by combining exemplary chairmanship—it was a privilege to serve under him on that Group—with a remarkable personal contribution to the theory and practice of corporate governance. My other mentor from the United States has been, my friend of longstanding, Robert A. G. Monks. Bob Monks' writings on corporate governance are essential texts and a tribute to his boundless energy and missionary zeal, given his full-time commitment to putting governance principles into practice in the marketplace. No one could fail to be inspired by Bob and Ira, to whom I owe very special thanks.

The Genesis of Corporate Governance

> Corporate governance has only recently emerged as a discipline in its own right, although the strands of political economy it embraces stretch back through centuries.[1]
>
> World Bank Group

Background

Governance is a word with a pedigree that dates back to Chaucer and in his day the word carried with it the connotation wise and responsible, which is appropriate. It means either the action or the method of governing and it is in that latter sense that it is used with reference to companies. Its Latin root, *'gubernare'* means to steer and a quotation which is worth keeping in mind in this context is: 'He that governs sits quietly at the stern and scarce is seen to stir.'[2] It appeals to me, because it suggests that governance need not and should not be heavy-handed. The governor should be able to keep the corporate ship on course with a minimum use of the tiller.

The Committee on the Financial Aspects of Corporate Governance, which I chaired, took as its definition of corporate governance, 'the system by which companies are directed and controlled'. Demb and Neubauer in their classic work, *The Corporate Board: Confronting the Paradoxes,*[3] define it as, 'the process by which corporations are made responsive to the rights and wishes of stakeholders'. The concept of process may be helpful, because it emphasizes the continually changing nature of the expectations which boards have to meet, while the issue of who are the stakeholders and what are their rights is one to which we shall return. I will, however, keep as my definition, 'the system by which companies are directed and controlled'.

The point which both definitions make is that companies and their boards work within boundaries. These boundaries are set by laws and regulations, by the providers of funds, by the shareholders in general meeting, by the constitutions of companies themselves and by public opinion. The influence of public opinion should not be underestimated, for it has been largely responsible for putting societal issues, such as the environment and human rights, on the governance agenda. The key issue to keep in mind is that the nature of the boundaries within which companies operate is continually changing. The task for boards and their chairmen is to be alert to the implications of these changes and to foresee their direction. The object of this book is to assist chairmen and directors to understand how these governance boundaries have arisen, how they may develop in the future, and what their impact has been, and is likely to be, on the workings of boards.

Governance origins

The East India Company

On the 31 December 1600, a Royal Charter was granted to The Company of Merchants of London trading into the East Indies. The Company began with 218 members and was governed by a Court of Directors, although the directors were referred to rather confusingly as 'committees'. The governance structure consisted of the General Court or Court of Proprietors and the Court of Directors. The Court of Proprietors was made up of all those with voting rights, the qualification for which in the early days was normally an investment of £200. It met infrequently, because it soon numbered several hundred, but it was the supreme authority. Its sanction was needed for the raising of funds and it elected the directors.

The Court of Directors was the executive body and was responsible for the running of the company, although its policy decisions had to be ratified by the Court of Proprietors. The Court of Directors consisted of the Governor, the Deputy Governor and twenty-four directors. The make-up of their Court was not dissimilar from that of the Court of the Bank of England in my time, with its Governor, Deputy Governor and sixteen directors. The East India Company's Court met frequently and had numerous subcommittees which looked after specific functions such as purchasing, sales, and correspondence.

The governance structure of the East India Company was therefore little different from that of a company of today. The Court of Proprietors were the shareholders in general meeting, the Court of Directors were the board assisted by appropriate subcommittees, and the Royal Charter laid down the boundaries within which the Company had to work. The Court of Directors carried out most of the classic functions of a board of today. It was they who selected the chief executive. In making their first appointment to that position, they chose someone in whom they had confidence, in spite of pressure of patronage to appoint someone less well-qualified. Their admirable policy on selecting their executives, as relevant now as it was then, was 'not to appoint any gentleman in any place of charge'.[4]

They were responsible for the financing of the Company's enterprises. The procedure was for the Court of Directors to recommend a new voyage to the Court of Proprietors. Provided they agreed, a subscription book was opened to raise the sum required. The directors were therefore directly accountable to the shareholders for capital expenditure. In addition, the Court of Directors set the strategic direction of the Company, for example, when they switched their trading focus from the East Indies to India itself, even if this was more by force of circumstance than by design.

Governance continuity

Not only was the governance structure of the East India Company comparable with that of companies today, but so were the issues which faced the board. Their shareholders differed in their motives for investing in the Company and in their time horizons. The short-term investors wanted a return on their money after each voyage, while others took a longer view. The board also had the problem of controlling its appointees, who were acting not only for the Company but also often for themselves, in distant stations and out of touch for long periods. This made the selection of the Company's captains and factors a crucial board responsibility.

The upshot of this reference to the way in which the most influential company in Britain was run some four hundred years ago is that its structure and the responsibilities of its board are clearly recognizable to those in charge of companies today. Corporate governance has therefore been with us since companies began to take their present form. Why then does it seem to have moved onto the business and political agenda only so relatively recently?

The basic governance issues are those of power and accountability. They involve where power lies in the corporate system and what degree of accountability there is for its exercise. The essential point is that the balance of power within the corporate system is continually shifting and it is these changes, especially in relation to shareholder-owned companies, which bring governance issues to the fore. To understand why corporate governance has become such a matter of debate today, it is necessary to look briefly at the manner in which it has developed, concentrating on the changing balance of power between the main players on the corporate stage, shareholders, boards of directors, and managers.

Governance developments

The agency problem

In the eighteenth century, Adam Smith drew attention in *The Wealth of Nations* to an important governance issue in his commentary on joint stock companies:

The directors of such companies however being the managers rather of other people's money than of their own, it cannot well be expected that they should watch over it with the same anxious vigilance which the partners in private copartnery frequently watch over their own. . . . Negligence and profusion, therefore, must always prevail, more or less, in the management of the affairs of such a company.[5]

The agency problem which Adam Smith identified has been and continues to be the subject of exhaustive study, because it is inherent in the relationship between the providers of capital and their agents who put that capital to use, that is to say between shareholders and boards. Adam Smith clearly did not have a great opinion of the majority of directors of joint stock companies of his day, nor of those who invested in them. He says of the latter, 'and when the spirit of faction happens not to prevail upon them, give themselves no trouble about it, but receive contentedly such half-yearly or yearly dividend as the directors think proper to make to them'.[6] Given passive investors and the relative size of the then joint stock market, the agency problem as Adam Smith described it, was not a major economic or political issue.

Nowadays, attention would be focused more on directors and executives pursuing their own interests, for example, by reinvesting in expanding their empires as opposed to increasing the return to their shareholders, rather than on their negligence and profusion—though those failings are still with us. The agency problem continues to be important in governance terms, because it has its influence on the structure and composition of boards, on the requirements for disclosure, and on the balance of power between shareholders and directors.

Company law

In the nineteenth century, there were two important measures of company law in Britain which are particularly relevant in terms of governance. The Joint Stock Companies Act of 1844 required all new businesses with more than twenty-five participants to be incorporated. This gave them a legal status and personality of their own and one which could be obtained simply by registering with the Registrar of Companies, as opposed to requiring an

Act of Parliament or Royal Charter. At the same time, companies had to file their constitutions and annual accounts with the Registrar, thereby providing a degree of disclosure.

Then came the Limited Liability Act of 1855, which limited the liability of shareholders to the amount of share capital which they had invested, should their company become bankrupt. The number of these incorporated or limited companies increased steadily in the nineteenth century. By 1914 around 65,000 were registered, a figure which had grown to about 200,000 by 1945. When this figure is compared with the more than 1,100,000 companies registered at Companies House today, one of the reasons for the relatively recent rise in interest in matters of corporate governance becomes clear.

The governance of all manner of companies is important and our Committee's report said: 'The Code of Best Practice is directed to the boards of directors of all listed companies registered in the UK, but we would encourage as many other companies as possible to aim at meeting its requirements.'[7] Nevertheless, this book focuses on the governance of publicly quoted companies and is written from a UK background. There are around 2650 UK registered companies listed on the London Stock Exchange and interestingly Switzerland and Britain are the only two countries where stock exchange capitalization exceeds GDP (Gross Domestic Product) and does so by a considerable margin.[8]

Ownership and management

The twentieth century debate on corporate governance really got off the ground when attention was drawn to the increasing separation of the ownership of companies from their management. The most influential statement of the consequences of this divide was made by Berle and Means in *The Modern Corporation and Private Property*.[9] Their thesis was that the separation of ownership from management had resulted in shareholders being unable to exercise any form of effective control over boards of directors, who were theoretically appointed by them to represent their interests. Berle and Means were also concerned at the increasing power of large corporations, power which might one day challenge that of the state and therefore needed to be controlled. The basic accountability issue, however, was not simply that ownership had become largely divorced from management, but that ownership was dispersed. It was the fragmentation of ownership that neutered the power of the shareholders. On the other hand, the fact that most holdings were relatively small meant that shareholders had no difficulty in selling their holdings, if they lost confidence in the way their company was being managed. They had the power to withdraw their custom. Nevertheless, the inability of the majority of shareholders to hold boards of directors accountable put the agency problem firmly on the governance agenda.

While Berle and Means are understandably cited as the authorities on this question of the separation of ownership from management, the Liberal Industrial Inquiry of 1926–28 in Britain, of which my father was a member, had reached much the same conclusion:

Private enterprise has been trying during the past fifty years to solve for itself the essential problem, which the Socialists in their day were trying to solve, namely, how to establish an efficient system of production in which management and responsibility are in different hands from those which provide the capital, run the risk and reap the profit . . . .[10]

The Inquiry, equally, drew attention to the weakness of boards of directors in too many companies whose ownership was, in their words, diffused: 'In such companies, . . . a director would consider himself greatly aggrieved if he were to be dropped merely because he was elderly, useless or without special qualifications for the work.'[11]

Although there was considerable debate about the consequences of the separation of ownership and management on both sides of the Atlantic, it was not followed through to the extent of proposing measures, whether statutory or voluntary, which could have affected the governance of companies. There are a number of reasons why this was perhaps so. One reason could have been that from a political point of view a real concern of the 1930s was lack of competition and the growth of monopoly power, as countries protected their industries behind trade barriers. This must have seemed a greater contributor to inefficiency and higher prices than disenfranchised shareholders. Another reason was that investors could always sell out, as has already been mentioned, and so they had no great cause to demand more control over the companies in which they had invested.

Finally, in Britain certainly, and to an extent in the United States, boards of directors were not seen as central to the way in which companies were run. Thus the inability of shareholders to appoint directors of their choice, as opposed to those put forward by the existing board on a co-option basis, does not appear to have been a burning issue. To return to the Liberal Industrial Inquiry:

We do not think that the Boards, as at present constituted, of Public Companies of diffused ownership are one of the strong points of private enterprise . . . . The truth is that a strong and possibly efficient management rather likes to have an ineffective Board which will know too little to have views or to interfere; and the ineffective Board enjoys its fees.[12]

In terms of the balance of power, it was executive management which was in the corporate driving seat, both in the UK and in the US, in the period between the two World Wars. Given the relative weakness of boards of directors, the fact that shareholders were not in a position to hold them accountable, or to exercise control over them, did not become the governance issue it might have been.

Somnolent boards

In the aftermath of the Second World War, it was understandable that corporate governance was on no one's agenda. It was a time of reconstruction worldwide, the problem was shortage of supplies and any remotely competent company could keep its shareholders satisfied. I did not, as a sales representative, have to sell Cadbury's chocolate to my customers in the early 1950s, I had to ration them. Equally, the pace of technical and market change was still relatively gentle and competition was not yet international in most sectors. The rising economic tide lifted all ships and there were no apparent reasons for intervening in a private enterprise system which was delivering looked-for results.

The comparative tranquillity of the corporate scene was rudely disturbed in the US by the collapse of Penn Central in 1970. Penn Central was the United States' largest railway company and it was indeed the sixth largest company in the country. A dramatic account of how the company went down, as experienced by an outside director of the company, appeared in an article in the 1976 autumn edition of the *Harvard Business Review*. It was written by Louis Cabot, a Harvard professor:

I served for one fateful year on the board of Penn Central. The education was fast, brutal and highly practical. Even today the lawsuits are not all settled and that education has cost me several times more than the price of a Harvard Business School tuition. At each Penn Central directors' meeting, which only lasted one and a half hours, we were presented with long lists of relatively small capital expenditures to approve, we were shown sketchy financial reports which were rarely discussed in any detail. The reports were not designed to be revealing, and we were asked not to take them away from the meeting. We always had an oral report by the Chief Executive Officer promising better results next month which never came true.

Louis Cabot did all the right things as an outside director, including writing to the chairman to say that this was no way to run a business. But before any of his letters had even been answered, Penn Central had collapsed and Louis Cabot was being sued along with the other directors. What is clear from his vivid description of board meetings at Penn Central is that the board simply failed to do its job. It was both uninformed and misinformed and it exercised no real control over the Chief Executive Officer (CEO). The fault lay with the chairman and the board, but primarily with the chairman, whose job it was to ensure that board members had the information which they needed to govern the company. Accurate and timely information are essential elements of board control.

The Securities and Exchange Commission (SEC) was so concerned by the misreporting of earnings by the Penn Central board and by the collapse of the company itself that it instituted an enquiry into how all this came about. Its official report was fiercely critical of the board's shortcomings and emphasized the need for board independence and for vigilant outside directors. The report included the statement, 'the somnolent Penn Central board . . . was typical of most giant corporations' boards in the postwar period'.[13]

The SEC's response to the Penn Central affair, and to concerns about improper foreign and domestic payments by US corporations, was to insist that boards must, through their outside board members, exercise effective oversight over management. In 1977, the SEC therefore approved a rule by the New York Stock Exchange that all US listed companies should establish audit committees composed solely of outside, independent directors. The regulatory reaction in the US to corporate failures and wrongdoing was to emphasize that governance was a basic board responsibility and that independent outside directors were an essential element in the make-up of boards, if boards were to be in a position to hold management properly accountable. The SEC's approach had a direct influence on the way in which the UK responded to similar governance problems nearer home.

The wake-up call

While the regulators were playing their part in raising governance standards, it was the market which really sounded the alarm for somnolent boards. The wake-up call came in the form of the threat of an unwanted takeover offer. The market's answer to poor board performance and lack of accountability to shareholders was to promote a free market in the control of companies and their assets. The logic behind the takeover approach to corporate governance was beguilingly simple and double-barrelled.

Takeovers were seen as solving problems of poor performance, because by definition the highest bidder would be able to generate the best return from the resources of the company over whose assets they had taken control. That was the first barrel. The second barrel was even more precisely targeted and was directed at ensuring that as far as possible takeovers were financed by debt. This would serve to strengthen accountability to shareholders. The new board team would have to concentrate on generating cash to service the debt. If they wanted funds to expand their business, they would have to convince their shareholders that their expansion proposals would add value to the enterprise. This would prevent boards from being able to use their internal financial resources for projects which might seem to be more in the interests of the executives than of those of the company at large, without having first acquired the assent of their shareholders.

More generally, the takeover threat was seen as alerting the boards not just of target companies to the need to achieve higher levels of performance, but those of all publicly quoted companies which might conceivably become targets.

Investor involvement

Predictably, boards reacted to the threat of being taken over by erecting defences of varying degrees of ingenuity and effectiveness. In addition, takeovers turned out in a number of cases to be little more than a costly and disruptive method of bringing about changes at the head of companies. A recent review of the governance effectiveness of takeovers has concluded: 'We have assessed that the market for corporate control is not a very effective way to discipline management. If target shareholders win, bidder share-holders break even or lose, and furthermore, efficiency gains are quite low; who pays the bill?'[14]

While the market in the control of assets continued to exert a discipline on boards, investors began to use their influence to bring about changes in top management or strategy by persuasion. Whereas the takeover tactic tended to cast investors and boards as adversaries, the involvement of investors with boards was aimed at aligning the interests of shareholders and boards through dialogue and debate.

This move by investors, both in the US and the UK, to address the twin issues of performance and accountability was based on a fundamental change in the balance of power between investors and boards. The frag-mented share ownership of the inter-war period was being replaced by a concentrated form of share ownership as an increasing proportion of shares became held by the investing institutions. In the UK the pension funds became particularly dominant. Around seventy-five to eighty per cent of the shares of British companies are now held by institutions,[15] with pension funds alone owning about thirty per cent. Interestingly, the number of individual shareholders in the UK has risen alongside this move towards concentration of ownership. This is the result of privatization issues being spread widely but thinly.

This change in the pattern of share ownership in favour of the investing institutions, such as pension funds and insurance companies, has encouraged the institutions to use their influence with boards for two reasons. First, as major shareholders they clearly have influence based on the power of their votes. Boards cannot disregard the views of important shareholders, especially if there is some degree of consensus between them over the action which individual boards need to take to raise their game. Second, there are now powerful incentives for institutional investors to use their influence to improve the performance of their portfolios. When they were not so dominant, they could sell out of companies in whose boards they had lost confidence. Now that collectively their holdings are so large, selling out is more difficult, since competing institutions are likely to have come to the same view about the companies whose shares they want to sell. In the jargon of the market, 'Exit' is giving place to 'Voice', as the way for investors to improve their returns. Or as Georg Siemens, one-time head of Deutsche Bank, said of the German banks when they found themselves locked into holding company shares with which they had been landed: 'If you cannot sell, you must care.' The institutions now had a financial incentive to care.

Even for institutions who manage indexed funds, and thereby own a cross section of the market, it is rational to intervene to improve the performance of companies in the index, provided that the expected value of the outcome is greater than the cost to the individual institution of intervening.

The Committee on the Financial Aspects of Corporate Governance

This was the way in which the corporate governance scene was evolving at the time that the Committee, which I chaired, was established, although the concentration of share ownership in the hands of the institutions was less marked than it is now. The Committee was set up in May 1991 by the Financial Reporting Council, which is responsible for accounting standards, the London Stock Exchange and the accountancy profession. Its terms of reference were to consider the following issues in relation to financial reporting and accountability and to make recommendations on good practice:

(1) the responsibilities of executive and non-executive directors for reviewing and reporting on performance to shareholders and other financially interested parties: and the frequency, clarity and form in which information should be provided;

(2) the case for audit committees of the board, including their composition and role;

(3) the principal responsibilities of auditors and the extent and value of the audit;

(4) the links between shareholders, boards and auditors;

(5) any other relevant matters.[16]

The reason why the three sponsoring bodies decided that consideration of these issues was needed was growing concern over the reliability of the reports and accounts of UK companies. The collapse of companies such as Coloroll and Polly Peck,[17] whose accounts prior to their failure appeared to give no clear indication of the true state of their finances, cast doubt on the trust which could be placed on reports and accounts and on the audit statements attached to them. This in turn, it was feared, could erode confidence in UK accounting practices and in the reputation of London as a financial centre.

The Committee had only just begun its work when wider issues of governance made the headlines, with the failure of the Bank of Credit and Commerce International and the unravelling of the affairs of Robert Maxwell. As a result, the Committee's Report and Code of Best Practice covered a wider field than its title might have indicated. The Committee published a draft report in May 1992, in order to seek comments on its preliminary approach to its task. It was unprepared for the size of the demand for the draft, 13,500 copies of which were finally distributed. This coverage was excellent in terms of stimulating the debate on corporate governance, even if it meant overspending the Committee's budget, as we could hardly charge for a draft!

The importance of the draft was that it attracted much well-considered and informed comment, which was reflected in the final recommendations. In addition, the level of support which the Committee's proposals received gave it a mandate to proceed. The issue here was that the Committee had been established by financial interests, but its recommendations, although they included recommendations to investors and the accountancy profession, centred on a Code of Best Practice addressed to boards of directors. Neither the Confederation of British Industry nor the Institute of Directors were formally involved in the formation of the Committee, yet it was their members who were being asked to follow the Committee's Code recommendations. The former chairman of the CBI Companies Committee and the President of the IOD were members of the Committee and both brought the experience and knowledge which they had gained in their respective organizations to the work of the Committee, but they were on the Committee as individuals and not as representatives. As the preface to the Committee's Report says of the response to the draft: 'While it has not been uncritical, the great majority of our respondents have supported the Committee's approach and it is this consensus which gives us a mandate to proceed. The Committee is being looked to for a lead, which we have a duty to provide.'[18]

The code approach

The impact of the Committee's Report and those of its successors on the work of boards and their chairmen is the subject of the next chapter. In terms of the development of corporate governance, the publication of a Code of Best Practice in this country helped to stimulate similar approaches worldwide. The international newsletter *Governance* had a headline in its February 2000 issue, 'Code Epidemic Hits Portugal'. Whether or not codes are contagious, many countries now have codes of corporate governance, since the establishment of sound governance practices is perceived to encourage both investment and corporate efficiency.

The next step has been the development of international governance codes, such as the report to the OECD by the Business Sector Advisory Group on Corporate Governance of which I was a member. This in turn led to the *OECD Principles of Corporate Governance*.[19] The World Bank, the IMF and the Commonwealth Association for Corporate Governance have all followed suit. The OECD report is particularly concerned with the role of corporate governance in improving competitiveness and in accessing capital in global markets. The CACG Guidelines of November 1999 quote James D. Wolfensohn of the World Bank as saying: 'The proper governance of companies will become as crucial to the world economy as the proper governing of countries.'[20] The Guidelines themselves stress the contribution which sound governance can make both to economic performance and to promoting integrity.

The final stage in the codification process has been the publication by major institutional investors of their own codes of best practice, which set out the standards which they expect from the boards of the companies in which they invest. This is an indication of how the balance of power has shifted since the 1930s when shareholders were relatively impotent, boards were somnolent and it was corporate executives who were in charge. In the late 1980s the growing power of institutional investors was evidenced in the US by the changes which they brought about in the leadership of large US corporations like General Motors, IBM, Westinghouse and Eastman Kodak. The changes took place when investor dissatisfaction put the outside directors on the boards of these companies under pressure to act. As a consequence, investors today have gained power, boards are exercising a greater degree of control over their enterprises and the role of outside directors has been strengthened.

The focus on governance

The increase in the influence of institutional investors reflects the remarkable rise in the funds for whose investment they are responsible. Pension funds have been one of the main contributors to this upsurge on the back of ageing populations and diminishing confidence in reliance on state retirement benefits. One figure from the US illustrates both the recent rate of increase in investment and its global nature. US holdings of foreign stocks which stood at a figure of around $250 billion in 1991 had risen to $1400 billion by 1999.[21]

A fundamental reason why corporate governance has so recently moved onto the economic and political agenda worldwide has been this rapid growth in international capital markets. Countries wishing to attract investment need to convince potential investors that reliable governance structures are in place, both at the state and at the corporate level. The other side of the same coin is that institutional investors, who can invest anywhere in the world, will look to place their funds where their standards of disclosure, of timely and accurate financial reporting, and of equal treatment of all shareholders are met. As the World Bank Report of August 1999 states: 'What makes corporate governance increasingly important in today's global market is the demand from growing businesses for external domestic and international capital in quantities and ways which would have been inconceivable just a decade ago.'[22]

There are other background reasons for the recent emergence of corporate governance as a major national and international issue. The corporate sector has grown in economic and social importance in the developed world as state economic control has shrunk. Companies have become larger and more international, thereby raising new questions over their accountability. Societal concerns over corporate activities are now wider in scope and more in evidence. While instances of fraud and failure may have sparked off corporate governance enquiries, as they did in Britain, an underlying unease over the role of companies in society was already surfacing and was a focus of media attention to a considerably greater degree than in the past. Arguably, the pace with which the recommendations of the UK's original Code of Best Practice were taken up, signalled that corporate boards sensed the need for a more explicit approach to governance and were looking for a lead.

Against this background to the way in which corporate governance has developed over time and the reasons for its recent and rapid emergence as a subject of international import, we turn to what these developments mean in practice to boards of directors and their chairmen.

Notes

1. The World Bank Group (1999). *Corporate Governance: A Framework for Implementation*, August, ii.
2. Cicero, *De Senectute*, translation.
3. Demb, Ada and Neubauer, F.-Friedrich (1992). *The Corporate Board: Confronting the Paradoxes*, Oxford: Oxford University Press, 187.
4. Keay, John (1993). *The Honourable Company*, London: Harper Collins, 14.
5. Smith, Adam (1838). *The Wealth of Nations*, London: Ward Lock, 586.
6. Ibid., 586.
7. Gee Publishing Ltd (1992). *Report of the Committee on the Financial Aspects of Corporate Governance* (ISBN 0 85258 915 8), para. 3.1.
8. Peters' Committee (1997). *Corporate Governance in the Netherlands*, 42.
9. Berle and Means (1932). *The Modern Corporation and Private Property*, New York: Macmillan.
10. Benn, Ernest (publisher) (1928). *Britain's Industrial Future*, London, 100.
11. Ibid., 90.
12. Ibid., 91.
13. Millstein, Ira (1998). *The Evolution of Corporate Governance in the United States*, World Economic Forum, 14.
14. Gugler, Klaus (ed.) (2001). *Corporate Governance and Economic Performance*, Oxford: Oxford University Press.
15. Department of Trade and Industry: Company Law Review Steering Group (2001). *Modern Company Law: Final Report*, Vol. 1, 141.
16. Gee Publishing Ltd (1992). *Report of the Committee on the Financial Aspects of Corporate Governance* (ISBN 0 85258 915 8), 61.
17. Polly Peck went from a market value of £1.75 billion to a deficit of nearly £400 million in four weeks.
18. Gee Publishing Ltd (1992). *Report of the Committee on the Financial Aspects of Corporate Governance* (ISBN 0 85258 915 8), 9.
19. OECD (1999). *OECD Principles of Corporate Governance*, Paris (ISBN 92 64 17126 6).
20. CACG (1999). *Principles for Corporate Governance in the Commonwealth*, New Zealand, November, inside front cover.
21. Monks, Robert A. G. (2001). *The New Global Investors*, Oxford: Capstone, 81.
22. World Bank Group (1999). *Corporate Governance: A Framework for Implementation*, August, 1.

2

Code Consequences for UK Boards

Good corporate governance is not just a matter of prescribing particular corporate structures and complying with a number of hard and fast rules.[1]

Hampel Committee

Code developments

The report of the Committee on the Financial Aspects of Corporate Governance with its Code of Best Practice was published in December 1992.[2] The report included recommendations to investors, accountants, and auditors, but at its heart was the Code of Best Practice, which was directed to the boards of all listed companies registered in the UK. The discussion which follows, therefore, deals primarily with the consequences of the development of governance codes for the chairmen and boards of UK listed companies.

The committee which I chaired stood down in May 1995 after completing a report on the degree of compliance with the committee's Code of Best Practice.[3] From then on subsequent committees took over responsibility for reporting and making recommendations on governance matters as they arose. The Study Group on Directors' Remuneration, usually referred to, after its chairman, as the Greenbury Committee, was set up in January 1995 on the initiative of the CBI, although it operated independently of its sponsor. The Committee was established in response to public and shareholder concerns over executive pay. This was a matter which was attracting increasing political attention and which could only be dealt with effectively by a committee largely made up of heads of major businesses, whose lead on the remuneration of directors was likely to be followed by their fellow chairmen. It published its report in July 1995.[4]

The Hampel Committee

Then in November 1995 the Committee on Corporate Governance was established by the chairman of the Financial Reporting Council under the chairmanship of Sir Ronald Hampel. It was sponsored by the London Stock Exchange, the Confederation of British Industry, the Consultative Committee of Accountancy Bodies, the National Association of Pension Funds, and the Association of British Insurers and thus had a broader basis of support than any of its predecessors. It had the task of reviewing previous governance recommendations, picking up any new issues which had arisen and pulling together all the existing recommendations, plus those of its own, into a single Combined Code.

The final report of the Hampel Committee was published in January 1998[5] and was followed by the Combined Code which came out in June 1998.[6] At this point, the London Stock Exchange published its new Listing Rule together with the related Principles of Good Governance and Code of Best Practice (the Combined Code). This Code supersedes all previous codes and thus is the code which ultimately determines the effect of the various corporate governance initiatives on the boards of UK listed companies. It adds new provisions to those which were already in place under the earlier two codes and it is helpful to be aware of the thinking which lay behind these changes and what it is that they involve for boards.

Code principles

While the Combined Code has added new provisions, the principles behind the approach to self-regulation, or what should more accurately be called market regulation, embodied in all the codes remains the same. The recommendations of the original 1992 Code of Best Practice were intended as guidelines and they were in the words of the report: 'to be followed by individuals and companies in the light of their own particular circumstances. They are responsible for ensuring that their actions meet the spirit of the Code and in interpreting it they should give precedence to substance over form.'[7] That approach has not changed. Equally, the Combined Code like its predecessors is not mandatory, nor is it unnecessarily prescriptive, for example, it is still a matter for boards to decide whether to split the two top posts. The only Code requirement is that they should justify a decision to combine them. The fundamental principle on which the whole code approach is based is that of disclosure, or transparency, a word more favoured than practised by the European Commission. It is up to boards to implement code proposals in ways which meet their individual needs and which carry the support of their shareholders.

Disclosure

What all codes have required is not compliance, but disclosure. Compliance itself is a matter between boards and their shareholders. The Combined Code draws a helpful distinction between principles and provisions and explains that the question to ask of principles is how companies have applied them, while the equivalent question over provisions is how far they have been complied with. Hence, under the Code, boards are now being asked to explain how the principles at the head of each section of the Code have been applied by their particular company. What is required is a narrative statement setting out the way in which individual boards have approached complying with the Code, thus getting away from a more formalistic response which simply registers assent or not to its proposals. While a narrative statement of this kind demands time and thought, it enables boards to express their approach to the principles of governance in their own way and it is an opportunity for them to use compliance with the Code as a means of strengthening the character and identity of their companies in the minds of their shareholders, their employees, and a wider public.

Other principles which are common to all of the published codes are the need to put substance above form in responding to them and the fact that they are drawn from best practice. None of the recommendations included in the codes are based on what the committees concerned considered companies should in theory be doing, all are rooted in the actions and experience of leading companies.

A single code

Finally, the principle that codes should apply to all listed companies, regardless of size, has been maintained throughout. There are two arguments against creating, for code purposes, a first and second division of companies based on size. The first is practical. Whatever measure is used, such as market capitalization for example, there would be movement between the divisions at the margin through time. The second argument is one of principle and is founded on the belief that shareholders are entitled to expect that the same standards of governance and accountability should apply to all companies, regardless of size, which offer their shares to the public.

The Combined Code and its predecessors took account of the fact that smaller quoted companies might find some of their recommendations difficult to comply with, and for this reason boards have always had the option of explaining why any given provision was not appropriate to their particular situation. CISCO, The City Group for Smaller Companies, is the organization which represents the interests of those quoted companies outside the FTSE 350. It has been consistently helpful in supporting the aims of governance codes, while providing advice to its members over the most appropriate way to follow them.[8] The Hampel Committee summed up, in its *Final Report*, how compliance with the Combined Code by smaller companies should be assessed: 'But we would urge those considering the governance arrangements of smaller listed companies to do so with flexibility and a proper regard for individual circumstances.'[9]

Code aims

The aims of codes of best practice are to contribute to board effectiveness and to corporate accountability. Board effectiveness can be judged by performance against appropriate benchmarks and accountability is measured by the degree to which boards respond to the needs of those they are there to serve. The two go together to the extent that, the more accountable a company is the more its standards of performance are set objectively from outside the enterprise. The *Final Report* referred to the contribution which corporate governance made to business prosperity and to accountability and went on to say: 'But the emphasis on accountability has tended to obscure a board's first responsibility—to enhance the prosperity of the business over time.'[10] It was certainly not the intention of any of the governance committees to distract attention from the board's leadership role and from the need for companies to succeed in consistently meeting their business objectives. I would not personally have remained involved in matters of corporate governance for the time I have, had I not firmly believed that its appropriate application assisted the cause of board effectiveness.

Clarity of role

A key way in which codes help boards in their leadership task is by prompting them to be clear about their role and their responsibilities. Evidence given to the committee which I chaired showed a degree of confusion over, for example, the respective responsibilities of directors and auditors in relation to financial reporting, and uncertainty over the division of respon-sibilities between boards and managers. The need, therefore, for a board formally to determine those matters which are specifically reserved to it for decision, provides the starting point in establishing its precise role. The introduction of governance codes has I am sure assisted boards to be clearer about their specific task.

Disclosure

The principle on which governance codes are based, as has already been said, is that of disclosure. The aim of codes is to encourage boards to explain how they direct and control their enterprises. This enables all those with rights and responsibilities towards businesses to be aware how individual com-panies are being led by their boards and consequently for them to be able to exercise their rights and responsibilities in an informed way. Disclosure is as much an opportunity for companies to establish their business aims and principles, as it is a means of enhancing their accountability. All else apart, openness is the basis of public trust in the corporate system. Justice Brandeis of the United States summed up the case for disclosure with his customary insight and authority when he wrote: 'Sunlight is said to be the best of disin-fectants; electric light the most efficient policeman.'[11]

Checks and balances

Another code aim, which follows on from disclosure, has been to heighten awareness by boards of the need for checks and balances in their governance systems. Both the 1992 Code of Best Practice and the Combined Code emphas-ize the need to ensure that no one individual has unfettered powers of decision. Meeting this provision entails consideration of the composition of boards and of how responsibilities should be shared between those at the head of companies. It also involves maintaining what the Combined Code refers to as: 'a sound system of internal control to safeguard shareholders' investment and the company's assets'.[12] The objective is to reduce the chances of fraud or failure and to draw attention to possible grounds for concern as early as possible, while making it clear that no control system can provide more than reasonable assurance that all is as it should be. Checks and balances are not, however, all about maintaining control. A balanced board, for example, which is not dominated by one individual or one set of inter-ests and whose members come from a range of backgrounds, is a means of ensuring that issues and options are thoroughly debated by the board and therefore that its final decisions are well thought through.

What codes aim to do is to provide boards with a checklist against which to review their governance structures and processes and to provide investors with an agenda for their dialogues with boards. The manner in which boards apply code principles and comply with code provisions has to be resolved between boards and their shareholders. The emergence of codes has placed decisions over the way in which companies are led and controlled where they should be, in the hands of the providers of capital and those who put that capital to use. In the wake of our committee's report and the publication of the Code of Best Practice in 1992, I was surprised how often I was appealed to both by board chairmen and by investors to adjudicate on whether the Code was being applied in the way in which our committee had intended. Quite apart from the practical impossibility of coming to a conclusion after hearing one side of the argument and having in any case no intention of becoming a professional referee, I always made it clear that the committee had not been established to lay down the law over how companies should be governed. Its task had been to make governance recommendations, which it was then for boards to implement in ways which made sense to them and to their share-holders. That standards of corporate governance in the UK have now become a responsibility of investors, as well as of boards, is to a significant extent due to the influence of codes.

Impact of codes on boards

The most obvious consequence of the publication of the 1992 Code of Best Practice was that it put corporate governance on the board agenda. Boards were asked to state in their reports and accounts how far they complied with the Code and to identify and give reasons for areas of non-compliance. They were encouraged as well to: 'make a general statement about the corporate governance of their enterprises, as some leading companies have already done'.[13] Clearly boards already had structures and processes in place for directing and controlling their companies, but it was unusual for boards to have brought together these elements, which tended to be seen as separate, and thereby to have reviewed their governance system as a whole. The need for the statement of compliance to form part of the report and accounts, and for the verifiable parts of it to be subject to review by the auditors, meant that all directors shared responsibility for it. Whatever the light in which boards regarded the introduction of the Code of Best Practice, they gave thought to the way in which their company should respond to it and this put governance firmly on the corporate map.

Independence

The 1992 Code of Best Practice's recommendations led boards in turn to consider their composition, the way in which board members were nominated, and the formation of board committees. The recommendation that boards should establish audit committees comprising three non-executive directors, the majority of whom should be independent, meant that complying companies needed a minimum of three outside directors, of whom two would have to be independent. The audit committee recommendation was central to the Code's response to concerns about board standards of reporting and control. It had the further and wider effect of influencing both the structure and composition of boards. It meant also that for the first time boards were asked to distinguish between their non-executive directors and decide which of them were independent. The Code left that judgement to boards themselves, but defined independence:

We recommend that the majority of non-executives on a board should be independent of the company. This means that apart from their directors' fees and shareholding, they should be independent of management and free from any business or other relationship which could materially interfere with the exercise of their independent judgement.[14]

The distinction between independent non-executive directors and those who had some actual or potential link with the company was no reflection on the value of the latter as board members. It simply reflected a difference in their distance from the company and therefore the degree to which they could be considered to be disinterested.

Non-executive directors

The 1992 Code of Best Practice had consequences for the way in which non-executive directors were selected by boards which complied with its recommendations. It recommended that they should be selected by a formal process and that both this process and their appointment should be a matter for the board as a whole. The evidence showed that at that time the most usual way for potential non-executive directors to be selected was through the good offices of chairmen. The object of the recommendation was to encourage boards to identify the kind of person who could recognizably add value to the existing board, thereby not confining the search to names which were already known to the board, and to involve all board members in the choice of those with whom they were going to be working as fellow directors.

A more general consequence of the Code of Best Practice was that it drew attention to the importance of the role of non-executive directors on boards and it strengthened their position in the corporate structure through recommending the establishment of audit and of remuneration committees. These committees were to be wholly or mainly made up of non-executive directors. This meant that the directors on them were involved in the affairs of the company beyond their attendance at board meetings and that they worked with senior managers as well as with executive directors. In addition, the report pointed out that non-executive directors could make a particular and important contribution to the board in reviewing the performance of the board and of the executive, and in taking a lead where potential conflicts between the interests of the executives and those of the shareholders could arise. At the same time, the report stressed that looking to non-executive directors to contribute in this way did not undermine the unitary nature of the board, since all decisions were ultimately the responsibility of the board as a whole.

Nevertheless, concerns were expressed that the Committee's approach could prove divisive, casting the non-executive directors as monitors and executive directors as the monitored. The Committee was conscious that its recommendations could be misconstrued along those lines, which was why it included this clarification of its approach: 'The emphasis in this report on the control function of non-executive directors is a consequence of our remit and should not in any way detract from the primary and positive contribution which they are expected to make, as equal board members, to the leadership of the company.'[15] The Hampel Committee report put any doubts about divisions on the board to rest and made clear the extent of the support for the UK form of unitary board.

Reporting and controls

An essential section in the 1992 Code of Best Practice, given its terms of reference, related to reporting and controls. This covered the board's duty in its reports to present a balanced and understandable assessment of the company's position and referred to the need for the opening statement, normally by the chairman, to represent the collective view of the board. The directors were also asked to explain the extent of their responsibility for preparing the accounts and to ensure that an objective and professional relationship was maintained with the auditors. The recommendation in this section which gave rise to difficulty was that: 'The directors should report on the effectiveness of the company's system of internal control.'[16] The main problem, definition apart, was whether a commitment to 'effectiveness' would unintentionally extend a board's legal liabilities. Alternative words such as 'appropriateness' or 'adequacy' were suggested, but they missed the point. What investors and others needed to know was not only that the board had an adequate or appropriate control system in place, but more importantly that they were satisfied with the way it was operating. The issue has been resolved, first as a result of the guidance of an accounting working group under the chairmanship of Paul Rutteman, which the Hampel Committee endorsed, and then definitively by the recommendations of the Turnbull Committee to which further reference will be made.

Governance responsibilities

Other recommendations included in the 1992 report drew the attention of boards to the need for a proper process of induction for newly appointed board members and for the provision of internal or external training for directors in the light of the weight of their responsibilities. Both of these matters were dealt with more specifically in the Hampel report. Finally, the report underlined the importance of the company secretary's role in being available to provide professional guidance to all board members over their governance duties and responsibilities. In attempting to adapt, not always happily, a corporate code to other types of governing body, the value of the company secretary's post is too often overlooked.

The impact of the 1992 Code of Best Practice and of the Combined Code, which is now the final authority in this field, on the boards of UK companies has primarily been to systematize the way in which they approach their governance responsibilities. Codes have identified the issues which boards are seen as needing to address and have provided them with guidance in doing so, in the light of the standards now expected of well-governed companies. As a result, there is a greater degree of uniformity between companies over their governance structures and processes. As the Hampel report concludes in assessing the impact of the 1992 code: '. . . it is generally accepted that implementation of the code's provisions has led to higher standards of governance and greater awareness of their importance.'[17]

The implications of the Combined Code

The Combined Code is divided into two sections. The first is directed to companies and the second to institutional shareholders. While the shareholder section is important in its own right, it is the Code's implications for companies which are dealt with here. Section 1 of the Code contains fourteen governance principles and boards are asked to report on the way in which they have applied them. The intention is that boards should have a free hand in explaining their governance policies in the light of these principles. The section then has forty-five provisions in respect of which boards are required to state whether they comply with them and to provide an explanation where they do not.

The main changes between the Combined Code and its precursors can be summarized in the order and under the headings in which they appear in the Code. The full code reference is given, but only such of the wording as relates to the essential changes.[18]

Directors

'Every director should receive appropriate training on the first occasion that he or she is appointed to the board of a listed company, and subsequently as necessary.' (A.1.6). This provision is a new one and firms up the references to the need for the training of directors in the 1992 report.

A decision to combine the posts of chairman and chief executive officer in one person should be publicly justified. Whether the posts are held by different people or the same person, there should be a strong and independent non-executive element on the board, with a recognised senior member other than the chairman to whom concerns can be conveyed. The chairman, chief executive and senior independent director should be identified in the annual report. (A.2.1)

Previously, there was no call to justify the combination of the two posts; the requirement was that, where they were combined, it was essential that there should be a strong and independent element on the board with a recognized senior member. The position of recognized senior member now applies even when the chairman and chief executive posts are not combined. This has implications which are discussed later, but it was introduced to meet the situation should other board members or shareholders have concerns relating to both the chairman and the chief executive.

'The board should include non-executive directors of sufficient calibre and number for their views to carry significant weight in the board's decisions. Non-executive directors should comprise not less than one-third of the board.' (A.3.1). Prior to the introduction of this provision, boards needed to have a minimum of three non-executive directors to meet the requirements of establishing a properly constituted audit committee. Ensuring that non-executive directors have at least one-third of the board seats, further strengthens the position of outside directors on unitary boards.

'Non-executive directors considered by the board to be independent should be identified in the annual report.' (A.3.2) There was no requirement previously for boards to identify in the annual report which of their non-executive directors they classed as independent. The 1992 code left it to boards to decide which directors met the criteria of independence, but added: 'Information about the relevant interests of directors should be disclosed in the Directors' Report.'[19] The object of that injunction, which was sparsely heeded, was to enable shareholders and others who were interested to arrive at their own judgements on director independence. The issue of the adequacy of information on directors and their interests has now been dealt with by the Combined Code in A.6.2.

Unless the board is small, a nomination committee should be established to make recommendations to the board on all new board appointments. A majority of the members of the committee should be non-executive directors and the chairman should be either the chairman of the board or a non-executive director. The chairman and members of the nomination committee should be identified in the annual report. (A.5.1)

The 1992 code offered nomination committees as one approach to making it clear how board appointments were made and to assist boards in making them, but did not include the setting up of nomination committees as a specific recommendation.

All directors should be subject to election by shareholders at the first opportunity after their appointment, and to re-election thereafter at intervals of no more than three years. The names of directors submitted for election or re-election should be accompanied by sufficient biographical details to enable shareholders to take an informed decision on their election. (A.6.2)

The question of insulation from election had not been dealt with before. While non-executive directors always came up for election, this was not always the case with executive directors.

Directors' remuneration

'The performance-related elements of remuneration should form a significant proportion of the total remuneration package of executive directors.' (B.1.4)

'Remuneration committees should consider what compensation commitments (including pension contributions) their directors' contracts of service, if any, would entail in the event of early termination.' (B.1.9)

These provisions provide new guidance on current remuneration issues, and include providing explicitly for compensation commitments.

To avoid potential conflicts of interest, boards of directors should set up remuneration committees of independent non-executive directors to make recommendations to the board, within agreed terms of reference, on the company's framework of executive remuneration and its cost; and to determine on their behalf specific remuneration packages for each of the executive directors including pension rights and any compensation payments. (B.2.1)

The board should report to the shareholders each year on remuneration.(B.3.1)

These provisions clarify the respective responsibilities of the board and the remuneration committee. The Greenbury recommendations on the subject gave the remuneration committee responsibilities which properly belonged to the board. It was constitutionally necessary to reaffirm the authority of the board and to make the relationship between boards and their committees clear. Boards are responsible for the terms of reference and membership of the committees they set up and it is to them that these committees report.

Relations with shareholders

'Companies should count all proxy votes and, except where a poll is called, indicate the level of proxies lodged on each resolution, and the balance for and against the resolution, after it has been dealt with on a show of hands.' (C.2.1). This provision is a further step in the direction of disclosure and is aimed at encouraging shareholder voting.

'Companies should propose a separate resolution at the AGM on each substantially separate issue and should in particular propose a resolution at the AGM relating to the report and accounts.' (C.2.2). This provision prevents different issues being bundled together in a single resolution and enables shareholders to know on precisely which issues they are being asked to vote.

'The chairman of the board should arrange for the chairmen of the audit, remuneration and nomination committees to be available to answer questions at the AGM.' (C.2.3). It is right that the chairmen of the main committees should be present at annual general meetings; it is equally right, in my view, for the chairman of the board to decide who should answer shareholder questions.

'Companies should arrange for the Notice of the AGM and related papers to be sent to shareholders at least 20 working days before the meeting.' (C.2.4). This is a further provision to encourage the involvement of shareholders in AGMs, and to ensure that they have the information which they need to enable them to take an active part in the proceedings.

Accountability and audit

'The board's responsibility to present a balanced and understandable assessment extends to interim and other price-sensitive public reports and reports to regulators as well as information required to be presented by statutory requirements.' (D.1.2). This is a new provision and emphasizes the responsibilities of boards for all reports which present the position of their companies to outside audiences and which therefore go out in their name.

'The directors should, at least annually, conduct a review of the effectiveness of the group's system of internal controls and should report to shareholders that they have done so. The review should cover all controls, including financial, operational and compliance controls and risk management.' (D.2.1). Authoritative guidance has now been published on how this provision and Principle D.2 of the Combined Code are to be applied by boards. This finally resolves the difficulties raised by the earlier recommendation that boards should report on the effectiveness of their system of internal control. The board's duty is to review their system and to report to shareholders that they have done so. How they should go about their review is set out in *Internal Control: Guidance for Directors on the Combined Code* (Report of the Turnbull Committee).[20]

The Head of Listing at the London Stock Exchange has written a Foreword to the report of the Internal Control Working Party chaired by Nigel Turnbull which summarizes its relationship to the Combined Code:

The Working Party's guidance is consistent with both the requirements of the Combined Code and of the related Listing Rule disclosure requirements, and clarifies to boards of listed companies what is expected of them. We consider that compliance with the guidance will constitute compliance with Combined Code provisions D.2.1 and D.2.2 and provide appropriate narrative disclosure of how Code principle D.2 has been applied. [21]

With the guidance on internal control finally in place, the stage has been reached when boards should be able to plan on the basis that the Combined Code will remain in force, with only minor changes as foreseen by the Hampel Committee.[22]

Although the list of new provisions looks long, their incorporation should not prove burdensome to boards which already comply with existing codes. Many of them clarify or firm up existing recommendations. The additions are mainly in the fields of remuneration and relations with shareholders. The pay of top executives remains a contentious issue and the new provisions reflect shareholder concerns over the need for pay to be linked to performance and for clarity over the responsibility for determining executive pay.

The provisions over shareholder relations are aimed at encouraging shareholder involvement in governance and making general meetings more useful both to shareholders and to boards. There remain, however, two more general and basic issues in relation to the governance role of codes which deserve consideration. They are the merits of self- or market-regulation as against statutory regulation, and the light in which boards should, or do, view published codes.

Statutory or self-regulation?

Clearly both statutory and self-regulation have their part to play in corporate governance. The issue is the balance between them and the aspects of governance for which each of them is appropriate. The balance will vary country by country and the UK has more of a tradition of voluntary regulation than its continental neighbours. The Takeover Code or the Code of Advertising Practice, for example, rule on matters which are statutorily controlled elsewhere in Europe. Their rulings are accepted, because those subject to them regard this form of regulation as preferable to a statutory equivalent. The advantages of non-statutory systems of this kind are normally their speed of judgement, their relatively low cost, and their ability to deal with new issues as they arise, none of which are attributes of statutory systems. A further benefit of the voluntary approach is that it can promote compliance, not just with the letter of the law, but with the intention behind it, thus setting a higher standard. Statutory systems, on the other hand, have the advantages of relative certainty, enforceability, and therefore of fairness, since their rules apply equally to all.

Code advantages

The main argument for codes of practice in the field of corporate governance is that important aspects of governance are not easily reduced to legally enforceable rules. The Combined Code, for example, refers to 'non-executive directors of sufficient calibre'.[23] This requires a qualitative judgement, which shareholders and financial commentators have shown themselves ready and able to make, but it would be difficult if not impossible to frame a legal regulation which could have the same effect. Quite apart from the need for qualitative judgement in a number of areas covered by codes, codes can in some instances be more effective than an equivalent law in achieving their purpose. For example, the Combined Code principle, which addresses whether the posts of chairman and chief executive should be combined, states: 'There should be a clear division of responsibilities at the head of the company which will ensure a balance of power and authority, such that no one individual has unfettered powers of decision.'[24]

If it was a legal requirement that companies should have both a chairman and a chief executive, the intent of the law could be bypassed by appointing a cipher in one or other post. The letter of the law would have been followed, but its purpose frustrated. No follow-up by investors would be possible, because the response would be that the board concerned had met its legal obligations. The Code reference to a clear division of responsibilities, however, enables shareholders or others to pursue the matter by asking precisely how responsibilities are divided and to press the point until they receive a satisfactory answer.

Code compliance

If a code is, so to speak, purely voluntary and has no teeth, the risk is that it will be followed by the well-intentioned and ignored by the less conscientious, those above all whom codes are drawn up to influence. The 1992 Code of Best Practice would not have achieved the degree of compliance which it did, if it had not had the authority of the London Stock Exchange behind it. The only obligation on listed companies was to disclose how far they complied with the Code and to explain areas of non-compliance. It would have been hard for any board to justify non-disclosure and in that sense the compliance requirement was not onerous.

The consequence of disclosure, however, was that it gave shareholders and informed opinion as the basis for judging, whether a company's governance structure was acceptable, or in need of strengthening in some way. Equally, it provided them with the information they required in order to enter into a constructive dialogue with the company concerned. Thus compliance with the disclosure requirement of the London Stock Exchange, enabled the Code to achieve its aims without having to be enforced by further sanctions. The power of the Code lay in opening up an informed debate between the principals, boards and their shareholders, and in setting the agenda for that debate.

I would suggest that the degree of market regulation, for which codes have been responsible through informed investor involvement, adequately meets present needs. Equally, the balance between market and statutory regulation looks about right, subject to the findings of the Company Law Review. The report of the 1992 Committee made the point that: 'Any further degree of regulation would, in any event, be more likely to be well directed, if it were to enforce what has already been shown to be workable and effective by those setting the standard.'[25] This was partly an encouragement to support the voluntary approach in order to avoid a greater degree of statutory regulation, but it also suggested that the latter, if it became inevitable, could benefit from the former; that is to say that the two approaches were not necessarily opposed. The one recommendation of the 1992 Code of Best Practice which could appropriately have been given statutory authority, would have been the one relating to the establishment of properly constituted audit committees. A functioning audit committee with clear terms of reference is now an essential part of the governance structure, not just of listed companies, but of most forms of organization.

Cause or effect?

It is worth concluding this discussion of the impact of codes on UK boards by touching on the question of how far codes were a response to demands for higher or more consistent standards of corporate governance and how far they were themselves drivers or setters of those standards. Looked at from a board point of view, to what extent were code recommendations, burdens laid on them by committees who had been given that task, and to what extent did they provide guidance to boards over issues which they needed to address, in order for their companies to maintain their market standing and reputation?

The first point is that the UK codes which have been published were drawn up as a result of the emergence of specific governance concerns to which boards needed to respond. This was particularly true of the 1992 Code of Best Practice and the recommendations of the Greenbury Committee. The Hampel Committee's Combined Code brought together the work of all three committees in a form which was aimed at enabling boards to obtain positive benefits from compliance. Codes were, therefore, primarily a response to issues facing boards, rather than being imposed on companies in order to raise governance standards in some general sense.

Second, all of the committees consulted widely, so that their recommendations largely grew out of the evidence presented to them by companies and their representative organizations. The 1992 Code of Best Practice was just that. All of its recommendations were derived from the governance systems of companies which were recognized as having been consistently successful. The standards set by the codes were those which were already in place in respected companies and the aims of all three codes could be described as that of spreading best practice and of enabling boards to learn from each other's experience. In addition, boards were being asked to satisfy their own shareholders over their systems of governance, not to report to some external regulatory authority.

Where companies have had some reason to regard the consequences of codes as being burdensome has been when they have been interpreted in an unnecessarily prescriptive manner. The codes were intended to be guidelines and to be implemented flexibly in ways which met the individual needs of companies and their shareholders. They were not framed as rigid rules and if they are treated as such, then they can become impositions. However, it is not then so much the codes themselves which are at fault, but the manner in which boards have been pressed to apply them. The need for flexibility and for a proper appreciation of the circumstances of individual companies has at times been lost sight of in the quest for rules and certainty, rather than the exercise of judgement.

International influence of UK codes

The final point on the origin and standing of the UK codes is the surprising degree to which they have influenced the approach to corporate governance issues internationally. Even some of the wording used in the governance codes of other countries seems to be derived from their UK equivalents. This surely supports the view that the UK codes were addressing practical governance problems, and providing needed guidance, rather than being well-meaning but basically uncalled-for interventions.

Notes

1. Gee Publishing Ltd (1998). *Final Report: Committee on Corporate Governance*, January (ISBN 1 86089 034 2), para. 1.11.
2. Gee Publishing Ltd (1992). *Report of the Committee on the Financial Aspects of Corporate Governance* (ISBN 0 85258 915 8).
3. Gee Publishing Ltd (1995). *Compliance with the Code of Best Practice*, May (ISBN 1 86089 006 7).
4. Gee Publishing Ltd (1995). *Directors' Remuneration*, July (ISBN 1 86089 036 9).
5. Gee Publishing Ltd (1998). *Final Report: Committee on Corporate Governance*, January (ISBN 1 86089 034 2).
6. Gee Publishing Ltd (1998). *The Combined Code*, June (ISBN 1 86089 036 9).
7. Gee Publishing Ltd (1992). *Report of the Committee on the Financial Aspects of Corporate Governance* (ISBN 0 85258 915 8), para. 3.10.

8. CISCO (1994). *Guidance for Smaller Companies.*

9. Gee Publishing Ltd (1998). *Final Report: Committee on Corporate Governance*, January (ISBN 1 86089 034 2), para. 1.10.

10. Ibid., para. 1.1.

11. Brandeis, Louis D., *Other People's Money and How the Bankers Use It* (London, Bedford Books, St Martin's Press), 89. The book was first published in 1914 and I am indebted to Robert Monks for tracking down the source of this notable, and so often misquoted, statement of the learned judge.

12. Gee Publishing Ltd (1998). *The Combined Code*, June (ISBN 1 86089 036 9), Principle D.2.

13. Gee Publishing Ltd (1992). *Report of the Committee on the Financial Aspects of Corporate Governance* (ISBN 0 85258 915 8), para. 3.8.

14. Ibid., para. 4.12.

15. Ibid., para. 4.10.

16. Ibid., para. 4.5.

17. Gee Publishing Ltd (1998). *Final Report: Committee on Corporate Governance*, January (ISBN 1 86089 034 2), para. 1.8.

18. Gee Publishing Ltd (1998). *The Combined Code*, June (ISBN 1 86089 036 9).

19. Gee Publishing Ltd (1992). *Report of the Committee on the Financial Aspects of Corporate Governance* (ISBN 0 85258 915 8), para. 4.12.

20. Institute of Chartered Accountants (1999). *Internal Control: Guidance for Directors on the Combined Code*, September.

21. Ibid., *Foreword.*

22. Gee Publishing Ltd (1998). *Final Report: Committee on Corporate Governance*, January (ISBN 1 86089 034 2), para. 1.25.

23. Gee Publishing Ltd (1998). *The Combined Code*, June (ISBN 1 86089 036 9), A.3.1.

24. Ibid., A.2.

25. Gee Publishing Ltd (1992). *Report of the Committee on the Financial Aspects of Corporate Governance* (ISBN 0 85258 915 8), para. 3.6.

3

The Board Task

If the board is not taking the company purposefully into the future, who is? It is because of boards' failure to create tomorrow's company out of today's that so many famous names in British Industry continue to disappear.

Sir John Harvey-Jones[1]

Leadership

In the quotation which heads this chapter, Sir John Harvey-Jones captures the essence of the board task. The board's function is to set the company's aims and objectives and to ensure that they are achieved. Codes of corporate governance are there to provide a framework, which will assist boards to meet the expectations of those they serve, but it is board leadership that generates the drive on which the growth of individual companies and of the economy as a whole depends.

The debate on corporate governance has focused on the role of boards of directors, because they are the bridge between those to whom the board is accountable and those who are accountable to the board. Boards are the link between shareholders and managers in publicly quoted companies and more widely between the providers of funds and those who put them to use. They are equally the link between companies and the outside world. This is why the board is, inescapably, the centre of the governance system. The board primarily looks outwards to those whose aims it has been elected to meet. Its task is to devise plans and policies to achieve those aims and to appoint and monitor executives to ensure that they are achieved.

However, a review of the role of boards carries with it a review of the role of their chairmen. Chairmen are responsible for the work of their boards and it is their job to get the best out of them. This is why their boards appointed them to the chair and it is the one responsibility which they cannot share or delegate. Boards are there to give leadership to their companies and they in

turn look to their chairmen for leadership. The reason why the responsibilities of chairmen and of their boards are intertwined is that the authority of
chairmen is derived from that of their boards. They speak for their boards
and it is the view of their boards which they represent.

Given the importance both of boards and of their chairmen to the governance of companies, it is perhaps surprising that existing corporate legislation
barely refers to either of them. Britain's Companies Act puts very little restric-
tion on the form in which UK companies structure the way in which they are
governed: 'British law gives greater flexibility to the founders and controllers
of companies to design and structure their businesses to suit their needs than
any other legal system of which we are aware.'[2]

Legislation is directed at the responsibilities of directors as individuals, rather
than at their collective duty as members of a board. Boards of directors as
governing bodies owe their existence to experience over the centuries, not to
statute. Their advantage was summed up by a classical author in around 200 BC,
when he wrote—'Nemo solis satus sapit'. In English, less polished than the Latin,
it means that no one on their own is wise enough.[3] To the benefits of collective
wisdom can be added those of the need to avoid too great concentrations of
power and to share the burden of responsibility at the head of an enterprise.

Boards provide a means of bringing a range of minds and of viewpoints,
backed by a variety of experience, to bear on the issues which confront companies. Boards are deliberative bodies and at their meetings ideas are formed
and turned into policies and plans of action, through debate. They are a
resource to which those who have the executive responsibility for running
a company can turn. They are also the source of authority of the executives.
Their authority in publicly quoted companies is legitimized, because the board
which appoints them to their executive positions has in its turn (with all its
limitations) been elected by, and derives its authority from, the shareholders.

The chairman's role

The responsibility for ensuring that boards provide the leadership which is
expected of them is that of their chairmen. Chairmen, however, have no legal
position; they are whoever the board elects to take the chair at a particular
meeting. Boards are not bound to continue with the same chairman for suc-
cessive meetings. In law, all directors have broadly equal responsibilities[4] and
chairmen are no more equal than any other board member. Chairmen are an
administrative convenience and a means of ensuring that board meetings
are properly conducted.

Like boards, chairmen are barely mentioned in Britain's Companies Act. Section 6 of the 1967 Act laid down that the chairman's emoluments should be disclosed in the company's annual accounts and the chairman's signature is required on certain formal documents. These precepts apart, the only other requirement of chairmen is that they should be on time, if they want to retain their position. For example, the Articles of Association of Cadbury Schweppes had this to say about how the chair should be taken at a General Meeting of the company:

The Chairman of the Board, if any, or in his absence the Deputy Chairman of the Board, if any, shall preside as Chairman at every General Meeting, but if there be no such Chairman or Deputy Chairman, or if neither of them be present within ten minutes after the time appointed for holding the meeting, or shall decline to take or shall retire from the chair, the Directors present shall choose one of their number to act as Chairman of such meeting, and if there be no Director chosen who shall be willing to act, the members present in person and entitled to vote shall choose one of their own number to act as Chairman at such meeting.

This is a tighter timetable than that suggested in Table A of the Companies Act, which is a cogent reason for chairmen to be familiar with the articles of their companies. Cadbury Schweppes had a similar article covering ordinary board meetings, but there the leeway given to the chairman was only five minutes, after which time the board chose one of those present to take the chair. Thus from a statutory point of view there is no necessity for a board to have a continuing chairman and the law is solely concerned with a chairman's pay and punctuality. The chairmanship could, for example, rotate among board members, just as in former days all directors of the Bank of England could expect in turn to become Governor.

Although board chairmen have no statutory position, the choice of who is to fill that post is crucial to board effectiveness. Broadening the point, when we attend a meeting of any kind, we can sense almost from the start whether the chairman is competent or not. Providing he or she is, the meeting will serve its purpose. If the chairman is not up to the task, it is improbable that the meeting will achieve anything but frustration and waste of that most precious of resources—time. Continuity and competence of chairmanship is vital to the contribution which boards make to their companies. The lead which boards are there to give to their companies, stems from the leadership which chairmen give to their boards. To quote from a speech of Sir John Harvey-Jones: 'It is through the board that the company takes its drumbeat from the chairman.'

Direction and management

The starting point in discussing the task of boards is to be clear where their duties begin and end. This is why the Combined Code, for example, recommends that boards should determine which matters lie solely within their authority and which are delegated to management. 'The board should have a formal schedule of matters specifically reserved to it for decision.'[5]

The distinction between direction and management is crucial. Direction is the task of the board and management is the task of the executives. Unless that division of duties is clearly drawn and clearly understood by everyone concerned, there will be confusion over where the power of decision lies and over who is accountable for decisions. The line between direction and management within a company will change through time and will vary between companies; what matters is that, at any given time, there should be no doubt about where it lies.

The most comprehensive and logical definition of the difference between direction and management is to be found in the works of Dr John Carver. In an essay on the theory of governance, he writes: 'Other than the Policy Governance® Model described in this article, there is no complete or conceptually coherent theory of governance in existence.'[6] In his Model, he distinguishes between the ends of an organization and the means by which those ends are achieved. It is the job of the board to set the ends, that is to say, to define what the company is in business for, and it is the job of the executive to decide the means by which those ends are best achieved. They must do so, however, within rules of conduct and limits of risk which are set by the board. The board is ultimately accountable both for the company's purpose and for the means of achieving it. The task, however, for which the board alone is responsible is the determination of corporate ends. It should, therefore, confine itself to that role and give managers the authority to devise means to those ends, while keeping within the boundaries of acceptable conduct which the board has defined. The distinction between ends and means is helpful conceptually in deciding where the job of direction stops and that of management begins. It leads on to a more general review of board functions.

Board functions

I would summarize the main functions of the board as follows:

- to define the company's purpose;
- to agree strategies and plans for achieving that purpose;

- to establish the company's policies;
- to appoint the chief executive;
- to monitor and assess the performance of the executive team;
- to assess their own performance.

Definition of purpose

The board represents the interests of the shareholders by setting the company's aims and by monitoring their achievement. It is, therefore, the function of the board to define the purpose of the company. The company's purpose can be defined in terms of the products or services it will offer, the markets it will enter, the financial targets it will meet, or some combination of all three.

One of the best known statements of corporate purpose is that of IBM, which is expressed in quite different terms because it is based on that corporation's three beliefs. These are, belief in respect for the individual, belief in giving the best customer service of any company in the world, and the belief that an organization should pursue all tasks with the idea that they can be accomplished in a superior fashion. These beliefs are set out in a book which Thomas Watson Jr, the second generation leader of the corporation, wrote in 1963.[7]

However a company's purpose is expressed, it is the job of the board to ensure that the aims of the enterprise are clear, that they are kept up-to-date and that they are backed by the commitment of those who are charged with carrying them out. It is for the board to provide the company with a sense of vision, as well as a sense of direction. If the company is to make the most of its opportunities, the board has to be the source of inspiration for the attainment of the goals which it sets. The board is also responsible for the manner in which a company achieves its goals and, therefore, for the kind of enterprise it is and that which it aspires to become.

Strategies, plans, and policies

If the board is to take the company purposefully into the future, it has to ensure that the company makes the most of its opportunities and that it is looking ahead to where those opportunities can best be found. It needs to determine not only the company's short and long term goals, but also the manner of their achievement. The board is, therefore, responsible for the strategy of the business and for agreeing the operating plans and targets required to turn the strategy into action. It does this in conjunction with the management with whom lies the responsibility for achieving the results. The company's strategy and action plans may well move backwards and forwards between the board and the management until final agreement is reached on their form. The outcome is thus a board/management dialogue, rather than the board passing on a set of instructions to those who have to execute them. In this way both board and management are committed to a jointly agreed strategy.

Policies relate to the manner in which the company is managed and the impact which its actions have, on those within the company, and on the world outside. Policies set the company's standards and promote its values. They sit within a statutory framework which is itself extending both in scope and in detail. Health and safety and equal opportunities are examples of areas where both regulations and the expectations of the community have required boards to draw up policies in more detail and with a wider coverage than in the past. They are also examples of areas of employee and public concern which are continually developing. This is a reminder that boards not only need to agree policies but also to keep them up-to-date.

Ethical standards form another much-debated policy field. The 1992 corp-orate governance report said: 'It is important that all employees should know what standards of conduct are expected of them. We regard it as good practice for boards of directors to draw up codes of ethics or statements of business practice and to publish them both internally and externally.'[8] The lead and example to ensure that such codes are taken seriously has to come from the top. Boards, therefore, have the dual role of framing codes of conduct and of living by them.

Further policy fields could be those relating to the environment, to com-munity activities, to the treatment of suppliers, to trading with the third world, or to human rights. It is for boards to decide which aspects of the way in which the company conducts its business would benefit from policy guid-ance. The task then is to see that relevant policies are framed, in conjunction with those to whom they are addressed, and that everyone whom they affect is aware of them. That, however, is not the end of a board's policy respons-ibilities. There is a need for boards to review their company's policies in order to maintain their relevance, a point already touched on. More crucially, it is part of the board's task to ensure that company policies are followed. It is not enough for boards to affirm well-intentioned policies of, for example, non-discrimination in employment. Boards need to assure themselves that their policies are lived up to at every level within their organizations.

Appointing and assessing the executives

The key to ensuring that the board's thinking and decisions are transformed into reality lies in appointing the right executives to the right posts. The vital appointment is that of the chief executive and the importance of the board's decision over who should be in executive charge of the business needs no emphasizing. It is the job of boards to appoint their chief executives and to ensure that they continue to measure up to the demands of their posts in a fast-changing world. Appointing and, if necessary, replacing the chief executive are not only crucial board functions, but they are extremely difficult and demanding ones. Chairmen, therefore, have a particular responsibility for seeing that every possible step is taken to make the best appointment in the first place and that thereafter boards formally review the progress of their chief executives and let them know regularly how their performance is rated. If they do not meet the standards set by the board, the board has to face up to replacing them. Chairmen—those who are not chief executives as well—have to take the lead in this review process. As a recent and rewarding book on how directors view their roles and responsibilities says, in relation to the dismissal of executives in general and chief executives in particular: 'The chairman's role is crucial here.'[9]

What is it that boards are reviewing? Boards appoint chief executives to manage their businesses and they are the only executives who are directly accountable to the board. Reviewing their performance follows directly on, therefore, from assessing how far the companies they manage have achieved the objectives which their boards have set. Assessing the progress of the company is the basis for assessing the chief executive and the assessment needs to be made against measures of attainment which have been agreed between the board and the chief executive. The better the board has done its job, the clearer are the criteria of success by which the chief executive will be judged. This comparison of aims and achievement is a continuing one on the part of the board and should not be treated just as an end of term report. Essentially, the objective of boards is to give every support they can to their chief executives and one aspect of that support is the opportunity which boards should provide for frank and open discussions with their chief executives. Who else can chief executives consult over how well they are doing their job? Chief executives should be able to see their boards as a continually available source of counsel and support, rather than mainly as a monitor and paymaster.

When it comes to assessing the performance of the executive members of the board, the non-executive directors have a particular contribution to make to the process, as a consequence of their independence from executive responsibility. They stand back from the day-to-day activities of the company and can view its aims and achievements objectively from the outside. They can also draw on their knowledge of performance standards set by other bodies with which they are involved. Any decisions arising from reviewing executive performance are those of the board as a whole, but the non-executive director input to those decisions is especially valuable. Whether assessing the chief executive or other members of the executive team, the review process should be seen not as an end in itself, but as a path to improvement.

The board as the driving force

The leadership role of the board was well and forcefully summed up by Kenneth Dayton in an article he wrote about his own company, Dayton Hudson, in the *Harvard Business Review*.[10] This is how he put it:

For this reason we state clearly in the board's position description that it is the board's function as representatives of the shareholders to be the primary force pressing the corporation to the realization of its opportunities and the fulfilment of its obligations to its shareholders, customers, employees, and the communities in which it operates.

Kenneth Dayton's account of the role of his board is striking for a number of reasons. First, his board has unusually set down what it sees as its job in the form of a position description. Second, the description defines the board's function as acting as the bridge between the shareholders and the executives; the company's aims are not its own but are those of its shareholders. Third, the board accepts that it has obligations beyond those which it owes to its shareholders. Finally, the board's function is to be 'the primary force pressing the corporation' to achieve its aims. It would be hard to find a stronger statement of board purpose or a clearer expression of the board's leadership role.

Accountability

In carrying out their functions to whom are boards accountable? The board is appointed by the shareholders and is accountable to them for the company's progress and actions. It is, therefore, as we have seen, the bridge between the owners and the managers of the company. Chairmen have the dual task of ensuring that their boards direct their companies effectively and that they retain the confidence of their shareholders. It is their job to keep the bridge in good repair. They are responsible for seeing that their boards hold the right balance between the interests of the shareholders and the aims of the executives, when the two are not identical.

Chairmen may at times have to remind their executive board members that the company does not belong to them. It is all to the good that executives should identify themselves as fully as possible with the enterprises in which they are working and from which they gain their livelihood. However, it is only too easy to slip from commitment to the company's aims, which is wholly admirable, to possessiveness over what those aims should be. It is also easy to pay insufficient regard to whether those aims would receive equally enthusiastic support from the shareholders, were they to be given the chance to express their views. It is for chairmen, as the link with the shareholders, to see that their boards frame the company's purpose with the interests of those who own shares in it firmly and continually in mind.

To whom does the board owe its duty?

The simple answer to this question is that boards owe their duty to their shareholders. The precise and legal answer is that directors, and therefore the boards of whom they are made up, owe their duty to the company. How real is the difference between these two concepts and does the difference matter? While serving the shareholder interest is a useful working definition of a board's duty, there are situations when it may cease to hold good. It is, therefore, necessary to consider how the law relating to companies and their shareholders has developed in this country.

First, it is clear that a company as a body corporate has a legal personality distinct from its members. A company is not, therefore, the same as its shareholders. In the leading case of *Saloman* v. *A Saloman & Co Ltd* (1897) AC22, Lord Macnaghten stated: 'The company is at law a different person altogether from the subscribers to the memorandum . . . the company is not in law the agent of the subscribers or trustee for them.'

That the company is neither the agent of the shareholders nor their trustee was made clear by the judgment of the Court of Appeal in 1908 in *The Gramophone and Typewriter Ltd* v. *Stanley*. Lord Justice Buckley dismissed the argument that in practice the shareholders could be considered to be the company with the words: 'It is so familiar that it would be a waste of time to dwell upon the difference between the corporation and the aggregate of all the corporators.' He then went on to make this important statement about the relationship between the board and the shareholders:

The directors are not servants to obey directions given by the shareholders as individuals; they are not agents appointed by and bound to serve the shareholders as their principals. They are persons who may by the regulations be entrusted with the control of the business, and if so entrusted they can be dispossessed from that control only by the statutory majority which can alter the articles. Directors are not, I think, bound to comply with the directions even of all the corporators acting as individuals.

Interestingly, the chairman of The Gramophone and Typewriter Limited is referred to by the court as chairman of the company, not as chairman of the board. This provides a certain measure of authority for referring to chairmen as chairmen of their companies, rather than simply as chairmen of their boards. Less encouragingly, the chairman had made some unwise public comments which were used by the Revenue against the company. They were, however, swept aside by Lord Justice Buckley as being 'only the expression of a layman for whose views the company is not responsible'. This might not be a good line of defence for chairmen or their companies today!

In effect, the shareholders of a company elect its directors and entrust them with the control of the company's affairs. From there on, the directors owe their duty to the company and in following that course they may take decisions which some or all of the shareholders consider not to be in their best interests. The recourse which the shareholders have in that situation is to exercise their powers in general meeting to vote in a new board of directors whom they consider will look after their interests more faithfully.

The distinction between a company and its shareholders

The distinction between a company and its shareholders was clearly drawn by Lord Evershed in 1947 in a case concerning compensation for the shareholders of Short Brothers on the compulsory acquisition of their shares in 1943: 'Shareholders are not in the eye of the law, part owners of the undertaking. The undertaking is something different from the totality of the shareholdings.'[11]

The outcome of the Short Brothers case was that the shareholders were entitled only to the market value of their shares on the day when they were acquired and not to their proportion of what the company as a whole might have been said to have been worth at that time to someone buying control of it. What shareholders own are shares. These shares acknowledge the investment which their holders have made in a company carrying on a business and confer certain rights and responsibilities on their owners. The owners are entitled to whatever dividends are declared and they have some security against the assets of the company should it be wound up. Owning shares in a company is not strictly the same as owning the business carried on by the company.

This distinction between the directors' duty to the company and to the shareholders is important if the views of the directors and the shareholders diverge over where the best interests of the company lie. The directors may regard a particular investment as serving the long-term interests of the company, even though it may be at some cost to profitability in the short term and so against the apparent short-term interests of the shareholders.

This example draws attention to the fact that interests differ among share-holders. Some are more concerned with trading in a company's shares than in holding them; others will differ over the relative importance which they attach to dividends and to capital appreciation. Shareholders are not a homo-geneous group with a common set of interests, as chairmen soon discover.

In the long-term versus short-term argument over the level of investment, the directors may well have a strong case in the interests of the company for overriding the immediate apparent interests of the shareholders or, if you like going counter to the decision which the majority of present shareholders might have made in a vote on the matter. The directors would argue that the shareholders would benefit in the longer run from an improvement in the earning power and capital value of the business as a result of the investment. In doing so, the directors will be taking account of the future needs of present shareholders and of the interests of future shareholders.

When it is a question of making an acquisition, shareholders in public companies do have the opportunity to express their views if the acquisition is of a certain size. A possibly more contentious issue arises over the choice between reinvesting in the business, perhaps taking it in a new direction, or returning cash to the shareholders through higher dividends. There is regret-tably ample evidence of the scale in the past with which boards invested in their own businesses at lower rates of return than shareholders could have earned had they been able to invest the same resources for themselves.[12]

There used to be a taxation argument in Britain for reinvestment because capital appreciation was taxed at a lower rate than income. That argument no longer holds, since income and capital are now taxed more evenly. It would be understandable for boards to see the continued growth and development of the business as a self-evident objective and one which commended itself to them. From their perspective it would mean being involved with an expand-ing enterprise and it could also be argued to be in the interests of the com-pany, on the basis that bigger was likely on balance to be better. It is, however, for the chairman and the board to test whether bigger is likely to be better from the shareholders' viewpoint and to weigh the case for investing share-holders funds on their behalf, against enabling them to invest their propor-tion of those funds themselves.

Conclusion

This section began by posing the question whether the difference between directors owing their duty to the shareholders or to the company was real and whether it mattered. The difference between shareholders as a body and the company was held to be real, and it certainly mattered financially to the shareholders in the Short Brothers case. It becomes real to boards of directors should they become concerned about the company as a going concern. At the point when a company moves into insolvency, the duty of the board is to the company's creditors not to its shareholders. They have now become the owners and it is their interests which the board has to safeguard.

Chairmen need, therefore, to be aware that the law distinguishes between the duties of directors to their companies and their responsibilities to their shareholders. The difference is most likely to surface over questions of timing. The board is entitled to take a long-term view of where the best interests of the company lie, even if that conflicts with what shareholders, or at least some of them, see as being in their immediate interests. The company is a continuing entity, while those holding shares in it will come and go. The board is charged with ensuring the continuity of the company, exceptional circumstances aside, but not necessarily in its existing form. In furtherance of that duty, it can take actions which will primarily benefit the company in the future and so advantage tomorrow's shareholders rather than today's. How far tomorrow's shareholders are the same as today's is a matter for the shareholders themselves.

Board review

The final responsibility on the earlier list of functions was that of boards assessing their own performance. It is accepted as a matter of course that individual executives will be evaluated and boards have just as much need as executives to have their performance assessed. The object in both cases is the same; it is to learn from past experience. The UK Hampel Committee approached the question tentatively, saying that performance appraisal by boards was 'an interesting development which boards might usefully consider in the interest of continuous improvement'. I believe that it is a development which it is necessary for boards to address to maintain their competitive edge and to meet the expectations of investors, some of whom have included it in their governance guidelines. CalPERS, the Californian public employees pension fund, states in its Governance Principles: 'No board can truly perform its overriding functions of establishing a company's strategic direction and then monitoring management's success without a system of evaluating itself.'[13] The issue, therefore, is not so much whether to carry out such an evaluation, as how best to do it and this is for chairmen and their boards to decide.

One approach is through a formal questionnaire, such as is described in an American report, entitled *Performance Evaluation of Chief Executive Officers, Boards, and Directors*.[14] It sets out a structured method for boards and board committees to assess how well they are discharging their responsibilities. It breaks down the evaluation of board performance into three segments: the performance of the board as a whole, the performance of the board leadership—board and committee chairmen—and the performance of the individual directors. It suggests that the assessment should be carried out annually, while majoring on one of the three headings each year. An advantage of this approach is that it requires boards to start by agreeing on the nature of their duties and responsibilities. A disadvantage is that it may relapse into a routine. Any worthwhile assessment needs to based on a fresh look at how the board is working, building on what has gone before but not too tied to it. A further point is that if questionnaires are used they should not be so detailed as to discourage the free expression of opinion. I have, for example, a UK board questionnaire which consists of forty-seven questions, each to be rated on a scale of 1–7.

As an alternative to boards reviewing their own performance, an external assessor can be used. The chairman of Southern New England Telephone, Alfred W. van Sinderen, describes in an interesting article how his board asked an outside consultant to conduct an independent evaluation of its effectiveness.[15] The evaluation proved to be of considerable benefit to board members and surfaced problems of which the board had not previously been aware. What the consultant, an academic, brought to the review process were objectivity and experience in working with boards.

My own preference is for a rather less structured approach and one which encourages debate between chairmen and board members. Board effectiveness depends so much on the way in which the members of a board work together, that I feel the evaluation process should be carried out collectively as far as possible. This can be achieved, if chairmen set aside a day away from distractions and encourage a free discussion around a prepared agenda. The agenda might start with the role of the board. Is there agreement among board members as to what its role is, and what it should be; is it equally clear to executive management? Are board members able to contribute to the strategic direction of the business, to the degree which they feel that they should? Do board members, especially the outside directors, receive the information they need, in the form in which they need it?

The next set of questions could be about the board itself, its size and make-up, and the adequacy of its plans for succession, moving on to the way in which the board works in practice and whether it spends its time to best advantage? This in turn might lead to a discussion of structural issues, like the role of committees and whether board members are satisfied with the division of duties between committees and the board. The final questions could be more personal such as, are board members confident that the company's control system offers them sufficient protection against risks to their reputations, and more generally how might they be able to get more satisfaction from their membership of the board?.

Open-ended board evaluations of this kind depend for their usefulness on the ability of chairmen to provide enough structure to keep the discussion on the rails, while encouraging board members to speak their minds freely on what are often sensitive and personal issues. The object is to strengthen relationships between board members, between board members and their chairmen, and between boards and management. While improving on past performance is one aim of the evaluation process, boards also need to assess what degree of improvement their competitive position requires. Their results in the market place are an objective measure of their success in directing the business and of the executive's success in managing it. But boards also need to judge whether they have set their company's sights high enough, in relation to their competitors and their opportunities. The outside world looks at a company's results year by year, but boards are concerned with continuity. Thus the board, in determining how well it has fulfilled its responsibilities, will need to assess how far it has maintained the momentum of the business and how well it has balanced the needs of the future against those of the present. These are judgements which the board alone can make in reviewing its record; it is the chairman's job to ensure that the board carries out such a review and that it puts the lessons learnt from it into practice.

Review of individual board members

In addition to the appraisal of the board's performance as a whole, chairmen can gain much from appraisal discussions with directors individually. Henry Wendt has described how, when chairman of SmithKline Beecham, he had an annual appraisal interview with each of his outside directors.[16] Their discussion covered such matters as attendance, grasp of key issues and especially level and quality of participation in board deliberations. Henry Wendt made the point that if an outside director does not participate effectively in discussions at the board, this diminishes the value of the board as a whole. SmithKline Beecham gave its outside directors specific assignments in relation to one of the company's business sectors and the way they discharged that responsibility added a further dimension to the appraisal.

Such discussions assist outside, non-executive directors to make a better contribution to the work of the board and they also have their part to play in decisions about changes in board membership. Although appraisals at SmithKline Beecham were confined to the outside directors, they could be at least as useful to executive directors, given that such directors have to resolve the tensions inherent in their dual roles as executives and as directors. They will be appraised by their chief executive in respect of their management task and it would seem logical for them to be appraised by their chairman in regard to their contribution as a member of the board of directors.

From a chairman's point of view, as I know from my own experience, any appraisal discussion with individual directors rapidly changes direction and becomes an appraisal of the chairman. Directors may well feel that the limitations on their ability to participate effectively in the board's work lie in the hands of the chairman. They may consider that the lack of timely, relevant information, or the way in which debates are handled and decisions made, make it difficult for them to contribute as well as they might.

Chairmen need to know what their directors feel is holding them back and what changes in board procedures or in their chairmanship would release their energies more effectively. Chairmen cannot improve their contribution to the working of their boards without this kind of honest and constructive feedback. Appraisal interviews with individual directors are an excellent way for chairmen to appraise themselves.

Conclusion

A fitting conclusion to this chapter is a check-list which Hugh Parker, who headed McKinsey in Britain, drew up as a means of measuring board effectiveness. It forms part of his invaluable advice to newly appointed chairmen.[17]

I have developed a check-list of six questions that I believe can be used by a chairman to test the effectiveness of his own board—and from that, as a starting-point, to decide what can be done to improve it.

Has the board recently (or indeed ever) devoted significant time and serious thought to the company's longer-term objectives, and to the strategic options open to it for achieving them? If so, have these deliberations resulted in a board consensus or decision on its future objectives and strategies, and have these been put in writing?

Has the board consciously thought about and reached formal conclusions on what is sometimes referred to as its basic 'corporate philosophy'—that is, its value system, its ethical and social responsibilities, its desired 'image' and so forth? If so, have these conclusions been codified or embodied in explicit statements of policy—for example, in respect of terms of employment etc.? Does the company have formal procedures for recording and promulgating major board decisions as policy guidelines for down-the-line managers?

Does the board periodically review the organizational structure of the company, and consider how this may have to change in future? Does it review and approve all senior appointments as a matter of course? Are adequate 'human resource development' programmes in place?

Does the board routinely receive all the information it needs to ensure that it is in effective control of the company and its management? Have there been any 'unpleasant surprises'—for example, unfavourable results or unforeseen crises—that could be attributed to lack of timely or accurate information?

Does the board routinely require the managing director to present his annual plans and budgets for their review and approval? Does the board regularly monitor the performance of the managing director and his immediate subordinate managers in term of actual results achieved against agreed plans and budgets?

When the board is required to take major decisions on questions of future objectives, strategies, policies, major investments, senior appointments etc., does it have adequate time and knowledge to make these decisions soundly—rather than finding itself overtaken by events and, in effect, obliged to rubber-stamp decisions already taken or commitments already made?

If the answers to all these questions are affirmative, it is safe to say that you have an effective board. If the answers are negative—or perhaps not clear—then you already have some indications of what needs to be done to strengthen your board.

Although boards now have code guidelines and principles to follow, this checklist stands the test of time in respect of the task which all boards shoulder, that of providing the degree of leadership which their companies have the right to expect.

Notes

1. Harvey-Jones, John (1988). *Making It Happen*, London: Collins, 162.
2. Department of Trade and Industry: Company Law Review Steering Group (2001). *Modern Company Law: Final Report*, Vol.1, para. 1.26.
3. Plautus, a Roman dramatist.
4. The law does take account of the qualifications and experience of individual directors in determining the standards which they are expected to meet.
5. Gee Publishing Ltd (1998). *The Combined Code*, June (ISBN 1 86089 036 9), A.1.2.
6. Carver, Dr John (2002). *On Board Leadership*, San Francisco: Jossey-Bass, 4.
7. Watson Jr, Thomas J. (1963). *A Business and its Beliefs*, New York: McGraw-Hill.
8. Gee Publishing Ltd (1992). *Report of the Committee on the Financial Aspects of Corporate Governance* (ISBN 0 85258 915 8), para. 4.29.

9. Stiles, Philip and Taylor, Bernard (2001). *Boards at Work*, Oxford: Oxford University Press, 78.
10. Dayton, K. N. (1984). 'Corporate Governance: the other side of the coin', *Harvard Business Review*, Jan/Feb.
11. *Short and Another* v. *Treasury Commissioners*, Court of Appeal, 1947.
12. Rappaport, Alfred (1986). *Creating Shareholder Value*, New York: The Free Press.
13. CalPERS (1998). *US Corporate Governance Core Principles and Guidelines*, 9.
14. National Association of Corporate Directors (1994). *Performance Evaluation of Chief Executive Officers, Boards, and Directors*.
15. van Sinderen, A. W. (1985). 'The Board looks at itself', *Directors & Boards*, Winter.
16. Wendt, Henry (1993). *Global Embrace*, New York: HarperBusiness.
17. Parker, Hugh (1990). *Letters to a New Chairman*, London: Director Publications, 12–14.

4

Board Membership

To have influence, individuals must think for themselves and be perceived
by others as concerned about the best interests of the organization as a
whole.

Inside the Boardroom[1]

Board composition

The unitary boards of British public companies are made up of executive and
non-executive directors. The potential competitive advantage of the unitary
structure lies in its combination of the depth of knowledge of the business
of the executive directors and the breadth of experience of the non-executive
directors. I prefer the term 'outside director', as used in the US, to 'non-
executive director', because it is a more precise description of their position
and of the attributes which they bring to a board. It also avoids describing
them by what they are not.

Clearly the effectiveness of a board depends on its composition, on its
balance of membership, and on the skill of its chairman. The views of chairmen, therefore, need to carry considerable weight in selecting members of
their boards, since it is their job to build them into an effective team, even
though the selection process itself is one which should involve the board as
a whole. In the light of the board task outlined in the previous chapter, what
considerations will board chairmen take into account in building their
boards, bearing in mind that the make-up of an individual company's board
needs to reflect the challenges which that particular company is either facing
or expecting to face?

Board size

The first balance which chairmen will wish to strike relates to the overall size
of their board. The balance is between a body which is small enough for there

to be true discussion and debate between members and one which is large enough to bring in the breadth of knowledge and experience which chairmen and their boards feel that they need. Sir Walter Puckey writing on board size says that in his experience

I have found that its most effective size for first-class participation and decision-making is between six and eight excluding the chairman and the secretary, who may or may not be a director. Too many board meetings display verbosity among a few and almost complete silence from the rest.[2]

Martin Lipton and Jay W. Lorsch, who have contributed so constructively to the debate on corporate governance in the US and internationally, argue persuasively for a reduction in the size of American boards. In their *Modest Proposal for Improved Corporate Governance* their recommendation is as follows: 'We believe that the size of a board should be limited to a maximum of ten directors (indeed we would favor boards of eight or nine) with a ratio of at least two independent directors to any director who has a connection with the company . . .'[3]

They reason that boards of this size enable the directors to get to know each other well enough for their discussions to be frank and searching and to allow every director to contribute to them. With this number it should also be possible for board members to reach a true consensus in coming to their decisions. It is worth adding that the 'modesty' of Lipton and Lorsch's proposals lies only in their not being backed by statute, not in their refreshingly radical nature.

Other authorities edge the figure up. Sir Walter Puckey quotes Harold Koontz as saying that it is sensible 'to limit a board to thirteen members in order to obtain the free discussion and deliberative interplay which board decisions require'.[4] At the upper end, Professor Northcote Parkinson's researches have conclusively demonstrated that what he refers to as the 'coefficient of inefficiency' is reached when the members of a body number between nineteen and twenty-two; at that point an inner cabinet is established, or establishes itself, to take over the functions of the original board or committee.

Common sense suggests that a board should be no larger than it needs to be to meet Harold Koontz's requirements of free discussion and deliberative interplay. Owner–managers establishing a board structure will want to begin with as small a board as possible, since the choice of the founding members is so critical. Lipton and Lorsch's limit of ten seems to me an admirable starting point for any consideration of board size. Those numbers will allow for effective debate and it is the job of chairmen to restrain the verbosity of the few and encourage the participation of the majority.

Board balance

Insiders and outsiders

Within whatever limits of size boards set for themselves, chairmen are looking for a balance of experience, backgrounds, and points of view on their
boards. The smaller the board the more crucial the choice of board members
becomes. The first balance to be struck on a unitary board is between executive and outside directors. The executive directors bring to the board their
inside knowledge of the workings of the business and the nature of its markets, while the outside directors bring their experience, knowledge, and independence of judgement. The outside directors further divide into those who
are independent according to the definition set out in Chapter 2, n. 14 and
those who are not. Lipton and Lorsch's advice is that independent outside
directors should outnumber other directors by two to one.

The trend in the UK has been for boards to become smaller and for the
proportions both of outside directors and of those outside directors who
are independent, to rise. On the first point, there have been some dramatic
reductions in the size of boards of individual companies, for example, the
board of Marks & Spencer numbered twenty-one in 1998 and has now come
down to fourteen. Figures quoted in *The Professional Board* for the top 150
companies showed that on average they had 11.4 directors on their boards.[5]
There was, however, a wide variation within that average, with 15 per cent of
companies having eight or less and 15 per cent having fifteen or more. Just
over half of the board members of those same companies were outside directors. This confirms that the proportion of outside directors to executive
directors has risen compared with ten years ago, when boards were more
likely to be made up of one-third outsiders to two-thirds insiders.

The proportion of outside directors who are independent has undoubtedly
risen, encouraged by the requirement to have independent directors on
board committees. The extent of the change is hard to measure, because the
distinction between outside directors as such and independent outside directors has only been made relatively recently. In 1987, the Bank of
England made a survey of the Times 1000 companies, as a follow-up to a
similar survey it had made in 1985.[6] It found that slightly less than one-quarter of the outside directors identified in the study were either former executives of the company or professional advisers to it. This compared with
almost one-third in the 1985 survey. That rise in the proportion of independent outside directors continued through the 1990s, although the definition of independence became tighter than the one used by the Bank of
England.

Balance of experience

Another aspect of balance is the need for boards to consider the range of experience and attributes which they are looking for from their outside directors. I was involved in the process of director selection as chairman of PRO NED[7] from 1985 to 1993. PRO NED was established in 1982 under the aegis of the Bank of England and sponsored by a group of institutions representative of industry and finance. PRO NED's mission was to promote recognition of the vital contribution which outside directors of the right calibre could make to company boards and to help companies find appropriate candidates for such appointments. I was struck by the narrow view which many chairmen took over the pool from which they felt their outside directors should be drawn. They were usually looking for someone with experience on the board of a comparable or larger company and preferably their chief executive.

While executive directors from other companies are clearly a valuable element in the mix of outside directors on a board, they are likely to have a similar mindset to the executive directors who are already in place. The reason for considering selecting outside directors from a wider variety of backgrounds is that they will bring a different perspective to the work of the board. This was perhaps less important in the past, when boards could afford to focus most of their attention on looking inwards at their business operations. Now boards, in a rapidly changing and more international world, are having to give much of their time to looking outwards at the whole range of external factors which affect their enterprises. They are increasingly expected to take into account and report on such issues as, the impact of their companies on the environment and on the communities with which they are involved.

Further balances

Two other aspects of balance relate to the requirements of board committees and to the increasingly global scale of corporate activities. On the first point, a booklet on audit committees published by the Institute of Chartered Accountants recommends that: 'The committee collectively requires an understanding (or access to those with understanding) of business risk management, internal control, accounting and financial reporting, and other knowledge depending on the circumstances of the company.'[8] While that does not mean that one of the outside directors has to be an accountant, the demands of the audit committee is a factor which chairmen will take into account in considering the balance of experience which they are looking for on their boards.

The degree to which companies spread their activities internationally raises the question of whether their board balance would be improved if it included a director from abroad, who could be either an executive director or an outside one. Boards of British companies are increasingly appointing directors from overseas to broaden their perspective on the business and social issues on their agendas.

The problem for chairmen is how to achieve the mix of backgrounds, experience, age, and personalities which they believe are necessary on their boards, while at the same time keeping them an effective and manageable size, in line with the advice with which the chapter started.

Board contribution

Executive directors

The sole reason for appointing any directors is the value which they will add to their board. This means that what will qualify executives to become board members are the qualities they can bring to the board's activities. Clearly their function in the company is relevant, but the argument for executives joining the board should not be solely on the grounds that they hold key executive posts. Rather, the argument should be the other way round, on the basis that only someone of board calibre should be the holder of such a key post. It is the wider attributes which executives are expected to bring to boards, rather than their management responsibilities, which make them board candidates. It is unfortunate that in Britain so much standing should be attached to directorships; the position in the US, where it is the executive office and its title that counts, is a healthier one. As a result of this concern with status, there is pressure to appoint executives as directors for reasons other than the qualities which they can bring to the board. Chairmen have to be resolute in agreeing to the appointment of executives to the board, not on grounds of seniority or as a reward for service, but on their merits as potential directors.

The dual role

Executive directors have the problem of a dual role within their companies. They are on both sides of the divide, discussed earlier, between direction and management. They have to take off their management hat when entering the board room and replace it with their directorial one. That is difficult enough, but they also need to be able to take their own stance on board matters, even if this means going against the views of the chief executive to whom they are responsible managerially, but with whom they are equal as directors. This duality of role has led to a questioning of the principles on which unitary boards in the UK are based. While at times executive directors are in an invidious position, for example, if the board issue is the future of their chief executive, a mix of executive and outside directors can be made to work well in my experience. The advantage over having the chief executive alone speaking for the management of the business is that the board has the opportunity to hear the views of other key executives and to raise matters with them. While chief executives will understandably meet with their executive colleagues before a board meeting to agree a common line, that process itself adds a breadth of view to the way in which the chief executive will then report on the state of the business, in the presence of their executive colleagues.

Board equality

There are, however, two points to make in relation to assisting executive directors to play their part as equal members of a board. First, if they have had the opportunity to become outside directors on the board of another company, they will have learnt from experience the essential differences between direction and management. They will equally have appreciated what it takes to become an effective member of a board team. Second, their ability to contribute to their own board rests largely in the hands of their chairman. It is for chairmen, by the way in which they handle their meetings, to affirm the equality of all board members, whether executive or outside directors, since they carry the same responsibilities. It is only when executive directors are confident that their standing in the boardroom is on an equal footing with that of their chief executive, that they are in a position to speak and to act as full directors.

Outside directors

When asked in a survey[9] what was their most important role, the outside directors taking part were virtually all agreed that it was 'providing an independent viewpoint'. Independence of mind and of judgement is the particular quality which outside directors bring to their boards. They bring their independent viewpoint to bear on issues of strategy and governance, and on the running of the business. In all the surveys I have seen, outside directors regard strategy as the field in which they feel that they should be able to make their greatest contribution. They place governance next and give a lower rating to operational issues. This makes it clear that outside directors see themselves as being on the board to assist in enhancing the prosperity of the business over time, equally and together with their executive colleagues. They play their part in improving the performance of the business primarily through their involvement in the formulation of strategy.[10]

Governance responsibilities

They also have an essential governance role by virtue of their independence and objectivity. Their governance role is built into the board's structure through the Combined Code's provision that boards should establish audit committees of at least three directors all of whom should be outside directors, the majority of them being independent.[11] In addition, as has already been mentioned, they are well placed to take the lead over issues where the interests of the executives and those of the shareholders might conflict and over assessing the performance of the executive team.

The principal point is that the executive directors are as responsible for the governance of their companies as the outside directors, and the outside directors are as responsible for the performance of the business as the executive board members. Outside directors are an integral part of the board team and the qualities and experience which they bring to the board should complement those of the executive directors. Sir Allen Sheppard, now Lord Sheppard, highlighted, as chairman of Grand Metropolitan, the contribution of outside directors to performance when at a PRO NED conference he said that their role was as much that of an accelerator as a brake.[12]

Attributes

This leads on to the question of what chairmen look for in selecting outside directors. Two important attributes which I have always looked for are commitment to the enterprise and time. Commitment is essential, if outside directors are to gain the full confidence of those in executive charge of the enterprise and for them to carry weight in board discussions. Time is equally vital. It is not enough to have time to attend scheduled meetings of the board and of its committees and to join in on away-days to discuss strategy. If a company runs into difficulties of any kind or becomes the target of a bid, the outside directors should be in a position to give whatever time is needed in order to resolve the challenges with which their board is faced. This is when their role is key, both because they stand further back from the action, and thus can take a broader view, and because they can take some of the load off the executives, who have, in such circumstances, to be able to concentrate totally on the running of the business.

I believe that outside directors add vitality to a board. They balance the knowledge of the business of the insiders with the supportive but critical objectivity of outsiders. They need to be able to challenge accepted thinking constructively. In doing so, they broaden a board's outlook and stand ready to question what those of us who have worked in one business all our lives may well take for granted. The participation of outside directors breathes fresh life into a board's discussions and brings out the best in the executive directors. A leaven of outsiders of the right kind is an essential ingredient in an effective board. As for the personal qualities that chairmen seek in their outside directors, Geoffrey Mills, an author of books on boards, quotes Angus Murray on the subject: 'A good non-executive director needs to have intellect, integrity and courage. Of these qualities, courage is the most important, for without it the other two characteristics are useless.'[13]

Representative directors

The issue of representative directors on boards became a matter of debate in Britain with the publication of the Bullock Report in 1977. The Report was not primarily concerned with the efficient running of companies, but with changing the balance of power within them. Its basic proposal was that employee representatives should be appointed to the boards of British companies. There were numerous weaknesses in the Report's recommendations, but the fundamental flaw was that representative directors have no place on a unitary board. It is not possible to square the idea of directors representing a particular interest with the concept of a unitary board, on which all directors have the same responsibilities and duties.

If employee directors had been appointed to unitary boards, as Bullock recommended, then either the directors would have ceased to be employee directors or their boards would have ceased to be unitary, because the two concepts are incompatible. If employee directors accept the same responsibilities as their fellow directors, they are no longer employee directors, but the board has retained its unitary nature. If, however, they remain employee directors then the board is no longer unitary. This is the reason why any direct representation of special interests is incompatible with the unitary board model.

An inevitable reaction to the Bullock proposals was that other interests advanced their claim to board representation, most notably consumer groups who saw shareholders and employees as likely to put the interests of producers before those of consumers. However, the appointment of directors representing any specific interest, environmentalists were another candidate, would undermine the unitary nature of the board. It would then have to become a forum for resolving differences between the interest groups represented on it—not a cheering prospect for chairmen.

What is clear is that a representational board, as postulated by Bullock, could not be the driving force in a company. This is not to say that the way in which interests should be represented in society and how the balance of power between them should be struck are not issues of importance; but they need to be considered separately from the manner in which the members of an effective board should be chosen. To the extent that the concern behind the Bullock proposals was that directors came from too narrow a social grouping, then the outside element on a board presents opportunities for widening the backgrounds from which directors are drawn. This in turn coincides with the need for boards to deal with a broader range of issues than in the past. There is, therefore, advantage to be gained from diversity in board membership, always provided that board members are appointed for the value they can add, not for the interests which they might be thought to represent.

The 3i experience

The 3i organization in Britain provides an excellent example of how a venture capital institution with a stake in a number of companies can strengthen the boards of those companies, without requiring representation on them. The group has established a bank of experienced directors, who are available to be nominated to company boards. Its booklet, *The Role and Contribution of an Independent Director*,[14] sets out the way in which companies, mainly those in which 3i has an investment, can draw on this resource. It opens with the statement: 'The independent director nominated by 3i has the same responsibilities and obligations to the company as the other directors.' There is no question of directors appointed through the good offices of 3i representing an interest other than that of the companies whose boards they have joined. They are nominated, but they are independent, and they are brought into a company with the straightforward aim of strengthening its board.

Board selection

Networks

The traditional way of selecting outside directors for British boards was by word of mouth and relied to a great extent on what the Americans dub the 'buddy system'. Chairmen would ask for suitable names from their board colleagues and possibly from their professional advisers. They would then put their preferred candidates to their boards, who would be more or less bound to accept them. The selection process would start with names, not with the task. Politicians, in my experience, have been the worst offenders in this regard, too often taking the view that the precise requirements of the post they were trying to fill were almost irrelevant. Provided, they said, they could find the right individual, he or she would then write their own job description. Politicians still search for names which they recognize, but at least public posts are now advertised which requires their search process to start with a job description.

The defects of finding board candidates through the old boy network are clear enough. It draws from the limited pool of those known to board members and their circle. Its aim is to find potential board members who are compatible with the existing directors, rather than focusing on the specific value which they are expected to add to the work of the board. They give boards made up in this way too much of the flavour of a club. When it comes to looking to financial or legal advisers for assistance in the process, they have no particular qualifications in board selection and, worse still, may indeed have favours to repay. Finally, directors who feel that they owe their place on boards to their chairmen have their independence diminished to that extent. It seems extraordinary that appointments to the board were so often treated in the past more casually than those to any level of management.

Nomination committees

This is why the Combined Code states that, 'There should be a formal and transparent procedure for the appointment of new directors to the board.'[15] The object of a formal procedure is to encourage chairmen and their boards to review their present board membership and to identify gaps in experience, background, age, or personality, the filling of which would strengthen the board team. The search for board candidates then becomes purposeful and is focused on the qualities which the board is looking for, rather than on names. The Combined Code provides that recommendations on board appointments should be made by a nomination committee, unless the board is small. A majority of the members of the committee should be outside directors and it should be chaired either by the board chairman or an outside director.

Nomination committees are now accepted practice and their involvement breaks the tie of personal patronage associated with selection by chairmen.

But old customs die hard and one of the findings in a recent study was that: 'In the majority of companies (80%), it is the Chairman who is principally involved in finding NexDs. In only half the companies surveyed are the Chief Executive and Board also involved in the process.'[16]

There is a balance to be struck here. I believe that the responsibility of chairmen for their board teams means that they should play a leading role in selecting the members of their teams. However, involving other board members in the choice of candidates strengthens the position of those who are appointed in two ways. First, it means that those who will be working with them as colleagues have had a say in their selection. Second, those appointed know that they have broad board support and do not owe their position primarily to their chairman.

Competitive selection

I learnt from my experience at PRO NED of the advantages of nomination committees and boards having a choice of candidates for outside directorships. An element of competition gives confidence to those who are chosen and this is particularly helpful to any who have not previously had company board experience. It also puts outside directors so chosen on an equal footing with their executive counterparts. Executive directors reach the board in competition with their fellow executives and they want to know that their outside directors were chosen in the same way, openly and on merit. Otherwise, new outside directors have to play themselves in to overcome any suspicion that they are joining as members of a board club.

Demand and supply

The final issue which is raised over the appointment of outside directors is whether there are enough candidates of the right calibre. It is true that the demands which are made on directors mean that the number of such posts that any individual can undertake are now fewer than they were. This applies as much to executive directors considering outside directorships, as to outside directors themselves. Provided chairmen and boards are prepared to look beyond the limited circle of those who are already on plc boards, there are a number of other sources of good candidates. These include the divisional directors of major companies, academics, and those with extensive management experience in the public and voluntary sectors. In addition, career patterns are changing. Partners in professional firms are retiring early, as are many managers, and are looking for an opportunity to put their knowledge and experience to good use.

It is not possible seriously to suggest that there is a shortage of potential outside directors when so few women are board members. The number with main board experience are in consequence limited, which is why it is necessary to look wider than at the existing board pool. The responsibilities which many women carry in voluntary organizations and in public life will have given them a different type of experience from that of the executives; as a result they can bring a particular kind of added value to a board. Now that boards are having to broaden their agendas and to spend more time on the external aspects of their activities, they will gain from having directors with a wider spectrum of viewpoints than in the past, in line with the wider interests which they are now being called upon to take into account. This is not diversity for its own sake, but for the contribution which it can make to board effectiveness.

Joining a board as an outside director offers challenge, interest, and a chance to contribute to the progress of an enterprise. There will continue to be enough able men and women who are willing to take up such posts, provided that the risks through litigation, especially to reputation, do not begin to outweigh the rewards, which should more adequately reflect the weight of their responsibilities than they commonly do at present.

The chairman's role

Chairmen are responsible for the effectiveness of their boards and my preference is for them to chair the nomination committees of their boards. This gives them a legitimate degree of influence without slipping back into patronage. Boards are teams and like other teams need to be made up of people with different attributes. This is why filling a board vacancy should begin with an assessment of what manner of person would add most to the capabilities of the existing board members. In addition, chairmen need to make a judgement on complementarity of character, as well as of experience and background. How far will potential candidates be able to combine standing up for their own individual opinions with being members of the board team? Boards have to find their own particular balance of challenge and collegiality and it is primarily for chairmen to determine where that should lie. Thus personalities matter.

Search process

Chairmen need also to decide how best to go about the search for board candidates. There is no reason why personal networks should not play a part, but they will be unlikely on their own to provide the required degree of choice. Executive search agencies provide a professional service and are able to cast their nets as wide as chairmen will allow. They are in a position to ascertain whether candidates are potentially interested, without chairmen having to approach them personally. Advertising for board members, as for example the Bank of England has done, has proved perhaps surprisingly successful mainly in the public and voluntary sectors, in the sense that it appears to have attracted a minimum number of oddballs and to have brought forward good applicants from unexpected quarters. There are also groups of companies prepared to encourage their ablest executives to join each other's boards, thus establishing a common pool of potential board members.

Need for judgement

A point which does concern me is that investor guidance on board membership, mainly related to outside directors and to which of those count as independent, is in danger of becoming too rigid. Their criteria on such matters as age, length of service as an outside director, and family relationships should be taken as guidelines, not as commandments. My view on this is coloured by my having transgressed most such guidelines myself. I was an outside director of the Bank of England for twenty-four years, I served on the same board as my brother, and as chairman I have persuaded directors to stay on the board beyond the usual span, because of the value of their wholly individual contributions. Independence is more a matter of character than of the elapse of time. Chairmen need to form their own judgements of the contribution which their board members make and, with the support of their boards, to stand by them. Provided that the nomination process is clear, that the reasons for selecting individual directors are explained, and that shareholders have confidence in the chairman, proposals for board membership will receive their support.

Chairmen can maintain the vitality of their boards and bring about necessary changes in their composition through terms of office. When a director's term of office is coming to an end, chairmen will review with the director concerned the issue of reappointment, taking into account their point of view and that of the board. Chairmen have to ensure that all directors contribute from their own particular standpoint, but that the board's decisions are arrived at collectively. It is for chairmen to hold their board teams together and to encourage diversity of opinion while maintaining singleness of purpose. The one absolute necessity, in terms of membership, is that all boards should include at least one director who can tell their chairmen when it is time for them to go!

Notes

1. Bowen, William C. (1994). *Inside the Boardroom*, New York: John Wiley & Sons.
2. Puckey, Sir Walter (1969). *The Board Room*, London: Hutchinson, 85.
3. Lipton, Martin and Lorsch, Jay W. (1992). 'A Modest Proposal for Improved Corporate Governance', *Business Lawyer*, Vol. 48, 59.
4. Puckey, Sir Walter (1969). *The Board Room*, London: Hutchinson, 86.
5. Bingham, Kit (2001). *The Professional Board*, London: Gee Publishing Ltd, 7.
6. *Bank of England Quarterly Bulletin*, May 1988, 242.
7. The Bank of England took the lead in sponsoring PRO NED; the other sponsors were British Institute of Management, British Merchant Banking and Securities Houses Association, British Bankers' Association, Confederation of British Industry, Institute of Chartered Accountants, Institutional Shareholders' Committee, London Stock Exchange and 3i plc. In 1994, the sponsors decided that PRO NED should stand on its own feet and no longer be dependent on sponsorship for its campaigning role; PRO NED, therefore, became part of Egon Zehnder, which enabled it to continue to promote best practice in relation to director appointments, but as part of a major international executive search organization.
8. Institute of Chartered Accountants (1997). *Audit Committees*, 8.
9. KPMG Peat Marwick (1994). *Survey of Non-Executive Directors*.
10. Gee Publishing Ltd (1998). *Final Report: Committee on Corporate Governance*, January (ISBN 1 86089 034 2), para. 3.8.
11. Gee Publishing Ltd (1998). *The Combined Code*, June, (ISBN 1 86089 036 9), D.3.1.
12. PRO NED (1991). *9th Annual Review*, September.
13. Mills, Geoffrey (1988). *Controlling Companies*, London: Unwin, 94.
14. 3i plc, *The Role and Contribution of an Independent Director*, Associate Directors Resources.
15. Gee Publishing Ltd (1998). *The Combined Code*, June (ISBN 1 86089 036 9), A.5.
16. *MORI Report* (1997). Carried out for GHN Executive Coaching, 4.

5

The Chairman and Board Structure

Whenever an institution malfunctions as consistently as boards of directors have in nearly every major fiasco of the last 40 or 50 years it is futile to blame men. It is the institution that malfunctions.

Peter Drucker[1]

Boards in the firing line

The quotation at the head of this chapter is taken from an article which Peter Drucker wrote in the *Wharton Magazine* in 1976. In it he said that boards all over the Western world were under attack and that the board had become an impotent and legal fiction. His broadside knew no bounds as, in the course of it, he claimed that Hermann Abs, the German banker, had sat on about one hundred and fifty boards at the same time! It is true that Dr Abs did hold some thirty supervisory board posts, until the law named after him enforced a limit of ten. Nevertheless, it was not uncommon for directors in the 1970s to hold more board posts than they could possibly do justice to, on top of which there were those somnolent boards referred to in the opening chapter whom the SEC pilloried. Peter Drucker's description of the standing of boards of directors at the time he was writing was both unflattering and to the point. Boards throughout the Western world were too often seen as not being in control of their companies and as having failed to prevent disasters or malpractices.

In Britain in the late 1970s, the Bank of England shared Peter Drucker's concerns about ineffective boards. Unusually for a central bank, the Bank of England kept a supervisory eye on the affairs of the City of London with a view to maintaining its international reputation and standing. When major British companies ran into financial difficulties, their first port of call would normally be the Bank to obtain guidance on how best to extricate themselves from their predicament. The Bank was able on such occasions to act as an impartial chairman and to bring together all those with a stake in the problem company, in order to attempt to find an acceptable way out of its difficulties. The Bank's summing-up, based on their experience of these calls for help, was that the root of the problem, in almost every case which came to their attention, was board failure.

This was the reason why, under the leadership of Sir Henry (later Lord) Benson, who was an adviser to the Governor, the Bank of England established PRO NED. The Bank reasoned that it was better to tackle the causes of failure rather than having to pick up the pieces afterwards. They found that the most common cause of the corporate problems they were called upon to help to resolve was that the boards concerned had allowed matters to drift. These boards were either not aware of the seriousness of their financial position, or they lacked the will to tackle the situation and simply hoped Micawber-like that something would turn up. The failure was not that of the institution but of the people who were meant to be in charge of it. A positive measure to reduce the risk of this kind of failure was, in the Bank's judgement, the appointment of competent, independent-minded, outside directors to corporate boards. Hence PRO NED's task, which was to persuade chairmen of the advantages of having capable, outside directors on their boards and to help them to find such people. While the board as an institution remained broadly unchanged on both sides of the Atlantic, its structure did alter. In the UK, its composition changed, as we have seen, with the appointment of more outside directors, more of whom were independent. In the US, committees of the board were formed, starting with audit committees. Audit committees gave boards a means of sharpening their systems of internal financial control and of improving their standards of financial reporting.

However, such governance changes as were made in the wake of Peter Drucker's scathing criticisms still left boards under attack for not running their businesses as efficiently as they should and more generally for not being adequately answerable either to their shareholders or to society at large. The charge that boards do not work as they should is widespread and is not confined to corporate boards; it includes the boards of not-for-profit organizations as well. This raises issues for chairmen. Are there, for example, better forms of board structure or process which would improve the functioning of boards?

Effectiveness and accountability

The starting point for any such enquiry, is to examine the criticisms levelled at the way boards work in the UK and the US and then to consider what action could be taken to meet those criticisms. The main criticisms of boards relate to their performance and to their accountability. Boards had long been indicted for their lack of performance, but their lack of accountability was put firmly on the governance agenda by Robert Monks and Nell Minow with their book *Power and Accountability*.[2] The quotation from the book printed on its jacket reads: 'Corporations determine far more than any other institution the air we breathe, the quality of the water we drink, even where we live. Yet they are not accountable to anyone.'

This carries the attack on from where Peter Drucker left off and the case made by the authors is that corporate power was constrained in the past by a combination of law, culture, and public opinion. They fear first that, in the US, restraints based on the law of a particular domicile are weakening in the 'race to the bottom' in regulatory terms between domiciles, the race being to attract companies to locate where the regulatory regime is feeblest. More generally, Monks and Minow are concerned that even those restraints will become increasingly ineffective as companies spread their activities internationally and no longer answer mainly to a single jurisdiction. The outcome of their analysis of the deficiencies of boards is that means have to be found to restore their effective accountability to shareholders, who must equally and in turn accept their governance responsibilities.

Under the heading of being insufficiently accountable, boards are charged with being self-perpetuating bodies, with drawing their membership from too narrow a section of the community, and with ignoring the interests of their shareholders and the wider interests of society. Thus the issue is one of board legitimacy, which in turn involves who is on the board and how they got there. The importance of how directors are selected relates to the role of the board as the source of authority within the company. The classical theory of the board is that the shareholders elect the directors and authorize them to run the company on their behalf. The board in its turn sets the aims of the enterprise and appoints managers to carry out those aims. The managers thus carry the authority of the board and the board that of the shareholders.

In practice, however, the shareholders of most public companies have little say in the appointment of directors, other than to nod through the nominations presented to them by the current board. They can vote against the names which come up for election at the AGM, but it is made difficult for them to put forward alternative candidates. Provided that a company produces acceptable results, its board can in practice become self-perpetuating. The result is that the legitimacy of the board as the appointee of the shareholders, and therefore as carrying their authority, is based on something of a fiction.

Whether the authority of directors and managers stems as directly from the shareholders as the textbooks say that it should, may not be thought to have much practical relevance. It is, however, all part of the charge that boards take too little account of the interests of their shareholders and are too far removed from shareholder influence. If board members feel that they owe their place on the board to their shareholders, they will be continually reminded of their responsibilities to them. If, in practice, they owe their place to their chairmen and fellow-directors, then they are more dependent on how they stand with their colleagues than with their shareholders.

The lack of a keen and consistent sense of accountability to the shareholders is a basic reason why many boards have failed to achieve the results that were expected of them. This lack of accountability stemmed in the past from the inability or unwillingness of shareholders to exert effective pressure on boards to take more account of their interests.

Self-perpetuating boards

A further consequence of boards being largely self-appointed is their tendency to draw their outside directors from their own limited circle. This goes back to the earlier discussion concerning the composition of boards. There are two arguments for enlarging the constituencies from which directors are selected. One is that boards would thereby become more effective through being able to exercise wider choice and the other is that companies would be helped to identify their aims more clearly with the interests of the communities of which they are a part. The two arguments overlap. For example, if there were more women on the boards of companies, a larger pool of potential directorial talent would be being tapped and the make-up of boards would come closer to that of society as a whole. It was argued in the US that a reason for boards failing in their duty to their companies was that their directors had too much in common with each other and were not therefore sufficiently critical in their judgement of performance.

There is clearly force in the argument that boards are self-perpetuating and that their members tend to come from similar backgrounds. It is, however, important to disentangle the arguments about the balance of power in society from those which are aimed at improving board effectiveness. On the latter point, strengthening the links between boards and shareholders and ensuring that there are sufficient independent-minded, outside directors on boards should have an invigorating effect on board performance.

Shareholder influence

There are actions which chairmen can take and are taking to enable shareholders to have more influence over the appointment of directors. One is to
provide shareholders with relevant information over existing board members, concerning their responsibilities and their experience, and equally to
provide the same information in respect of those who are up for appointment to the board at the AGM. This puts shareholders in a position to assess
why those directors are being nominated and the value which they are
expected to add to the board. They can then make an informed decision on
how to cast their votes. Shareholders in their turn have an opportunity to let
chairmen know their views on those coming up for election, either by speaking at the AGM or by writing their comments on their proxy forms. As a
chairman, I used to see a summary of such comments, which were instructive and often entertaining. Individual shareholders probably have more
influence than they imagine and should always be prepared to let chairmen
know what they think of their companies and of the way in which they
are run.

Individual shareholders who are dissatisfied with a board's performance
can sell their shares. The institutions collectively cannot, because they own
such a high proportion of the shares of UK companies. In addition, those
institutions which track an index are automatically invested in the companies which make up that particular index. The institutions, therefore, have
between them every incentive to accept their responsibilities as shareholders
and to use their powers to ensure, in their own interests, that the companies
in which they have invested their clients' money are properly directed and
controlled. To this end they have increasingly recognized the importance of
the way in which directors are selected and boards are made up.

The Institutional Shareholders' Committee published its guidance on *The
Role and Duties of Directors* in 1991 in response to approaches which they
had received from companies and their advisers over what it was that the
institutions expected from the boards of the companies in which they had
invested.[3] The Committee followed this up with a companion statement of
guidance entitled *The Responsibilities of Institutional Shareholders in the UK*,
which dealt with the reverse side of the same coin—what boards were
entitled to expect from their institutional investors.[4] This document specifically recommended that institutional investors should take a positive interest
in the composition of boards of directors. It stated:

The composition of a company's Board must be a matter of legitimate concern to
shareholders. They have the opportunity to confirm all appointments to the Board

which are initiated by the existing directors, and there is a growing acceptance that a properly balanced Board is essential to the well-being of a company. Institutions individually, or where appropriate collectively, are increasingly prepared to suggest change to remedy perceived weaknesses and where necessary to encourage Boards to appoint an adequate number of independent non-executive directors. Institutional shareholders seek to identify serious deficiencies at an early stage, and to initiate appropriate action.

That acceptance by the institutions of their responsibilities over board appointments has been taken further by the Combined Code's recommendation to institutional investors over the way in which they should evaluate the governance arrangements of companies, 'particularly those relating to board structure and composition.'[5]

Board models

Investor involvement in board structure and composition is a clear step in the direction of making boards more accountable to their shareholders. It is a move towards improving both the effectiveness and the accountability of boards, the two issues which lie at the heart of criticisms of the board as an institution. It leaves open, however, the question of whether the unitary board, in the form in which it has become established in Britain and in those countries which follow the same pattern of governance, is the best model on offer. Are there other forms of board which might have structural or procedural advantages over the UK type of unitary board?

The difference between US and UK boards, however, lies more in their composition than in their structure, although that difference has significant consequences for the way in which they work. The board of a US corporation is made up mainly of outside directors and the chief executive officer (CEO) is always a member. The CEO will usually be the chairman and thus will have a major say in the selection of outside directors. CEOs may include other executives on their boards, such as the Chief Financial Officer, the President, or the Chief Operating Officer. The result is that the levers of power—patronage, chairmanship and access to information—are normally in the hands of the CEO. Jonathan Charkham, who is the authority on comparative corporate governance, has described the composition and workings of US boards in his book *Keeping Good Company*.[6] He illustrates his analysis by including Herzel and Shepro's description of a typical US board meeting: 'The CEO would probably be the chairman of the meeting and completely in charge. Generally, he controls both the agenda and the flow of information to the directors. He dominates the meeting and the board plays a quite secondary role.'[7]

Herzel and Shepro go on to say that very little attention is paid to directors by shareholders, the market, or the press. Although, therefore, both the UK and the US have the same board model, they function very differently. In the UK, the board is in charge, it is essentially a collegiate body reaching its decisions by consensus, and the CEO reports to it. In the US, the CEO is normally in charge supported by the board. Of course, the way in which any individual board functions in either country depends on personalities and the character of the company concerned. The point is that the unitary board model is adaptable and so companies in either country can shape the model to suit their culture and customs. The difference between the ways in which the model works in both countries can be accommodated within basically the same unitary structure.

Two-tier boards

The alternative board model in Europe is the two-tier board, which was developed in its present form in Germany, although its origins go back to the Dutch trading companies of the seventeenth century. A two-tier board fulfils the same basic functions as a unitary board, but it does so through a clear separation between the task of monitoring and that of management. The supervisory board (*Aufsichtsrat*) oversees the direction of the business and the management board (*Vorstand*) is responsible for the running of the company. The supervisory board controls the management board through appointing its members and through its statutory right to have the final say in major decisions affecting the company. The structure rigorously separates the control function from the management function, and members of the one board cannot be members of the other. This separation is enshrined in law and the legal responsibilities of the two sets of board members are different.

The supervisory board system dates back to Bismarck and 1870, when the Companies Act Amendment Act made supervisory boards compulsory for joint stock companies.[8] Further legislation in 1937 clarified and formalized the distinction between the control function of the supervisory board and the executive responsibilities of the management board.[9] The supervisory board system was introduced to strengthen the control of shareholders, particularly the banks, over the companies in which they had invested. Shareholdings are more concentrated in Germany than in the UK and most quoted companies have at least one major shareholder, often a family or another company. Banks play an important part in governance as investors, lenders, and through the votes of individual shareholders for which they hold proxies. They are, therefore, well represented on supervisory boards.

It is sometimes argued that US boards with their preponderance of outside directors are moving towards creating a de facto two-tier structure, with a predominantly outside board performing the supervisory function and with an executive committee chaired by the CEO standing in for the management board. This is not an accurate analogy and there are a number of basic differences between a unitary board—even if most of its members are outside directors—and a supervisory board.

First, the unitary board, however many outside directors it has on it, remains in full control of every aspect of the company's activities. It initiates action and it is responsible for ensuring that the action which it has initiated is carried out. All its directors, whether executive or outside directors, share the same aims and the same responsibilities. The supervisory board, on the other hand, may have to approve management action, but it is primarily a monitoring body not an initiatory one. The tasks and duties of the two boards are different in line with their different legal responsibilities. Second, the CEO at least will be on a unitary board, so the board combines executive and outside directors, which the supervisory board is not allowed to do by law. Third, the kind of people who are outside members of a unitary board will be different from those who are members of a supervisory board. This is leaving on one side the question of employee board members. This distinction arises because the members as a whole of an operating board will require a different set of attributes from those that will be looked for from the members of a strictly monitoring body. Even from a monitoring point of view, German supervisory boards often include bankers, whose primary involvement in the company is as lenders rather than as shareholders. They, therefore, may face conflicts of interest and thus could not be classified as independent, in the sense that the majority of outside directors of unitary boards are.

It is, of course, possible for British boards to adopt a two-tier structure, given the freedom companies have under the Companies Act to organize themselves as they will. The board could be made up entirely of outside directors, including the chairman, while the CEO chaired a wholly executive management board. It would not, however, be recognized as a two-tier board in European terms, because the directors of both boards would have the same legal responsibilities. It would still be a unitary board, but one that had chosen to divide its duties between two bodies.

Employee representation

At this point it would be as well to clear up any misunderstandings about the relationship between two-tier boards and the representation of employee interests. Germany provides the clearest example of the two-tier link between employees and boards, although supervisory boards in the Netherlands also provide for employee interests to be taken into account, but do so less directly. The need for employee involvement became an issue in Germany after the First World War, when it was seen as a means of heading off threats of industrial strife. It resulted in two works councillors becoming members of the *Aufsichtsrat*, until that arrangement was abolished under the Nazi regime. The concept was revived after the Second World War in a series of measures, culminating in the 1976 Co-determination Act. This Act laid down the proportion of employee to shareholder representatives and required one of the directors on the management board to be responsible for labour relations.

When the question of giving employees a greater say in the conduct of the enterprises in which they worked became a live political issue in Germany, the two-tier structure provided a means of meeting that aim at the highest level of governance. It enabled the interests of employees to be represented on the supervisory board without involving them directly in the management control of the business. It also helped to fulfil the legal requirement for German boards to promote the interests of the company as a whole. These are described in Sir Geoffrey Owen's booklet, *The Future of Britain's Boards of Directors—Two Tiers or One?* as comprising, 'its own survival and the continued fulfilment of its functional responsibilities towards shareholders, employees, suppliers, customers, state and society'.[10] The two-tier board system has thus provided a channel for employee representation at board level, but that was not why it was devised. The arguments for separating the functions of supervision and those of management are independent from those concerned with ways of representing the employee interest.

Similarly, the question of board representation of employees is independent of whether boards are unitary or two-tier. Employee directors sit on unitary boards in Sweden. In Britain, both British Steel and the Post Office had employee directors on their boards and the Chrysler Corporation has done the same in the US. The other way round, supervisory boards in the Netherlands do not have directors representing the employee interest on them, although all nominations to the board have to be acceptable both to the employees and to the shareholders. I firmly believe that effective employee participation is of real value to companies and that the ideas and talents of the workforce are usually their most under-used asset. I doubt, however, that the board is the best level at which to involve employees, an issue to which we will return.

Positive features of the two-tier structure

The main advantage of the two-tier board structure is its clarity of purpose. The functions of supervision and of management are kept absolutely distinct and they are carried out by different people. The dividing line between direction, which is the task of the unitary board and turning direction into action, which is the task of its executive management is less easy to draw and to maintain precisely. When some of the same people are involved in both, the distinction can become further blurred. Directors of supervisory and of management boards know exactly what their respective legal duties are, whereas executive directors on a unitary board have a dual role. As a result of having clear guidelines, both supervisory and management boards can concentrate their attention on their key tasks; their reporting relationships are well-defined, as are the information needs of the supervisory board.

Shareholders appoint members of the supervisory board, other than the employee members, and they are more clearly representative of particular constituencies than their outside director counterparts on unitary boards. The supervisory board appoints the members of the management board, therefore the linkage between the owners, the supervisors, and the managers is clear and understood. The directors of both boards derive their authority from those who appoint them.

The supervisory board is also in a position to take an entirely independent view of the actions of management, since there is no overlap of membership between the two boards. Unitary board members owe their loyalty to their company, but they also have loyalties to their board colleagues; at times those two loyalties may pull against each other. There should be no such conflict of loyalties for supervisory board members.

As a last point, the two-tier board structure is able to accommodate the representation of interests other than those of the shareholders, without interfering with the responsibility of the management for the running of the business. To the extent that the representation of interests becomes an issue for boards, then the two-tier structure is better designed to deal with it than the unitary structure.

Operating differences

There are significant operating differences between the two types of board structure. The first is that unitary boards are responsible for providing drive and leadership to their companies. In the two-tier structure, it is the management board which is in the driving seat. The management board is responsible not only for the running of the business but for developing its strategy as well. The supervisory board may comment on, or suggest alternatives to, the plans for the future of the business put forward by the management board, but the initiative lies with the latter. Supervisory boards normally meet quarterly and so their ability to exert a positive influence on the management board and on the actual operations of the company is necessarily limited, although there are informal ways of keeping at least the chairman of the supervisory board informed between meetings. Unitary boards meet more frequently and the combined energies of all board members can be focused on raising the level of attainment of their companies.

The second difference in operating practice is that there is little opportunity for interaction between the two boards in the development of plans and policies. This follows from the strict separation of responsibilities between them and from the relative infrequency of supervisory board meetings. In a unitary board, strategies, plans, and policies are developed over time, through debate and argument, within the board and between the board and senior management. This method of hammering out decisions through a dialogue, between those who form policy and those who put it into effect, is one of the strengths of the unitary approach.

The track record

European companies have been successful under both types of board structure and variants of them, so there are no obvious conclusions to be drawn from comparing on a wholesale basis the results of companies run by unitary boards and by two-tier boards. It would be difficult in any case to isolate that part of a company's performance which could be solely attributed to its form of board. It is equally hard to differentiate between the effectiveness of a form of organization and the abilities of the people who make it work.

Criticism in Germany of their board system has focused not on the two-tier structure itself, but on the membership of supervisory boards and on the way they operate. It is said that some directors simply sit on too many supervisory boards and some are insufficiently professional in their approach to their directorial duties. There are doubts too about the ability of supervisory boards, meeting relatively infrequently, to keep up with fast-moving commercial and financial markets. The late Dr Ellen Schneider-Lenné said in her Stockton Lecture, 'If you asked me whether the German two-tier board system is better than the British unitary board, do not expect too much praise of the German system. In my opinion a well-composed unitary board will perform at least as well as a two-tier board.'[11]

It is because broad-brush comparisons can tell us little, that two publications on the workings of different types of board structure are of particular value to the corporate governance debate. *The Corporate Board* by Demb and Neubauer[12] is based on research carried out at the International Institute for Management Development in Lausanne, involving interviews with seventy-one directors serving on more than five hundred boards in eight countries. Its conclusions are, therefore, drawn from practical experience across national boundaries. The authors' research brings out that the views of directors over the role of the board are remarkably uniform, regardless of country or culture. Their views, however, over how boards should be involved in governance are remarkably diverse. The significant point is that this diversity of view applied even when directors were on the same board, or operated within the same national setting.

Jonathan Charkham's *Keeping Good Company*,[13] to which reference has already been made, gives an admirably lucid account of board systems in the UK, the US, Japan, France, and Germany. His book explains the governance framework within which boards in these different countries operate and the nature of the checks and balances to which they are subject. It describes the variety of ways in which companies are directed and controlled, as seen from the outside. *The Corporate Board* complements this approach by looking at governance from within, from the viewpoint of board members themselves.

After considering how other board systems work, there remains the question of whether there are lessons to be drawn from the workings of two-tier boards, which could be relevant to the chairmen of unitary boards.

Conclusions

Adopt the two-tier system?

The first conclusion which I would draw would be that there would be nothing to be gained by attempting to impose a common two-tier structure across the European Union in the name of harmonization. This is partly because such structural advantages as the two-tier model has do not seem to be decisive in terms of either effectiveness or accountability. It is also because two-tier boards and unitary boards are but parts of integrated business systems, which have evolved to suit their particular economic and social environments. A great deal more than the structure of the board would have to be changed to graft the two-tier approach successfully on to a company previously run by a unitary board. A further point is that it is simple to change the boxes on an organization chart, but quite a different matter to change the way in which people work. The trap over trying to alter board systems by fiat is that the structure may change to comply with the law, but the chances are that the working of the system will carry on as before.

The two systems coexist in France and Switzerland, with the majority of companies in both countries opting for the unitary model. Thus the only argument for structural harmonization would seem to be one of bureaucratic tidiness rather than for any practical benefits which it might bring. Convergence in the processes of governance is in any case being brought about, as we shall see, by market forces and this is irrespective of structure. It is nevertheless worth noting that, in Britain, the Labour Party included a reference to two-tier boards in its 1994 strategy statement, which read as follows: 'We believe that a supervisory board could provide a valuable forum for focus on longer-term strategy of the company, and we will provide a statutory basis for a two-tier board structure for those larger companies who choose to adopt it.'[14]

The statement seemed to fail to appreciate that strategy is not the province of the supervisory board in a two-tier structure. It did, however, recognize that there was no statutory basis for unitary boards either and, probably as a result, nothing further was heard on the issue of board reform until the setting-up of the Company Law Review Steering Group in 1998.

Clarify the board's role

There are, however, two features of the two-tier system worth taking note of—the clarity of its design and the separation of duties between the two boards. The aim should be to reflect as far as possible these positive features of the two-tier model within the unitary structure. Taking clarity of design and purpose first, the unitary board provides scope for confusion over what the duties of directors to the company entail, over where the division lies between direction and management, and over the combined responsibilities of executive directors for direction and for management. All of which implies that time devoted by chairmen, to ensuring the agreement of their boards as regards their functions and how they should be carried out, will be well spent.

Equally, there should be formal methods of induction for newly-appointed board members, rather than the expectation that they will pick the job up as they go along. The fact that the unitary structure is less well-defined than the two-tier structure means that more effort has to be put into pinning down exactly what the role of a unitary board member is. This requires debate and agreement among the members of any particular board, since there is no universal blueprint, and achieving this understanding is clearly the chairman's task.

Strengthen board independence

Dealing next with the separation of duties, the members of a supervisory board are well-placed to carry out their monitoring function on behalf of the shareholders, because of their independence from management. Their only link with management is that they appoint the members of the management board, and to that extent they have some commitment to their appointees. The supervisory directors can exercise full control over the management proposals which come to them, because they are not in any way committed to those proposals in advance. A problem which can arise with unitary boards is that by the time projects reach board level for approval, the executive commitment to them may be such that the outside board members can hardly do other than go along with them.

Actions which chairmen are able to take to strengthen the independence of decision of a unitary board, in the interests of the shareholders, include having sufficient independent directors of the right kind on the board and making sure that the board's power of decision is not pre-empted. Pre-emption can be avoided by ensuring that proposals come to the board at an early enough stage in the decision-making process. This again is a responsibility of the chairman. At times a persuasive executive case for a single course of action is put to a board, as if there were no rational alternative. The presentation may include other less compelling options, in order to steer board members towards the preferred solution. For outside directors to challenge the executive directors, at this stage in the decision-making process, could result in confrontation and/or an unacceptable degree of delay. The only way for chairmen to prevent pre-emption of this kind is to ensure that proposed lines of action and their alternatives are discussed in principle at the board, well before a major management commitment is made to any of them.

What counts is the way boards work

The basic structure of the unitary board does not seem to me to be in question. The issues arise over the membership of unitary boards and over the way in which they function. Unitary boards have shown themselves capable of directing businesses competently, of setting high standards of conduct, of being responsive to shareholders, and of taking account of society's needs. In sum, in spite of inevitable individual failures, unitary boards have proved both effective and accountable, the two fields in which boards have been under attack. To be effective and accountable, any board, whatever its structure, has to be properly led by its chairman, to be well-composed in Dr Ellen Schneider-Lenné's words, and to be made up of directors who are both committed to the aims of their enterprise and who can devote enough time to meet the demands imposed by their increasingly arduous duties.

It is the responsibility of the shareholders, and particularly of the main institutions among them, to assure themselves that the companies in which they have invested other people's money are headed by effective boards and to hold them to account for their performance. It is the responsibility of chairmen to ensure that their boards match up to the legitimate expectations of their shareholders.

Notes

1. Drucker, Peter (1976). 'The Bored Board', *The Wharton Magazine*, Fall, Vol. 1/1.
2. Monks, Robert A. G. and Minow, Nell (1991). *Power and Accountability*, New York: HarperBusiness.
3. Institutional Shareholders' Committee (1991). *The Role and Duties of Directors*, April.
4. Institutional Shareholders' Committee (1991). *The Responsibilities of Institutional Shareholders in the UK*, December.
5. Gee Publishing Ltd (1998). *The Combined Code*, June (ISBN 1 86089 036 9), Principle E.3.
6. Charkham, Jonathan (1994). *Keeping Good Company*, Oxford: Oxford University Press.
7. Ibid., 182.
8. Hopt, Klaus J., Vandenhoek and Rupprecht (1979). *The Functions of the Supervisory Board*.
9. Owen, Sir Geoffrey (1995). *The Future of Britain's Boards of Directors—Two Tiers or One?*, Centre for Economic Performance.
10. Ibid., 11.
11. Schneider-Lenné, Dr Ellen (1992). 'The Governance of Good Business', *Stockton Lecture*.
12. Demb, Ada and Neubauer, F.-Friedrich (1992). *The Corporate Board*, Oxford: Oxford University Press.
13. Charkham, Jonathan (1994). *Keeping Good Company*, Oxford: Oxford University Press.
14. Labour Party (1994). *Winning for Britain—Labour's Strategy for Success*.

6

Taking the Chair

The effort made by a chairman to ensure that meetings are properly conducted may well be the most valuable contribution he makes to the good of his company.

Stanley Dixon[1]

The primary task of chairmen is to chair their boards. This is what they have been appointed to do and, however the duties at the top of a company may be divided, chairing the board is their responsibility alone. The law may only be concerned with the need for there to be a chairman, but board members are concerned with finding the most competent chairman they can, for the good of the company and to ensure that the time which they spend at meetings should be as productive as possible. I agree with Stanley Dixon's conclusion with which this chapter opens, and chairmen of any kind of organization will find his notes on the art of chairing a meeting helpful. Taking the chair at board meetings is the aspect of the job of chairmen which is furthest from the public eye, but the one where their personal contribution is decisive.

It is decisive because to obtain full value from a meeting of any kind is a difficult task. While diligent preparation beforehand by the chairman is essential, there is no way of knowing in advance just how a meeting will develop. We are talking about a collective process and a dynamic one. Everything turns on the way in which people react to the ideas under discussion and to each other. The job of the chairman is to encourage board members to give of their individual best in a cooperative cause.

Conductors of orchestras surely have a fair amount in common with board chairmen. Conductors, however, at least have a score to work to, from which they expect their orchestras to be working as well. Chairmen have to be their own composers and they cannot be sure in advance what tunes their soloists will play, or whether they will perform at all. Where the analogy is certainly to the point is that chairmen, like conductors, are responsible for the success of the performance and to succeed they have to be in control from start to finish. As another authority on chairing committees, John Tropman, has pointed out: 'Committees in trouble have several directors directing at the same time from the same seat.'[2]

Meetings of the board

Aims of the meeting

The aim of a board meeting is for the board to arrive at the soundest conclusions it can on those matters with which it has to deal. This requires all board members to contribute as pertinently as they are able to the discussion. The resource which chairmen have to handle is the time and the talents of their board members. If they can encourage their directors to participate in the board's work to the best of their ability, then the board will be giving the company the leadership that it deserves and board members will feel that their valuable time has been well spent.

The opportunity which a board meeting offers is that of debating the issues before it and of arriving, through collective effort, at better conclusions—better from the company's point of view—than would have been possible without that debate. The board is a deliberative council and it is also the top decision-making body in the company; therefore only those matters which need to go to the summit should be taken there. Equally, a summit commands a wide view and it is precisely this breadth of view which a board should bring to the matters under scrutiny.

The aim which chairmen have continually in mind is that of coming to the best conclusion in the circumstances, not simply reaching an acceptable conclusion. To achieve this, chairmen have to control the discussion in order to keep it to the point, while at the same time encouraging board members who feel they have something worth saying to take part in the debate. This is a difficult balance to hold, because interventions which may not appear to be quite on target may nevertheless be picked up by others and developed usefully. It is from the to-and-fro of discussion that new ways for taking it forward will emerge. The purpose of a board meeting is to enable board members to build on each other's analyses and ideas. The chairman's task is to keep the discussion moving forward until it has achieved all that it can, then to bring matters to a conclusion and to ensure that the conclusion is acted upon.

Place of meeting

It may seem strange to move straight from the purpose of a board meeting to the subject of where meetings should be held. But given that this is the meeting of the company's summit, every effort should be made to ensure that such meetings are as productive as possible. What I find quite extraordinary is how often board meetings are held in inadequate places under unsuitable conditions. I have attended board meetings in rooms which were not properly ventilated, so that the choice was between fresh air and intrusive noise, or quiet and stuffiness leading inexorably to somnolence. I have sat at rectangular board tables, where those on the wings on the same side of the table could never see each other, nor hear each other for half of the time. There is a curious tendency for those who find it hardest to hear to gravitate to the extremities of any meeting table. It seems to me absurd to invest in the services of the best board members you can muster and then to fail to invest in providing them with productive surroundings in which to meet.

When I joined the Court of the Bank of England, we numbered eighteen. We met every Thursday and there were twelve outside directors, four executive directors, and the Governor and the Deputy Governor. We sat in order of appointment on each side of a long rectangular table, with the most recently appointed director ready at midday to move to the doors, through which he (the first woman director joined the Court in 1993) would announce Bank Rate. The announcement was usually 'No Change', but at my first meeting we did, momentously for me, agree a change. I did not, however, enjoy a brief moment of fame in proclaiming it, because those of us who were appointed at the same time sat in alphabetical order, and having a name at the top end of that order, for once worked against me. The Bank's board layout puzzled me, because the length of the table made hearing and taking part in the proceedings difficult. The reason for it was supplied, however, when a senior director, who clearly thought that I was being somewhat too free with my opinions for a new director, said to me, kindly but firmly, 'When I joined the Court, we had to stand up if we had anything to say'. Standing up to speak not only exercised a certain discipline on loquacity, but it also meant that everyone could hear what was said. It was only when the third Governor, under whom I served, took office that the rectangular table was changed for an oval one.

The rules are straightforward. Board members should be able to see each other and hear each other without effort. If microphones are necessary, either the board is too big or the layout is unsuitable. To get the most out of a debate, it is essential for the participants to be able to see each other.

How people express themselves is often as important as what they have to say, because facial expressions and gestures communicate just as words do. Equally, it is only by watching speakers, as well as listening to them, that you can decide when they are coming to the end of what they have to say, or have reached the point when they perhaps ought to be so doing. For chairmen to be in control they have to be in a position to see all the participants, which is why I prefer oval or round tables, or a horseshoe arrangement of seating.

The room should be quiet and the ventilation good. If you want board members to give of their best, you make it as easy as possible for them to concentrate on the matters in hand, from the beginning to the end of the meeting. I favour having no breaks so that the meeting can continue without interruption, with board members helping themselves to whatever refreshments will keep them alert and involved, but with no other distractions.

Board members are individuals and it is up to the board chairman and the board secretary to give thought as to where each should sit and to ascertain their preferences—do they prefer to sit always in the same place or between the same people, or would they rather move around? I took to arriving early at meetings of one board of which I was a member, in order to change the place names if necessary, so as not to have to sit next to a dedicated smoker of Gauloises. In the end I sorted the matter out with the board secretary and nowadays that particular problem would no longer arise.

Many of these matters may sound as if they are of small account, but they are not. Chairmen and board secretaries have only to reflect on the cost of board meetings, in terms of the people involved and of their value to the company, to understand why they need to apply themselves imaginatively to providing their boards with a good working environment.

As a separate point, there are a variety of aids to communication which board members may want to use, from overhead projectors to screens for films or videos. As companies become less anchored to their home base and more international, there will be an increasing demand for video conference facilities. What matters is that any such systems should carry out their respective functions efficiently and unobtrusively. They are there to assist discussion and involvement and not to detract from them by failing to work, or by requiring a rearrangement of people or furniture before they can be brought into action. As a member of the UK board of IBM, I had the privilege of meeting in a board room where all such devices were built in and were an integral part of the design of the meeting place. Again, this seems to me to be a thoroughly justified investment.

Timing of meetings

There is less to be said on timing, other than that meetings should be started on time and that there should be an agreed aim as to when they should finish. An Australian bank had as good a system for starting boards on time as I have yet come across. They paid a fee for attendance at meetings and the total fees for all board members were put ready beforehand on the board table. As soon as the hour for the meeting struck, the amount on the table was divided between those who were then present. After a point, meetings become progressively less effective, and two-and-a-half to three hours is probably as long as it is reasonable to expect board members to play their part in the proceedings enthusiastically and to the full. If a board meeting needs to be longer than that, it is sensible to continue with a second, separate meeting.

As important as the total time for the meeting is the time spent on each agenda item. At one series of meetings which I chaired, the secretary used to put an indicative number of minutes against each item on the agenda. That is attempting to impose too strict a pattern on the proceedings, although it is useful for secretaries to keep a check on how much time their boards spend on specific issues, like strategy, as an input to the board appraisal process. Most chairmen will, in any case, start their meetings with a rough idea of the time to be spent on each of the main items, leaving anything else to be dealt with in whatever time remains. I find it logical to clear matters of report first and then to move on to matters of substance in their order of priority.

Agenda

This leads on to the agenda. The board secretary and the chairman prepare the agenda in consultation with the chief executive, who will know what decisions are required of the board in order not to hold up the progress of the business. Setting the agenda is one of the ways in which chairmen exercise control over the meeting. It is important that the matters to be discussed at a board meeting are signalled by the agenda. This gives directors the chance to reflect on them in advance. It also means that directors who are going to miss meetings can let the chairman know beforehand what their views are on the subjects up for discussion. Directors could feel justifiably aggrieved if matters which were not on the agenda, and on which they had views to express, were dealt with in their absence.

Agenda items for board meetings come under three main headings. There are matters of report which keep the board informed about the company's progress. Such reports deal with matters which are the responsibility of the management, not the board, but they are essential to the board in the carrying-out of its monitoring function. Periodic reports on sales, profits, shares of market, and cash flow come under this heading. The reported figures may have implications which are proper matters for board debate, but it is for chairmen to keep the debate to those grounds and not to allow it to stray into advice from the outside directors to the management on how they should do their job.

As an example, having spent my working life in the food industry, I appreciate only too well the fascination which consumer advertising holds for board members. It is a subject on which everyone is expert; yet the death-knell to good advertising—that is, advertising which will achieve its purpose— is to allow board members any say whatsoever in its execution. That is a management function. But there is a policy aspect to advertising, which is a proper matter for the board to discuss and on which to rule. For advertising is part of the public face of a company and it has consequences for the company's identity and for the way in which the company is perceived by the community.

Therefore, a board should be aware of the advertising which is going out in the name of the company and it is entitled to take a view on whether the overall impact of that advertising is in keeping with the standards of the company. Advertising policy is a matter for the board; advertising execution is the responsibility of management. The line between policy and execution is not always easy to draw in practice, but it is up to the chairman to protect the management from board interference in matters which have been delegated to them.

After matters of report come matters for decision. They may be formalities like sealings, or they may be issues of critical importance like a bid for another company, the raising of funds or an appointment to a key post. The chairman will know which of these decisions have to be taken at any particular meeting and will ensure that board members are equally aware of the time constraints. There is a good deal to be said for having a preliminary discussion of an important issue and so drawing all the points of view on it from around the board table into the open. Board members then come to the next meeting prepared to bring the matter to a conclusion, but having reflected in the meantime on what was said by others the first time round.

This leads on to a third heading, which is the general one, of matters which need airing, or on which the executives are looking to the board for a steer. It might be, for example, that pressure was being brought to bear on the company over an environmental issue. This would not be a matter for the board to deal with itself. It would, however, be for the board to advise what order of importance should be attached to the demands being made on the company, and whether the matter should run its normal managerial course or whether some special form of response was required.

One particular task which should never be given to boards is that of drafting. The board's advice on drafts is invaluable and I have never known a written statement which was not improved as a result of submitting it to the board and listening to their views. Drafting itself, however, is best done by an individual. When companies have a statement of note to make publicly, it should be drafted by one person, preferably by the chairman, with the advice and help of whomsoever they choose.

Board information

In deciding on the board agenda, the board secretary and the chairman also agree what information board members should receive in support of the items on it. The board's absolute requirement for timely and relevant information has already been stressed; without it no board can be in control. Reports should be presented in a consistent form to save the time of board members and to enable straightforward comparisons to be made, against the past or against forecast. The presentation of information can always be improved and board members need to be encouraged to express their views on presentation to the secretary or to the finance director. For example, it is confusing if the figures read chronologically from left to right in one report and from right to left in another, even if that is in line with accounting conventions. When reports are going to the board, the sole test is whether they convey the essential information clearly and concisely to those to whom they are addressed.

In providing board members with the information which they require in order to take decisions, the same considerations apply. The particular point to keep in mind under this heading is that the outside members of the board should not be at an unnecessary disadvantage to the executive members. This may mean giving them some additional background information on why, for example, the company has reached the point where a particular decision is necessary.

Board reports have to be understandable to the non-expert and should provide only the information which is needed to debate the relevant issue intelligently and to come to a judgement on it. Anything more risks obscuring the key points and reduces the chance of the document being read in full. Rudyard Kipling cut every word out of his writings which he judged to be unnecessary; this meant that he intended every word he left in to be read.

He should be the model for those who draft board papers. Equally, the chairman should take it for granted that board papers have been thoroughly studied before the meeting. Nothing deadens a discussion as effectively as opening it with a rehearsal of what the majority of board members have already read.

It is part of the job of chairmen to go through the board papers, as if they were outside directors, to ensure that they provide board members with all the information which they need for the proper discharge of their responsibilities. The reason why this is one of a chairman's essential functions is that the gap between executive and outside directors is one of knowledge and understanding of the business. If outside directors are to play a full part in board proceedings, they must have whatever information is necessary to reduce their disadvantage in this regard to a minimum. It is the responsibility of chairmen to ensure that this happens, but equally it is the responsibility of outside directors to ensure that their chairmen are aware what information they require and in what form.

A recent Australian book on boards makes the point that outside directors should not rely solely on the information which is handed out to them. 'Other means of private research independent of management, such as reading, will increasingly be required.'[3] Quite so.

The course of the meeting

The chairman needs to decide with the chief executive and the board secretary what it is that the board meeting has to achieve. What decisions are required, by when, and on what matters are the management looking to the board for a lead? The chairman's objective is to arrive at the best outcome in respect of each deliberative item on the agenda and to do so by drawing on the collective wisdom of those sitting round the board table. The chairman will ask the appropriate director to introduce each item for discussion and then open the matter up for debate. The chairman's job is to keep the discussion on track, without discouraging the introduction of lateral ideas which may stimulate new lines of thought.

The Bishop of Ely in preaching at the memorial service for a widely-admired Cambridge don said of him: 'A committee's time, with him in the chair, was not time to be wasted, the Chairman's task [being] to hold it to the question needing resolution now (his perception of where that question lay was perhaps his own distinctive brilliance).' That sums up the chairman's task admirably. The chairman has to perceive what needs to be resolved and to keep the discussion moving—moving forward towards that resolution.

This demands an unrelenting concentration on what is being said and it also means making certain that valid points which have been raised are not passed by, just because the main stream of the discussion has taken a different course. Sound points can easily slip from sight as a discussion proceeds, but they need to be addressed and to be built on, and it is for chairmen to see that they are. Equally, chairmen have to avoid valuable time being wasted through misunderstandings. These can arise either from unequal knowledge between directors of the subject in hand, or from the failure of board members to make their points clearly. Chairmen are in the best position to sense both what a speaker meant and how it might have been interpreted by fellow board members. A timely intervention by the chairman can avoid those discussions at cross purposes, which are entirely unproductive and, perhaps because of that, can generate quite unnecessary heat. A way of preventing an issue becoming a debate or argument between individuals on a board is to stick to the helpful convention that directors either speak to the board as a whole, or they address their comments through the chair. This maintains the chairman's control over the proceedings.

Chairmen who want to make the best use of the abilities of their boards aim to promote an atmosphere of openness at board meetings and to make certain that all directors are equally encouraged to express their views. Openness and equality between board members are essential to a thorough debate and chairmen have to work persistently for their achievement. This is particularly so when there are executives, in addition to the chief executive, on a board.

In a management meeting presided over by the chief executive, the executives are being chaired by the person to whom they report and this affects the nature of the discussion at such meetings. The danger is that executive directors may treat a board meeting as if it were a management meeting. It is for chairmen to encourage the executive members of their boards to express their views on issues which do not fall naturally within their bailiwick. The challenge for chairmen is to draw on the differences between the viewpoints of their executive and outside directors, while maintaining their unity as a board team. Interestingly, what most surveys of director opinion reveal is that chief executives would prefer their outside directors to focus on matters of governance, rather than on the formulation of strategy, while this is precisely the area where, in their turn, outside directors consider that they could contribute most, but feel that they are not encouraged to do so by their executive colleagues.

A vigorous description of the way in which outside and executive directors can interact profitably and effectively appeared in the 1990 annual report of

Grand Metropolitan plc. It was written by Sir John Harvey-Jones, the company's deputy chairman and read as follows:

I suspect it is not necessary to say that the non-executives of Grand Metropolitan are a fiercely independent bunch who are never backward in coming forward. Your Chairman and our executive colleagues are not exactly shrinking violets, so our meetings are lively and robust events.

All of us believe that this forceful and open debate helps the Board reach the best possible conclusions. We enjoy the discussions, but serious differences of view are expressed and thrashed out and, in my experience, at some time or other each one of us has contributed to swaying the debate and influencing the company's direction.[4]

The chairman of the Grand Metropolitan board had clearly achieved the aim of enabling both executive and outside directors to speak their minds freely and constructively on a basis of boardroom equality.

I found an interesting comment on this matter of establishing the equality of board members in a booklet, published in 1963, on *The Committee Concept and Business*:

This leads to a neglected but particularly important reason why the chairman of a business committee must be a man of outstanding calibre. Only through his own values, personality and skill can he develop and sustain a high level of morale and mutual respect amongst members in a committee, irrespective of status or the authority relationships which apply outside the committee.[5]

For directors to feel that everyone is equal in the boardroom they have to acquire trust and confidence in their chairman and in the board. Trust and confidence are built on openness and on the willingness of all board members to say what they think, even if it may be critical of colleagues and of their proposals. Openness between board members is not only fundamental to the working of an effective board, it also sets the tone for relationships throughout the company.

Sir Walter Puckey wrote: 'Complete freedom to speak under a reasonably independent chairman is a precious asset.'[6] Complete freedom to speak is the goal to which chairmen, who appreciate the value of board debate, are always working.

Board decisions

When there are matters before the board that require a decision, then that is the end which the chairman will have in view in controlling the discussion. Chairmen are not necessarily working to achieve consensus, although consensus strengthens decisions; they are seeking the best possible decisions in the interests of their company, and those may be decisions which do not command universal support. Chairmen determine when to bring discussions to an end and they sum up where their boards stand, if there is a need to do so. It may be that there is insufficient agreement to reach a conclusion, in which case the chairman has to decide how to achieve the breadth of agreement which will be needed, if the matter is to be settled at the next meeting.

Voting is an unsatisfactory way of resolving an issue over which a board is divided, to quote Sir Walter Puckey again, 'Voting is a concession to weak chairmanship'.[7] I have known a chairman end every discussion by going round the board table asking each director for their view; this is an equally weak form of chairmanship. It is for chairmen to judge the feeling of the meeting and to put propositions to their fellow board members which reflect that feeling. Chairmen are there to give a lead, not to count heads.

Minutes

The decisions arrived at by the board are recorded in the minutes. They are the authority for action and therefore their wording is important. Their wording is also important because they constitute, along with any board papers filed with the minutes, the record of the meeting. A nice judgement is required over how full a record should be kept. The Cadbury board minutes, prior to the merger between Cadbury and Schweppes, only recorded decisions and not discussion, and directors' initials were put against all minutes requiring action. Directors received copies of the minutes which had their initials on them, and those minutes were both their marching orders and their authority for action.

There are times, however, when it could be important for future directors to have some background to a decision, such as how the need for the decision arose in the first place. This may best be done by filing a background brief with the minutes, rather than by extending the minutes.

Individual directors may ask for their dissension to a decision to be recorded in the minutes. This does not alter the responsibility of all members to support decisions arrived at in the board, regardless of their personal views. But it suggests either that the directors concerned see the need to protect their position, or that they may at a later stage use their dissent to undermine someone else's position. Whatever the reason, a recorded dissent is a signal which chairmen will take seriously.

The possibility that the minutes of the board might be used in evidence against it, by one of the authorities with jurisdiction over companies, has tended to make minutes briefer and less informative than they were when they were written for internal use only. From the point of view of anyone interested in business history, this is a loss. But it is the inevitable result of the greater degree of external control now exercised over companies and the more frequent incidence of legal suits. Chairmen's selective memoirs are no substitute for well-drafted minutes backed by the board papers to which they refer.

Chairmen and company secretaries are right to take considerable care over the minutes, which should be circulated as promptly as practicable. The perfunctory way in which minutes are usually dealt with at the beginning of board meetings reflects little appreciation of the time spent in preparing them.

The chairman's approach

Up to this point, I have referred to chairmen rather as if they were impartial judges, listening to the points of view expressed, keeping the discussion relevant, and then summing up the board's conclusions. The chairman has to be impartial in the sense of seeing that all board members who have something worth saying say it and that executive rank or seniority do not undermine the equality of all directors. This is why chairmen normally refrain from expressing their views on an issue, until other board members have had the opportunity to express theirs.

Chairmen, however, are as equal as other board members and as entitled to have their own views on the matters under discussion; to that extent they are partial and take part in the debate. To the degree that chairmen are looked to as representing their companies as well as their boards, they are bound to have their own views on corporate decisions which they may find themselves having to defend or promote publicly. How do they square their own convictions on a particular matter with their task as chairmen to ensure an entirely open debate?

The two positions are reconcilable, provided that chairmen enter the debate prepared to accept their board's judgement and that they are seeking through debate the best possible outcome for the issues under discussion. These provisos are necessary because there are chairmen who regard their boards as rubber stamps. They know what decisions they want to arrive at before the meeting starts, and the directors foregather simply to endorse the conclusions of the chairman or the chief executive.

At one such board, an outside director who queried an acquisition proposal was told that, if the directors were going to get into that kind of detail, board meetings would have to start at breakfast time! Such chairmen do not believe that discussion at the board can contribute anything to executive decisions; their boards are ornamental and serve no useful, deliberative purpose. Autocratic chairmanship of that kind turns the board into an executive committee.

As chairman, I held views with varying degrees of tenacity on most of the issues coming before the board. I also believed that subjecting those views to debate at the board would result in their being improved upon and usually modified. It is only through a thorough debate that you can be sure that all the options have surfaced. However apparently clear-cut an executive proposal may seem, new angles to it nearly always emerge when it is discussed at the board. If the original executive proposition comes through intact, then it has been well tested and its initiator can be confident of its merits.

I mentioned in passing the importance of bringing all the options to the surface. One of my concerns as chairman was to encourage the executives to consider every possible way of tackling a problem, however much that might involve challenging cherished beliefs. The danger is that somewhere in the process of framing executive proposals an idea will be thought to be too radical—'the chairman will never wear it'. There is no way of knowing what chairmen will wear until you try it on them, and I suspect that too often imaginative proposals are not aired for fear that they may offend the chairman's or the company's accepted tenets. This is an important reason why chairmen should encourage openness of debate.

What if the chairman or the chief executive disagree with a proposal which is coming before the board? Clearly it depends on how fundamental the disagreement is. If the issue was one about which the chairman or the chief executive felt so strongly that they would resign should the board go against them, then they must make their position clear before the discussion starts. In that extreme instance, the debate will be about their position rather than the issue which gave rise to it.

The much more common situation is that there is simply a difference of view prior to the matter being discussed at the board. For example, in my former company, it may be that the finance director is proposing that the company should raise more funds and I, as chairman, have doubts about whether this is an opportune time to do so. I would tell the finance director in advance that I was not convinced by his proposal, so that he knew where I stood. He would then put his proposal to the board and I, as a board member, would have the opportunity to express my views on it along with, but after, everyone else. But it has to be clear that, in disagreeing with the finance director, I will, as chairman, accept the board's view when we have argued the matter out. Interventions by chairmen cannot be reconciled with their duty to encourage an open debate, if they put their views so forcibly at the outset as to pre-empt discussion.

The outcome of a finely balanced debate can be affected by the order in which those for or against a proposal speak; and the decision by chairmen when to bring individual board members into a particular debate is one aspect of their control of the meeting. This, in turn, makes the point that chairmen need to know their board members as individuals and as much as possible about the way in which their minds work. Some may have to be encouraged to express their views, even on an issue where their experience is likely to be relevant, others may have to be restrained. It is not only that the opinions of particular board members may be of value at a given point in a debate, they may also have the ability to stimulate new ideas in others.

This stress on the way in which an effective board works as a collective explains why the composition of the board is so crucial. A potential outside director could have just the right career experience, but be unsuitable because of his or her personality. The chairman has to judge in putting forward the name, say, of a particularly forceful person, whether their participation would encourage discussion among other board members or kill it.

The longer board members have been together, the more they will have established their own methods of working as a group and the more important it may become to add new members who will be constructively critical of established views. Because the personal chemistry of board members is so crucial, it is difficult for unitary boards to accommodate new members who are wished on them, for example, as representatives of outside interests. New directors need to be nominated and appointed with the involvement and agreement of all the existing board members.

Committees of the board

One of the ways in which chairmen prevent board meetings from becoming overloaded, and either going on too long or requiring discussion to be curtailed, is by setting up appropriate committees of the board. Many boards appoint finance committees to go through the detail of financial proposals which are beyond the authority of the executives, and to make recommendations on them to the full board. This meets the test of focusing the board's attention on those issues with which it alone can deal and leaving any preliminary work to be carried out below board level. The key to the effective functioning of board committees is that their chairmen should ensure that they stick strictly to their terms of reference and these in turn should be carefully drawn up by the board. A finance committee, for example, should concern itself with the financial consequences of executive proposals, not with the merits of the proposals themselves which are for the board to assess. Equally, the committee has no remit to interfere with the management of the business, or to second-guess the finance director. Its task is to assist the board in coming to its conclusions, except where it has delegated authority to agree specific levels of capital expenditure.

One reason for forming board committees is to make the board's job more manageable; another is to enable the outside directors to play their full part in the governance of the company. It takes outside directors some time to get the feel of a company and of the people who make it up, if their only point of contact is through meetings of the board. Committees of the board provide outside directors with a structure through which to gain a better grasp of the business and one which gives them a role beyond attending board meetings. The provisions of the Combined Code have now made board committees an integral part of the process of direction and control.

Provision A.5.1 states that a nomination committee should be established to make recommendations to the board on all new board appointments, unless the board is small.[8] Provision B.2.1. states that boards should set up remuneration committees to recommend to the board the framework for executive remuneration and its cost: and to determine on their behalf specific remuneration packages for the executive directors.[9] Provision D.3.1. states that the board should establish an audit committee with written terms of reference which deal clearly with its authority and duties.[10] The Code also sets out who should be members of these three committees and requires the chairman of the board to arrange for their chairmen to be available to answer questions at the AGM.[11] It is appropriate to refer in rather more detail to each of the three committees, given the role which they play in the corporate governance system.

Audit committees

Audit committees are there to provide an assurance to shareholders—and to chairmen—that an essential aspect of a board's duties will be rigorously discharged. Since 1978, the New York Stock Exchange has required all listed companies to have audit committees made up solely of independent outside directors. The American Treadway Commission, in its 1987 report, concluded that audit committees played a crucial role in ensuring the integrity of US corporate financial reporting. Even where they may have been formed mainly to meet listing requirements, rather than from conviction, American experience has shown that audit committees soon proved their worth and developed into essential committees of the board.

The Combined Code provides that audit committees should be made up of at least three outside directors, the majority of whom should be independent and that their names should appear in the report and accounts. There is no shortage of useful guidance on the duties of audit committees and those which I have read are included in the bibliography. A straightforward set of terms of reference for an audit committee are outlined in Patrick Dunne of 3i's informative and entertaining book, *Running Board Meetings*; they are to:

- review the financial statements before publication
- consult with external and internal auditors (if there are any) regarding any matters arising in the course of the audit which should be brought to the board's attention
- report to the board on the adequacy of internal systems and financial controls
- report to the board on the scope of the external audit
- recommend to the board the appointment and remuneration of the external auditors.[12]

While an understanding of the requirements of financial reporting and internal control is clearly helpful, audit committee members are there to ask appropriate questions, to pick up any whiff of possible weaknesses in the company's systems, and to oversee the audit process; they are not there to audit the auditors. What they need to have is enough understanding of audit matters to know what questions to ask and how to evaluate the answers. The American Bar Association's *Corporate Director's Guidebook* is quoted as saying that the most important qualifications for an audit committee member remain, 'common sense, general intelligence and independent cast of mind'.[13] Those are qualities which chairmen will be looking for in their outside directors in any case, and they represent a sound basis for picking candidates for audit committees.

An issue which was raised with the corporate governance committee, which I chaired, related to the services, which auditing firms may provide in fields other than auditing, such as, consulting or tax advice. It was argued that, if the provision by an auditing firm of these services to a company became too significant in comparison with their audit business, this would cast doubt on their objectivity as auditors. One proposal, that was put to the committee, and which now has to be back on the governance agenda, was that auditors should be 'quarantined', that is to say that audit firms should be debarred from providing any other types of service to their audit clients. Our committee was not then—ten years ago—persuaded that any potential gains in objectivity would outweigh the limitations such a ban would impose on the freedom of companies to choose their most cost-effective sources of advice. Instead, the committee recommended that fees paid to auditors for non-audit work worldwide should be fully disclosed in the accounts. With this information, shareholders would be able to come to their own judgements over the independence of the auditors whose appointment they were asked to approve.

One of the purposes of an audit committee is to provide an accepted and regular channel of communication between the auditors and the outside directors. This enables auditors to alert board members informally to matters which they may be well advised to keep their eye on, although they do not yet qualify for inclusion in the management letter or in the audit report itself. There is inevitably a tension between auditors and directors over their respective responsibilities and therefore their potential liabilities in the face of failure or fraud. The audit committee provides a forum for reaching agreement on the ground rules in these matters. In the days before audit committees, the auditors would meet with the whole board. This was a formal occasion and gave no opportunity for the kind of exchange of views which can take place through an audit committee. The responsibility for establishing and maintaining a professional relationship between boards and their auditors rests with the audit committee.

The terms of reference of an audit committee are key, if the board is to retain full collective responsibility for financial reporting and control, and if the committee is not to involve itself in too much detail. To avoid this, it may be helpful to include a short sentence in the terms of reference defining what the audit committee is not there to do—that is to say to delve into the management of the business. The terms of reference of an audit committee which I chaired ended with the following statement: 'The Audit Committee shall not be responsible for reviewing executive decisions nor for monitoring the efficiency of the management.'

More fundamentally, however, concerns about the ability of audit committees to meet the expectations of shareholders and regulators, and about auditor independence, will have to be seriously addressed in light of the collapse in 2001 of Enron, the US energy trading company, and of continuing instances of financial misreporting. Accounting standards need to be tightened internationally and the existence of audit committees and internal audit departments are not of themselves sufficient safeguards, especially if there are doubts about the independence of auditors. The effectiveness of an audit committee depends critically on its chairman, but also on its membership, and on the diligence with which it carries out its duties. In the UK, in common with most countries, companies in the financial sector are accountable to regulators as well as to shareholders. The Financial Services Authority has made it clear that chairmen of the audit committees of UK banks will be held responsible for any instances of audit failure. The head of the audit committee of a large British bank reportedly spends two days a week on audit committee work and is paid accordingly.[14] This goes way beyond what would have been expected up to now of an audit committee chairman, even of a financial services company. It suggests that if audit committees are to provide the degree of assurance that boards and investors are looking for, their members will have to devote considerably more time to their duties and to be appropriately rewarded for so doing. The watchwords for the corporate audit process remain independence and vigilance.

Nomination committees

The Combined Code states that a majority of the members of a nomination committee should be outside directors and that the chairman should be either the chairman of the board or an outside director. I believe that the chairman of the board should wherever possible chair this committee, since it is chairmen who are responsible for the working of their boards and who should therefore play a leading part in selecting their team. This is in contrast to other board committees, where the independence of board chairmen is preserved through their not having been party to the discussions and decisions of committees, when the recommendations of those committees come to the board.

The Code gives no guidance on the size of a nomination committee. The Institute of Chartered Secretaries and Administrators recommends a chairman and a committee of three, with large boards considering the addition of more members.[15] Their task under the Code is to recommend all new appointments to the board. In addition, however, the committee is the appropriate body to review the structure and composition of the board, and above all to plan for succession. Succession planning is an understandably sensitive matter and only too easy to put off or to leave to furtive discussions in corridors. The advantage of involving the nomination committee is that succession plans for the top posts in the company become a regular, perhaps half-yearly, item on the agenda. At least the discussion then takes place, rather than being postponed through embarrassment and uncertainty.

I imagine that the size of the committee was left open, partly because it is not crucial and partly because it may vary with the matters under discussion. When, in Cadbury Schweppes, a decision was needed over my successor as

chairman, all the outside directors were formed into a nomination committee under the chairmanship of the deputy chairman and that seems appropriate in that kind of case. Recommendations from a nomination committee
not only put to rest any question of personal patronage over the appointment
of directors, but they also share out the responsibility for not reappointing
directors, who might have assumed that they would be reappointed.
Nomination committees can strengthen the chairman's hand as well when
appointments, which have the support of the board, do not necessarily fit a
particular set of institutional investor guidelines.

Nomination committees may, in addition, be the most appropriate bodies
to oversee the arrangements for the induction of new board members. The
Institute of Chartered Secretaries and Administrators have published a commendably clear booklet on *The Appointment and Induction of Directors*.[16] An
equally useful and informative guide, but this time for those considering
whether to take up an outside directorship, is Egon Zehnder's publication—
What a Non-executive Director Needs to Know.[17]

Remuneration committees

The Code provides for remuneration committees to be made up exclusively
of independent, outside directors. On numbers, the Institute of Chartered
Secretaries and Administrators recommends a committee of three, but going
up to four or five for companies with larger boards.[18] The committee's job is
to agree with the board the company's framework of executive remuneration
and its cost and to determine specific remuneration packages for each of the
executive directors. They consult with the chairman and/or chief executive
over their proposals and are entitled to whatever advice they feel they need
from within or without the company. They are equally entitled to the sympathy of all board members for taking on one of the most invidious and
time-consuming duties with which board committees are charged.

In the first place, the pay of executive directors has become complex and
their remuneration packages are made up of a number of elements, varying
in their time frame and in the degree to which they are dependent on corporate results of one kind or another. This is why the committee's work is both
onerous and time consuming. It is also by definition invidious, because committee members are determining the remuneration of their colleagues. Quite
apart from that, they face criticism of cheeseparing if executive directors
leave for higher offers elsewhere and criticism for generosity at the expense
of the shareholders, if they are thought to be paying over the odds. Sadly,
in Britain, pay attracts more public attention than do the results to which pay

is related. A final problem is the lack of accepted benchmarks. There used to be relatively stable relationships between pay at the top and the pay of the average employee; these differentials seem to be culturally determined, in that they were different in different countries. Those relationships no longer hold and the divide between the 'stars' and the rest has grown wider. Globalization has confused the situation further by widening the scope for comparing rewards for particular posts. International comparisons are only valid if all the other factors, like tax, are taken into account and they are often not relevant to those who choose to cite them.

In the face of all these difficulties, there is some firm ground on which committee members can stand. First, the more demonstrably pay is related to performance, the better both for the recipients and for the shareholders. Second, the reverse side of that coin, the less that is paid for failure whether by keeping contracts short or through mitigation, the less contentious the parting. Understandably and rightly, the contrast between loss to employees and shareholders and generosity to directors who presided over that loss is unacceptable.

Finally, the one benchmark which remuneration committees can and should take into account in setting the level of pay of top executives is how their remuneration fits into the pay structure of the company as a whole. The results which companies achieve are due to the efforts of all those who have contributed to them. There, therefore, needs to be an acceptable relationship between the pay of the average employee, that of the different levels of management and that of the executive directors. The commitment of everyone in a company is strengthened if the reward system appears fair for all ranks in an organization, a point to which we will return.

Board committees

When audit committees were first proposed, it was argued by some chairmen of UK companies that there was a danger that they would usurp the function of the board and that the board as a whole should perform the audit function. The problem with this view was that boards did not have the time to fulfil the duties of an audit committee effectively and that board meetings did not provide a fruitful forum for dialogue between auditors and directors, as those of us who sat in on such meetings will testify. The same reservations were expressed when further board committees were proposed. The concern was that these committees might become inner cabinets of the board, thus weakening the board's authority.

There is no reason why board committees should undermine the position of the board in any way, provided that their status as committees of the board is rigorously maintained. They are established by the board. Their terms of reference and membership are set by the board. They report their recommendations to the board, which is responsible for deciding on their implementation. Board committees have no powers of their own, except where the board has delegated powers to them. Authority, therefore, remains with the board, which is responsible for ensuring that the terms of reference of their committees are clear and that they are reviewed annually. It is up to the chairmen of board committees to keep their committees within their bounds.

The chairman's authority

Chairmen are put in charge of boards by their colleagues to ensure that board meetings will be run efficiently and that their time will not be wasted. Board members expect the chairman to exercise the degree of control needed to complete the board agenda in the accepted time and to arrive at the best conclusions of which the board is collectively capable. As long as chairmen use their authority impartially, with a view to expediting the business of the board, they will have the full support of their colleagues. Where the remaining directors can help is by keeping their fellow board members in line informally, so that it does not always fall to the chairman to enforce discipline.

The difference between the authority of chairmen and that of chief executives is that chairmen carry the authority of the board, while chief executives carry the authority delegated to them by the board. Chairmen exercise their authority on behalf of the board; chief executives have personal authority in line with the terms of their appointment. One of the responsibilities of chairmen is to represent the board between meetings when necessary. Chairmen hold their position through retaining the confidence of their boards.

What board members are looking for from their chairmen is that they should command their respect. Chairmen win the respect of their boards by preparing for meetings conscientiously and by their concentration and control during meetings. They have to be ready to listen carefully to everything that is said, and listening is an underrated accomplishment. They need to extract from a discussion what it is that the speakers really mean, which points are relevant to the matter in hand, and how they can be used to come not just to a conclusion, but to as good a conclusion as possible. Chairmen who can lead their boards, rather than driving them, to arrive at balanced judgements will have earned the respect of their colleagues. The final requirement is that chairmen should not take themselves entirely seriously—a certain sense of the absurd is in order.

Notes

1. Dixon, Stanley (1975/76). 'The Art of Chairing a Meeting', *Accountants Digest*, Winter.
2. Tropman, John E. (1980). 'The Effective Committee Chair, a Primer', *Directors & Boards*, Summer.
3. Moodie, Ann Maree (2001). *The Twenty-First Century Board*, Sydney: Australian Institute of Corporate Directors, p. 20.
4. Grand Metropolitan plc, *Annual Report*, 1990.
5. Brodie, M. B. (1963). *The Committee Concept and Business*, Henley Administrative Staff College.
6. Puckey, Sir Walter (1969). *The Board Room*, London: Hutchinson, 106.
7. Ibid., 198.
8. Gee Publishing Ltd (1998). *The Combined Code*, June (ISBN 1 86089 036 9), 15.
9. Ibid., 19.
10. Ibid., 23.
11. Ibid., C.2.3.
12. Dunne, Patrick (1997). *Running Board Meetings*, London: Kogan Page, 90.
13. Barnette, Curtis H. (1999). 'Realistic Expectations for Audit Committees', *Directors & Boards*, Winter.
14. *The Economist*, February 9–15, 2002.
15. Institute of Chartered Secretaries and Administrators (1998). *Terms of Reference: Nomination Committee*, October.
16. Institute of Chartered Secretaries and Administrators (1998). *The Appointment and Induction of Directors*, April.
17. Egon Zehnder International (1999). *What a Non-executive Director Needs to Know*.
18. Institute of Chartered Secretaries and Administrators (1998). *Terms of Reference: Remuneration Committee*, October.

7

The Chairman and the Chief Executive

There are probably as many ways of being a chairman as there are chairmen themselves.

The Role of the Chairman[1]

The chairman's role

The role of a chairman is a personal one. It will vary with individual chairmen, with the boards for which they are responsible, with their chief executives if they do not hold both posts, and with their companies. It will also vary through time. There is no straightforward job description to which chairmen can work. Chairmen have to decide for themselves just what they are able to do for their boards and for their board colleagues, which no one else can and just what it is that their boards expect of them. My interest in writing on this subject is to promote more discussion about the varied aspects of the chairman's role and the ways in which they can be undertaken. It is for individual chairmen to judge which of the issues thus raised are relevant, as far as they are concerned, and what personal balance to strike between the different duties which chairmen carry out.

The chairman's title

As I explained in the preface, I use the word 'chairman' in its accepted dictionary sense to include men and women equally. It is, of course, for individuals who take the chair of any organization to determine how they wish to be addressed. Holders of the post in British companies have in general retained the title of chairman, whether a man or a woman is in the chair. Whether they call themselves chairman or some variant of that title is a personal matter. What may be more relevant to the outside world is whether they add a description, such as 'executive' or 'non-executive', because that signals how they see their role. Problems arise when the signal is misleading.

Heidrick and Struggles published a survey in 1987 which addressed this question of the way in which chairmen described their relationship with their board colleagues:

'Non executive chairman', 'executive chairman', 'chairman and chief executive'— different titles but do they in fact signify different and separate responsibilities? Our survey showed that titles can be very misleading. Many of those chairmen surveyed who are acknowledged to run very successful companies and are thought to be non executive are anything but that. We found that they are either plainly or overtly regarded as executive by their subordinates or they are in effect the chief executive because of the degree of control they exercise over the nominated chief executive.

Even in the very large companies where the appointment of the chairman is handled through long-established and formal procedures, we found that the chairmen are fully executive in all but name.

We also found a similar, but reversed, position in those companies which genuinely had a non executive or part time chairman. In those circumstances, and in the overwhelming majority of cases, the chief executive was in effect the executive chairman.[2]

These conclusions seem to me to be too sweeping, since there has to be a fundamental difference between combining and dividing the jobs of chairman and chief executive, even taking into account that different individuals will split the work between them differently. What is significant is that this passage brings out how much confusion there is about the role of the chairman and the way it should be described. The object of attaching labels to the chairman's title is to clarify their position to those in the company and to those outside it. If those labels then turn out to be misleading or plain inaccurate, it is better to drop them.

I would suggest that there are two distinctions which matter, by which I mean that they convey useful information to all concerned about the chairman's role in any particular company. The first is whether the jobs of the chairman and the chief executive are separate or combined, and the second is whether chairmen spend most or only part of their time with the companies whose boards they chair. These are straightforward facts and assist in understanding the part which individual chairmen play in their companies.

On the executive/non-executive issue, J. G. Beevor was surely right when he wrote: 'No chairman is wholly non-executive'.[3] In its textbook sense, the term 'executive' means having the executive authority to put decisions into effect. Executives, therefore, have people who report to them and to whom they can give instructions. By that test, I was a non-executive chairman of Cadbury Schweppes, since the only person directly responsible to me was my secretary and it was the chief executive who issued all instructions. I had a functional or 'dotted line' relationship with the company secretary and with the finance director, in order to fulfil my responsibilities for the work of the board and for the financial state of the business, but they both reported directly to the chief executive.

Although I was non-executive in the sense of not having the authority to give management instructions of any kind, I do not think that the label 'non-executive chairman' would have been helpful, either inside or outside the company. My main job was as chairman of the company in which I had spent my working life and thus I carried more responsibility for the business than the description 'non-executive' would have implied. Hugh Parker's view is that: 'any chairman who calls himself—or allows himself to be called—a 'non-executive chairman' comes perilously close to being a non chairman.' [4]

Equally, on the question of time. I spent most but not all of my time on my duties as chairman of Cadbury Schweppes. I was not, however, and no chairman can be, a 'part-time chairman'. We remain chairmen of our boards, irrespective of the day of the week, of the time of day, or of any other chairmanships which we may hold. My conclusion is that the realistic solution is to stick to two titles. Chairmen are either, chairmen and chief executives, or chairmen, *tout court*.

Relationships

There are two more general aspects of the chairman's role which need to be kept in mind. First, chairmen are the leaders of their board teams and so their role cannot be defined in isolation from the roles of the other members of the team. Chairmen are concerned with the effectiveness of their boards as a whole and their task is to provide whatever form of leadership is needed to bring out the best in their board teams. Second, the team members will change through time as will the challenges facing their companies; thus the role of their chairmen does not remain fixed from appointment to retirement. Chairmen themselves change too as they gather experience or move towards handing over to a successor. One of the fundamental questions about the composition of boards is whether they include directors who can talk openly to chairmen about their chairmanship.

I am conscious of the importance of seeing board relationships as a whole and of the way in which the pattern of a chairman's job changes through time, because I have worked in a number of different combinations of posts at the head of a company. I was chairman and managing director of Cadbury Group Ltd from 1965 to 1969, at which point Cadbury and Schweppes merged. I then became deputy chairman and managing director of Cadbury Schweppes Ltd, until I succeeded Lord Watkinson as chairman in 1974.

During my fifteen years as chairman of Cadbury Schweppes plc, I shared the responsibility for the development of the business with two chief executives and three deputy chairmen, one of whom was also chief executive.

Although I have practical experience of different ways of splitting the top jobs, it is in the narrow context of one business as it grew. My comments, therefore, on the relationship between chairmen and their board colleagues are no more than that. They are comments to provoke thought and discussion, in the hope that such discussion will help chairmen decide what division of responsibilities at the top will best meet the needs of their particular situation. While the focus is on the separation or combination of the posts of chairman and of chief executive, that does not mean that the importance of other board positions, especially that of the deputy chairman, should be overlooked.

It is logical, however, to concentrate in this chapter on the respective roles of chairmen and of chief executives before broadening the discussion to include the whole of the top team. The relationship between chairmen and chief executives has become an issue in its own right in the debate on governance in Britain and is even being questioned in the US, where the combination of the two top posts has long been taken for granted.

Checks and balances

The Committee on the Financial Aspects of Corporate Governance emphasized, in its report, the crucial part which chairmen play in securing good corporate governance and went on to say:

Given the importance and particular nature of the chairman's role, it should in principle be separate from that of the chief executive. If the two roles are combined in one person, it represents a considerable concentration of power. *We recommend*, therefore, that there should be a clearly accepted division of responsibilities at the head of a company, which will ensure a balance of power and authority, such that no one individual has unfettered powers of decision. Where the chairman is also the chief executive, it is essential that there should be a strong and independent element on the board.[5]

The Committee was fully aware that what mattered was the board structure in its entirety and not solely whether the two top posts were combined. One of the more vocal criticisms of the Committee's recommendations was, however, that it should have made their separation mandatory for listed companies. This may primarily have reflected the lessons learnt by investors during a recession, but it also revealed a new and welcome interest in the importance of governance structures. A sound corporate structure cannot of itself ensure commercial success, but one without appropriate checks and balances increases the risk of disaster. What are, therefore, the respective roles of chairmen and of chief executives and how do they fit together at the head of a business?

Combined or separate?

The chairman/chief executive

The most unambiguous definition of the position of chairman is when it is combined with that of chief executive. There is then no question of a division of responsibilities and what needs to be established is the relationship between the board and the chairman/chief executive.

In discussing the advantages and disadvantages of combining the posts, there are some background points to keep in mind. One is that, taking British companies as a whole, it remains the most favoured approach to defining the top job, although there has been a marked drop in the number of public companies which combine the roles since the appearance of governance codes. In 1989, half of *The Times* top 1000 companies designated their senior director as chairman and chief executive, by 1994 fewer than one-quarter did so. However, it would be normal in a smaller company for whoever is running the enterprise to combine both roles. Given that there are roughly fifteen hundred times as many private as public companies in Britain, one person at the head of the business has to be the most common arrangement.

This runs on to a second point which is that most companies are founded by an individual, who is likely to be the owner and the manager. All being well, they remain in charge of their businesses as they grow, being responsible for their direction and their management. In that sense they are chairmen/chief executives. At some stage in the development of the business, reasons can arise for wanting to differentiate between the two posts, such as the introduction of outside sources of finance, ownership and management becoming divorced, or the founder wishing to take more of a back seat.

This may sound as though the reason for splitting the top posts is largely a question of size. Clearly growth and reaching the point where one person at the head of a business finds the load too great is often a trigger for dividing the leadership responsibilities. Family businesses, however, whatever their size may equally benefit from bringing in an outside chairman. Here the advantage is their objectivity in relation to family issues and their experience in other fields, like finance. The difference which size makes is that the outside chairmen of small to medium-sized family businesses may formally

spend only a strictly limited amount of time with their companies, like chairing a monthly board meeting, but they are available for disinterested and
independent advice when called upon.

Heading the company

Whatever the reason, dividing the responsibilities for heading a company
means dividing a position which was originally a unity. This concept of unity
at the top is of crucial importance in considering how the job might be
divided. It is an issue which should never be lost sight of and to which we will
return. At this stage, the point which is being registered is simply that the two
top posts are naturally combined in one person in the formative stages of a
company's development.

The extract from the 1992 Committee Report referring to the chairman's
role has already been quoted (page 104). Following it, reference was made to
the criticism that the Committee should have made separation of the two
posts mandatory for listed companies. The Committee's code was entitled the
Code of Best Practice and that is precisely what it was. In 1991, twenty-eight
companies out of the FTSE 100 combined the role of chairman and chief executive.[6] Many of those companies were universally well-regarded and therefore
there was no evidence to support the claim that best practice required the separation of the two posts. On the other hand, in the wake of Maxwell, the dan-
gers of the concentration of power if one person held both positions, without
effective checks and balances at board level, were only too clear. The pressure
to separate the two posts came mainly from institutional investors. This was
precisely the manner in which codes were intended to work. They are neither
mandatory nor unduly prescriptive; they set out principles which it is up to
boards to follow in ways which make sense to them and to their shareholders.
This allows boards to opt for appointing a chairman/chief executive, provided
that they can satisfy their shareholders that they have good cause to do so.
To proscribe that option would be unwarranted.

The checks and balances included in the 1992 Code of Best Practice are significant. First, there needs to be a clearly accepted division of responsibilities
at the head of the company such that no one individual has unfettered powers of decision. Second, where the chairman is also the chief executive, it is
essential that there should be a strong and independent element on the
board, with a recognized senior member. The recommendation that one of
the outside directors should be designated as the person to whom directors
or senior executives could turn in the event of concerns about the leadership
of the company was new, but not original. It has always fallen to the outside
directors to sort out problems related to their chairman/chief executive,

should they arise. Unless, however, one of the outside directors was the accepted person to whom other board members would turn in time of trouble, there could be a period of indecision with no one taking the lead to the detriment of the company.

Leadership

When it comes to the practical argument for retaining the position of the founder of a company and combining the role of the chairman with that of the chief executive, it is, at its simplest, that the combination provides the company with the strongest possible leadership. There is no ambiguity about who is head of the enterprise. For those in the company and for those outside it, who have a direct or indirect interest in its affairs, the source of authority is clear. One person is responsible for ensuring that the board frames the company's strategy and the policies which accompany it, and the same person is responsible for putting these into effect. The accountability of the chairman/chief executive is unequivocal.

To take a British example, this appears to have been the argument advanced by the board of Guinness, when they appointed their chief executive as their chairman after the acquisition of the Distillers company in 1986. The board had originally agreed to appoint an independent chairman of the highest standing, once the acquisition had gone through, but then appear to have taken the view that only a unified command at the top of the combined company could achieve the targeted, post-acquisition results. The subsequent acceptance by the shareholders in general meeting of the board's decision to go back on their commitment to appoint an independent chairman meant, either that they were convinced by the argument that the necessary leadership could only be exercised by one person, or that they did not wish to face a confrontation.

Reasons for combining the roles

The arguments, therefore, on the side of combining the roles of the chairman and of the chief executive are that it is common practice, that it is the way in which companies are run by their founders, and that it provides undisputed leadership internally and externally. Lastly, we are not simply discussing the narrow question of whether there should be one or two people at the head of an enterprise. Either way they are part of a board. Thus it is the way in which the board as a whole works, which sets the framework for those at its head. It is the counterbalance provided by the other board members which will determine whether or not the combination of the two posts confers an unacceptable degree of power on one person.

Chairman but not chief executive

There are a number of arguments for separating the roles of chairman and of chief executive. First, that different mixes of ability and experience are required for the two posts. Second, that it is up to the chairman to build the board team, a task which takes time and commitment. Third, that putting the two positions together concentrates a great deal of power in the hands of one person. Finally, that the combination makes it more difficult for the board to carry out its supervisory function.

Differences between the roles

On the first argument, the two posts call, I would suggest, for somewhat different qualities and strengths. Both the chairman and the chief executive need to have the capacity to lead, but leadership of the board is not the same as the leadership required to turn the board's decisions into action. Given that the board's job is to define the purpose of the company and how it is to be achieved, its chairman needs to have strategic sense, the ability to analyse the competitive environment and the capacity to stand back from the business of today.

There is an understandable difference in time horizons between a chairman, who assumes a responsibility for the long-term survival of the enterprise, and a chief executive, who appreciates that, unless this year's budget is delivered, there may be no long-term future for the chairman to consider. The chief executive, in carrying out the board's strategy, has above all to have the ability to make the right things happen. Of course, one person can be excellent both at strategy and at putting strategy into effect, as all successful commanders have been, but most of us are better at one than the other, or become better at one than the other.

Antony Jay of 'Yes Minister' fame, whose writings on management should be better known, draws a forceful distinction between the roles of the chairman and of the chief executive in his book, *Corporation Man*:

> The difference is so profound that it is practically impossible to discharge both duties properly at the same time. The present and the future do not run in harness: their demands and emphases move at a different pace and sometimes pull in opposite directions, and it is rarely satisfactory if the conflict takes place in a single man's mind. If one man tries to do both jobs, one of them is likely to go by default. [7]

The job which most probably will go by default is that of creating tomorrow's company out of today's. Separating the roles, therefore, provides a safeguard against the future being mortgaged to the present. It also presents an opportunity to appoint people with different strengths, and perhaps of different ages and backgrounds, to the top two posts, thereby spreading the workload between them and drawing on a wider range of attributes than would be possible with a single appointment.

The chairman's task

Next comes the chairman's responsibility for the composition of the board and for the way in which it operates. Directing an enterprise through a board is a more difficult form of governance than is commonly supposed. It is a fundamental error to regard committees of any kind as natural forms of governance or to believe that if you sit competent people of goodwill around a boardroom table, they will function as an effective board. Boards have to be pieced together and then made to work. Building an effective board takes time and patience on the part of board members, but especially on the part of their chairman. It is the chairman's task to turn a group of capable individuals into an effective board team. This demands application and an understanding of the nature and motivations, and strengths and weaknesses, of all members of the board. It means spending time with each director to appreciate how they see their roles as board members and in turn assisting them to contribute as incisively as possible to the work of the board. The object is to enable board members to work together as a team, in order that they may achieve as a group what would be beyond them separately. This requires a talent for listening, for leading, and for inspiring, and the time to do so.

All this is particularly true of a unitary board. Its potential advantages are its singleness of purpose and its capacity to integrate inside knowledge and outside experience in the service of an enterprise. Turning that potential into reality is the job of the chairman. Chairmen have to win agreement on the purpose of their boards and on how executive and outside directors can best work together in pursuit of that purpose. Members of an effective board work together as a team, but retain their independence of judgement; they also balance their loyalties to each other and to the board. These are some of the tensions at work within a board and without the right degree of tension boards would be too comfortable and complacent to do their job. It is for chairmen to manage these tensions constructively. As Clutterbuck and Waine point out in *The Independent Board Director*: 'Getting the balance of creative, positive conflict right is one of the chairman's most difficult tasks.'[8] There has to be a balance on a board between individuality and collegiality, and between continuity and change. It is chairmen who are responsible for finding these crucial points of balance.

As more is expected of boards and demanded of directors, the scale of the chairman's job as team leader has grown with those expectations and demands. I believe that the size of the task of building and heading a first division board are underrated, as is the difference which a competent and committed chairman can make to board effectiveness. It is asking a great deal of a chief executive to discharge the full responsibilities of a board chairman in parallel with running the business. The test for those who combine the top posts is how much of their time do they devote to coaching their board team?

Concentration of power

The third argument concerns the concentration of power and this has to be addressed, because of the way in which companies are governed in practice rather than in theory. Shareholders, in the normal course of events, have little control over the actions of the board which they have appointed, or in whose appointment they have acquiesced. The safeguard on which they are relying is that the board keeps their interests in mind and monitors the management to that effect. This safeguard is, however, structurally weakened if the chairman of the board is also responsible as chief executive for the management of the business.

The separation of the two roles builds in a check and a balance. Chairmen are responsible for ensuring that their boards take account of the interests of the shareholders and that they carry out their supervisory functions conscientiously. Chairmen, who are also chief executives, have to be scrupulously clear in their own minds when they are acting as the one and when as the other, as they move between the two roles. It can be done and it is done, but it is less demanding on all concerned to divide the roles rather than the individual.

When someone who holds both positions is determined on a course of action, which perhaps entails high risks for the company, who is to challenge their judgement? Their executive directors are their subordinates away from the board meeting and so it falls to the outside directors on the board to question the possible consequences of what is being proposed. It is not always easy for those outside the business to do this rigorously, since chief executives have the staff resources of the company behind them in making their case, whether or not the staff share the possible doubts of the outsiders.

The power of the chairman added to the power of the chief executive presents a formidable combination. This is recognized by those who hold both posts. For example, Lord Blakenham when he was chairman and chief executive of the Pearson group is quoted as saying:

I believe being chairman and chief executive is not an ideal arrangement, although it suits the type of group we have. It is easier to justify if you have a strong board of outside directors than if you have two or three rather cosy directors. If you combine chairman with chief executive and do not have a strong board he becomes too powerful within the group.[9]

That represents a balanced view of the whole question of whether or not the roles should be combined and focuses on the necessary safeguards if they are, first, that chairmen should themselves be conscious that the arrangement is not ideal and, second, that the combination demands a strong board. The importance of the second safeguard is that it is the job of the board as a whole, not just that of the deputy chairman or of the outside directors, to ensure that the chairman/chief executive's power is harnessed for the good of the company.

The more fundamental question is how efficiently can a board carry out its duty to monitor and, if necessary, to replace the chief executive, when the chief executive is also its chairman? The understanding that one among the outside directors is recognized as the senior ensures that there is a designated director with whom board members can register their concerns about the competence of a chairman/chief executive. This should help to avoid the delay and uncertainty which stood in the way of dealing with this kind of critical situation in the past. It also means that there is a board member who can take the lead in appraising the chairman/chief executive, a process that chief executives can hardly be expected as chairmen to undertake for themselves.

The same kind of difficulties arise over succession. When the time comes for chairmen/chief executives to retire, the task of their replacement is more difficult to handle than the retirement of one or the other. Chairmen would normally take the lead over the appointment of the successor to the chief executive, and one of their responsibilities is to see that there are potential successors. Equally, it is for the board, and particularly for the outside members of the board, to arrange for the chairman's succession. Chairmen/chief executives are in a position to have a major say in their own departure and over who should succeed them. This may not result either in a timely retirement or in a satisfactory handover. It is significant that Harold Geneen, who was highly successful in building up ITT, but had little time for boards of directors, should have failed so conspicuously in the matter of his own succession. This comes out clearly in Robert Schoenberg's book on Geneen's remarkable career. He dominated ITT for twenty years and increased its sales nearly thirty times to make it a major international company. But his business empire fell apart when he retired, too late and having failed to bring on a successor.

The conclusion is that there needs to be someone on the board who is in a position to tell chairmen/chief executives when the time has come for them to go, and to make sure, in the meantime, that responsibility is being handed on to potential successors.

Responsibility for the board

The final argument is in a sense an extension of the same point. It is that chairmen, whose primary responsibility is ensuring that the board works as it should, will find it easier to discharge this responsibility in full than chairmen/chief executives. For chairmen/chief executives this is only part of their job and not the part on which their performance will be judged outside the board. What is at stake is not solely the board's supervisory role—the single head having the responsibility as chairman of monitoring their own actions as chief executive—though that is an important element in the argument as far as shareholders are concerned. It also applies to the board's initiatory role, to its constructive questioning of policies and plans and its contribution to strategic thinking, let alone to taking the lead in assessing the performance of the board.

The board is a deliberative body and its deliberations take a different shape from those of a management committee. As has already been discussed, its members have equal duties and responsibilities and it is for chairmen to see that board members, executive and outside directors alike, participate in board debates on equal terms with their colleagues. When the relationship between the board members and the chairman is only through the board, then executive directors are clear that they are not in a management forum and that they are expected to act as full directors of the company. If the chief executive is in the chair, then both the chief executive and the executive directors have to be conscious that their relationship has changed; at the board meeting the chief executive is no longer their executive head, but *primus inter pares*, first among equals.

In addition, the course of discussion at a board is not the same as it would be in a management committee. The management proposals which come to the board have probably been thrashed out at an executive committee chaired by the chief executive. If the chief executive is then in the chair at the board, it requires a deliberate effort on their part not to have a rerun of the executive committee discussion. The chief executive could also be forgiven for feeling that all the critical points had already been argued out and that the board discussion should therefore be kept as brief as it decently could be.

If, on the other hand, the chief executive and the executives on the board have to present their proposals to a chairman and to outside directors, who were not party to the discussions leading up to the presentation, their approach will not be the same as it was to their fellow-managers. They will be putting their proposals to informed outsiders and will need to think through how their ideas and plans will look to competent colleagues, who do not automatically share the same assumptions. This is likely to add a useful dimension to the proposals themselves and to the grounds for advancing them, quite apart from any modifications to them or new lines of thinking about them, which may arise from the board debate.

Separation of the posts

I am in favour of separating the posts of chairman and chief executive, wherever it is feasible to do so. The small company which has just brought in outside investors can benefit from having an outside chairman, who may spend relatively little time in the company, but who chairs the board and takes responsibility for the company's external relationships, while the managing director concentrates entirely on the running of the business, the job which he or she knows best and does best. In large companies, there is more than enough work to be done at the top for it to be usefully spread between chairmen, chief executives, and deputy chairmen.

The arguments which convince me from my experience that the chairman should not also be the chief executive are that the two jobs call for a different mix of abilities and perhaps of temperaments, and that building and leading a board is a skilled and time-consuming job in its own right. I have also already made clear that I believe chairmanship to be a more demanding and specialized role than is generally appreciated.

I accept that people are more important than structures, so that the right people can make most organizational patterns work. But this is not to say that structures are unimportant. The objective should be to design structures which make it as easy as possible for the holders of office to do what is expected of them. Combining the two posts requires chairmen/chief executives to remind themselves continually which of the two hats they are wearing, or ought to be wearing. Why land an individual with that problem of self-identification, when it can be avoided by giving both the chairman and the chief executive separate responsibilities, so minimizing the likelihood of conflicts of interest?

The US CEO/chairman

An argument on the side of combining the two posts is that around 80 per cent of US public companies are run by CEOs who are also chairmen. There are, however, a number of points to take into account in comparing American and British boards and chairmen. In the first place, the way in which the balance is held between the power of the chief executive and that of the board may owe more to history and culture than to organizational theory. The combined CEO/chairman in the US mirrors the President's position as Head of State and Commander-in Chief. There is an American tradition of, and respect for, personal authority and leadership, within the bounds set by the Constitution.

The British Prime Minister chairs a cabinet, which is collectively responsible for governing the country. The cabinet is presumed to arrive at its decisions through debate, if not consensus, with the Prime Minister first among ministers, just as chairmen are first among equals on the board. I accept that some Prime Ministers have become more presidential than ministerial and that one cannot press the political/business analogy far, but there is a historical difference in the significance which our two countries attach to individual and collective leadership.

More practically, there is probably a greater difference in the way in which companies are directed and controlled in Britain and the US than would appear from the fact that we use the same governance terms. In Britain, boards are the source of authority. They appoint the chief executive who reports to them and looks to them for advice and support. Chief executives have to carry their boards with them, but they represent a resource on which they can draw. Assuming that the posts are split, they can talk to their chairmen on equal terms and share the burden of leading their companies, but it is the board which is in charge and whose confidence chief executives must therefore retain. Chief executives are not normally in a position to choose the outside members of their board, who they can expect to bring an independent point of view to bear on their proposals and plans and to provide a degree of constructive challenge. Clearly all boards are different, as are all chief executives, but in general the balance of power lies more with the board than with the chief executive.

In the US, the CEO/chairman would be likely to have more of a say in board membership and to that extent the board would be less independent of the CEO than a UK board. The CEO reports to the board and needs to retain their confidence but would probably not see outside board members as a resource to the same extent as their UK counterpart. In an arresting article entitled, 'What can American Boards learn from the British?', Hugh Parker wrote: 'It has even been said that some US CEOs now regard their board as just another department within the corporate structure that needs to be "managed".'[10] That may be an extreme position, but CEO/chairmen could be described as looking to their boards to back their plans and policies, while chairmen as such look to their boards to play their part in formulating plans and policies.

Moving closer?

The traditional governance pattern in the US was, however, altered by the proposal that boards should select one of their independent, outside directors as a 'lead director'. Lipton and Lorsch, in their 'Modest Proposal for Improved Corporate Governance', to which reference has already been made, outline their role as follows: 'We believe that the CEO/chairman should consult with this lead director on the following matters: the selection of board committee members and chairpersons; the board's meeting agendas; the adequacy of information directors receive; and the effectiveness of the board meeting process.'[11]

That is already moving towards a more collegiate style of leadership and it also enables the board to know who is going to take charge, should the CEO/chairman be in trouble or fail to perform. It goes a long way to meet the issues of checks and balances and of the board's role as supervisor and assessor of executive performance. Where the gap remains is over the chairman's responsibility for building the board team and for getting the best out of meetings of the board, since it is the CEO/chairman, not the lead director, who is in the chair. Given the limited time that CEO/chairmen are able to devote to the responsibilities of chairmanship, this still means that their boards and the way in which they work will inevitably differ from those where an independent chairman is at their head.

Another sign that UK and US board practices may be edging closer appeared in a recent American publication, which suggested that the values and expectations of society are changing the rules under which companies operate. In *The New Rules of Corporate Conduct*, Ian Wilson compares what he refers to as the 'Industrial Age Paradigm' with the 'New Rules Paradigm'. When it comes to the composition and structure of boards, his view is that the New Rules will require board members to be nominated by the board not management, require there to be a clear majority of true independent directors subject to term limits, and require the posts of chairman and of CEO to be separate.[12] Interestingly, General Motors did divide the top posts in 1993 when they replaced the CEO/chairman with a new CEO, Jack Smith, and nominated an independent director of great experience, John Smale, as chairman of the board. The General Motors' Guidelines which the board published the following year, specifically laid down that there would in future be a degree of independent board leadership in the form, either of a separate chairman or of a lead director. Institutional investors have pressed the boards of other US corporations to follow these guidelines and in doing so are bringing about a change in the relationship between boards and chief executives in the US.

Although on both sides of the Atlantic we refer to boards and to chairmen, it is as well to recognize that the differences which exist at present between their roles tend to be concealed by the words we use in common. In addition, boards are a part of a wider governance framework and any comparison of the way in which they work has to be made within that context. Nevertheless, there is now greater agreement between investors in Britain, the US and internationally on what constitutes good governance and on the part that boards and their chairmen play in delivering it.

Division of responsibilities

Corporate leadership

There have been considerable changes in the chairman's role in the UK in the last ten years. Fewer companies now combine the posts of chairman and chief executive. As a result, the demand for chairmen has grown. The majority of them are outside directors and many head more than one board. This has always seemed to me to be a logical development and one which offers a number of advantages. It means that a group of experienced executives have acquired, or are acquiring, the appropriate skills of chairmanship and are concentrating on chairing boards as their calling, rather than on managing businesses. They can offer their services as chairmen not only to companies, but to all manner of voluntary and public sector organizations as well, where competent chairmanship may be just as important and more likely to be wanting.

The fit between outside chairmen, who are only involved in the companies they chair for part of their time, and full-time chief executives has to be easier to manage than if chairmen spend most of their time with one company. Outside chairmen of this kind can carry out the essential task of chairmanship—responsibility for the board—without taking on duties which might otherwise be undertaken by the chief executive or other members of the executive team. In this way the best use can be made of the time and respective abilities of the partnership at the top. The danger of complementarity edging into competition is reduced, both because of limits to the chairman's time and because of the chairman's implied decision to retire from executive management.

What determines the split?

How should the separation of responsibilities be arrived at? The precise division will turn on the inclinations and skills of the people concerned, and on the time which chairmen are prepared, or able, to give to their companies. Then there are such practical considerations to be taken into account as which of them was in place first. The natural split is that the chairman is in charge of the board and all its works, while the chief executive is respons- ible for everything outside the board. Under this division, all management instructions are issued by the chief executive, so that there is no doubt within the company as to who is in charge managerially. The chairman is neverthe- less ultimately accountable for the company's actions and so has a right to be consulted and to be kept informed by the chief executive. The chairman carries the authority of the board, while the chief executive is specifically given executive authority by the board to put its decisions into effect.

I find this particular division of duties logical, because it is the one to which I have worked in the past. Variations on it are equally workable, given two conditions. First, that the chairman and the chief executive see their jobs as complementary and not as competing. Each is responsible for a part of what was once one job, so they have to ensure that their responsibilities match to make up a coherent whole. It is their ability to combine together to form an effective partnership at the head of the company which is crucial. Any whiff of competition between the chairman and the chief executive undermines the foundation of their relationship and will cause confusion down the line. This leads on to the second condition which is that the two individuals have to establish trust in each other.

Need for definition

I accept that defining the chairman's role as being responsible for the board and the chief executive's as being responsible for the business leaves open a wide range of duties which could be undertaken either by the chairman or the chief executive, or shared between them. For example, who represents the company to which external audiences? How far is strategy a matter for the board and thus the chairman and how far a matter for management with the chief executive in the lead? The reality is that more is shared than is divided, since both the board and the executive are jointly involved in the running of the business. Nevertheless, it is still essential for chairmen and chief executives to start by agreeing on their respective roles, in order to establish a basis for the sharing of responsibilities.

Apart from anything else, the board has to know what the chairman and the chief executive have agreed between them and endorse it. I worked as chairman with two chief executives and in both cases I wrote down what I saw as my role, which we then debated between us, modified as necessary and agreed. Neither of them followed suit in terms of putting a description of their job down on paper, largely because it was not necessary. We needed an agreed statement for one of the positions, anything not included in that was the province of the other. The advantage of having both a chairman and a chief executive is that the burden of responsibilities at the head of a business can be shared. Both have to be accountable for their areas of responsibility, but it is the quality of their joint leadership of the company which counts. The basis of their relationship needs to be defined at the outset, but from there on it will develop in line with their personalities and the demands of the business.

The right match

Selecting a chairman

On finding the right combination of people to share the top job, it will normally be the case that either the chief executive or the chairman will be in place. Assuming that it is the chairman who is retiring, the nomination committee has the job of selecting a successor. Provided the retirement has been foreseen, the committee will have identified one, or preferably two, potential candidates for the chairman's post. They are likely to start with the outside members of the board. An existing director has some knowledge of the business and of the executives who manage it. In addition, chief executives will know their other board members and so can form an opinion over how well they could work with one of them. As chairman, it seemed to me prudent to have two outside board members who could take over the chair. The reason for wanting more than one possible successor is that situations and circumstances can change, sometimes rapidly and unexpectedly, and your first choice may leave the board and no longer be available at the critical moment. It is also helpful for the chief executive, when the time comes, to have the chance to express a preference.

A question which arises is how far to signal to a new outside director that an element in their selection was the possibility that they might succeed to the chair. I have not personally found any difficulty with being open with a board candidate over this possibility. With the agreement of the chief executive, I explained to a prospective outside director that he would be our preferred choice as my successor, but that of course it would be for the board to make the decision when the time came. He joined the board on that basis, with no commitment over the succession; a commitment we were not in a position to make. In due course he succeeded me and admirably managed the transition from a largely full-time chairman who had spent his working life in the business to a highly experienced professional chairman, who was already chairman of another major company.

On the other hand, the expectations of outside directors in the matter of succeeding to the chair can be a source of difficulty. I found myself, as an outside director of another company, faced with sorting out a situation where more than one of the board members believed that they had been brought on to the board with a promise of the chairman's seat in due course. The problem was that nods and winks were claimed to have been given, but the winker was no longer on hand. Muddle apart, the advantage, as I say, of being able to choose from existing board members is that they are known figures and they have a certain grasp of the company and its competitive situation. If there are no acceptable aspirants on the board, the new chairman coming from outside cannot be expected to have any knowledge of the business. Joining a chief executive who is in place and who perforce will be the new chairman's main source of information and understanding will call for commitment to making the partnership work from them both and sensitivity over how to do so.

Selecting a chief executive

What about the situation the other way round, when the issue is finding a new chief executive who can work with an existing chairman? A particular instance is when the previous chief executive has moved into the chairman's seat. The selection process will go ahead to find a new chief executive from within or from outside the company. New appointees from within the company will have previously been their chairmen's subordinates. This means that they will have to bury a former relationship and grow a new one, which is likely to prove a difficult task for them and for the new chairman. More difficult still is the challenge to chairmen who have been chief executives to accept that, as chairmen, they have entered a new and different career. An essential step for them to take, in establishing the fresh basis on which they will be working with those who have succeeded to their posts, is to agree how much time they will devote to their role as chairmen.

Ideally, chief executives who become chairmen will do so in companies other than their own where their previous position will be irrelevant. The more usual course, however, is that they will take the chair in their existing company. That move gives them both the time and the standing to join the boards of other companies, which may in due course lead to other chairmanships. Joining the boards of other organizations, of whatever nature, will provide opportunities for them both to gain experience and to give their successors breathing space.

Sharing power

While separating the posts of chairmen and chief executives has principle and logic behind it and spreads the load at the head of the company, a load that has grown and continues to grow, its success depends on the way in which two people share power between them. It was doubts about their ability to find someone with whom they could work in harness that led many chairmen/chief executives to retain both posts. The success of the split turns on the building of a working relationship between two individuals who have held powerful positions and who wish to continue to do so—or they would have opted for a quieter life.

The issue is as much a question of personalities, and of the effort which both partners are prepared to put into making the partnership work, as it is to do with structure. It may, therefore, seem perverse to emphasize the importance of defining the roles as clearly as possible at the outset, when what matters is the way in which the relationship between two people develops. It is precisely because there is so much common ground between the two posts that the mapping of their respective territories should be the starting point. In addition, it is essential for the board and the executive managers to have as clear a picture as possible of the way in which those in the two key positions in the company intend to divide their duties between them. Of course the relationship will develop and change, but the firmer the initial ground rules the more logical will be that development and the more predictable it will be from the point of view of those working with the chairman and the chief executive.

All of this underlines the importance of having a succession policy in place for chairmen and for chief executives and for keeping it under review. An advantage of having a formal nomination committee is that it provides a forum for carrying out such reviews and for doing so regularly, not hurriedly when the need arises. The past record of boards in managing the succession to the top posts in their companies has not been impressive. Investors have a legitimate interest in knowing what processes boards have in place for dealing with the matter of succession and who is responsible for their implementation.

Conclusion

In conclusion, the point to hold onto is that chairmen and chief executives divide the leadership of their companies between them. These two elements of the leadership task must add up to a coherent whole. It is the relationship between their roles which matters. In an excellent paper on just this subject, John Roberts and Philip Stiles wrote:

Some of those that we talked to suggested that one logic of the separation of the roles of chairman and chief executive was simply the sheer scale of the task in a growing organisation; there is work for two at this level in a public company. But it is immediately obvious that the division of responsibilities for the board and business does not and cannot in practice delineate respective domains of autonomous action for the individuals involved. Instead the separation of the roles has to be understood as the creation of a pivotal relationship between what are arguably the two most powerful figures in a company.[13]

This perceptive conclusion underlines the size of the task at the head of a company, but it also makes the point that we need to see the relationship between the two most powerful figures in a company in a wider context. Vitally important though the posts of chairman and of chief executive are, they are part of the broader governance structure of a company. The individuals concerned have to be in touch with each other as often as is necessary to maintain their unity of purpose and to build a relationship of trust. Both jobs are at times lonely and chairmen will be the only people with whom chief executives can share certain problems and vice versa. An important aspect of the role of chairmen is to support their chief executives. Their relationship, however, is part of the network of relationships between board members and senior executives and should not be to the detriment of all those other links. Their thinking needs to be shared, so that other board members, who are less frequently in touch, do not feel left out of the development of policies and plans for which they are collectively responsible. Chairmen and chief executives are leaders of teams and it is the competence and cohesion of their teams which counts. Those two posts do not stand on their own.

The decisions over whether the two top posts should be separate or combined is a means to an end. The end is to ensure that as many companies as possible are directed by effective and accountable boards. An effective board is one which gives the company the leadership it needs and in which the responsibilities for directing the enterprise are shared. The division of responsibilities ensures accountability and that the company is not overly dependent on one person. The responsibility for making certain that companies are headed by effective boards lies with their shareholders. It is for them to determine whether they are prepared to accept, in particular circumstances, that the chairman should also be the chief executive. Equally, where the posts are split, they need to be confident that those holding the top posts can work together constructively and divide their responsibilities in such a way as to provide that essential unity of leadership.

Notes

1. Heidrick and Struggles International (1987). *The Role of the Chairman*, 6.
2. Ibid., 12.

3. Beevor, J. G. (1975). *The Effective Board, A Chairman's View*, BIM Paper, OPN 15, 10.
4. Parker, Hugh (1990). *Letters to a New Chairman*, London: Director Publications, 17.
5. Gee Publishing Ltd (1992). *Report of the Committee on the Financial Aspects of Corporate Governance* (ISBN, 0 85258 915 8), para. 4.9.
6. Davison, Ian Hay (2001). 'Is Better Corporate Governance Working?', *P D Leake Lecture*, October.
7. Jay, Antony (1972). *Corporation Man*, London: Jonathan Cape, 99.
8. Clutterbuck, David and Waine, Peter (1994). *The Independent Board Director*, London: McGraw-Hill, 105.
9. Bose, Mihir (1989). 'Pearson's Formula for Growth', *Director*, September.
10. Parker, Hugh (1994). 'What can American Boards learn from the British?', *Directors & Boards*, Spring.
11. Lipton, Martin and Lorsch, Jay W. (1992). 'A Modest Proposal for Improved Corporate Governance', *The Business Lawyer*, 48: 70.
12. Wilson, Ian (2000). *The New Rules of Corporate Conduct*, Westport, CT: Quorum Books, 53.
13. Roberts, John and Stiles, Philip (1999). 'The Relationship between Chairmen and Chief Executives: Competitive or Complementary Roles?', *Long Range Planning*, 32/1: 39.

8

The Chairman and the Top Team

The main job of team-building lies with the chairman.
The Independent Board Director[1]

The previous chapter focused on the relationship between the post of the chairman and that of the chief executive. While this is the key relationship at board level, chairmen work with and through their other board colleagues. Their links with other members of the top team are, therefore, important, starting with those who may deputize for them.

Deputies

The deputy chairman

In large companies there may be more than one deputy chairman, but for simplicity I will refer to the deputy chairmanship as a single post. There is a significant difference between the appellation of vice-chairman, which is usually a courtesy title, and that of deputy chairman. The deputy chairman stands in for the chairman and the potential importance of the deputy chairman's role seems to have been largely overlooked in the literature on boards. The new development, which should have the effect of reinforcing the deputy chairman's position, is the recommendation in the Combined Code that boards should recognize one of their outside directors as the senior independent director.[2] The 1992 Code of Best Practice recommended that where the chairman is also the chief executive, 'there should be a strong and independent element on the board with a recognised senior member'.[3]

The Combined Code has taken that recommendation a step further and applied it whether or not the two top posts are combined. This is presumably to cover the possibility that board members might have cause for concern over the conduct of both the chairman and the chief executive. How significant the position of the senior independent director will turn out to be, where there is both a chairman and a chief executive, unless it is combined with the deputy chairmanship, experience will tell. The logical arrangement is surely that the senior independent director should also be the deputy chairman. This adds substance to the deputy chairman's role and gives it added authority. It also meets the proposal by some institutional investors that the post of senior independent director should carry specific duties. The straightforward conclusion is that the senior independent director is the natural choice for the deputy chairmanship. I will therefore treat the two positions as one.

An advantage of combining the deputy chairman and senior independent director positions is that it avoids creating an extra post at board level and with it the possibility of overlap and confusion between the two roles. This places the deputy chairman in a position to play a leading part in the board team, whether the chairman and the chief executive are one and the same person, or two people. If there is both a chairman and a chief executive, then the deputy chairman completes the triumvirate which constitutes the team at the top.

The responsibilities of the deputy chairman/senior independent director

As members of the top team, deputy chairmen share the work which falls to the head of the company. Provided that deputy chairmen are party to the thinking of their chairmen and their chief executives, they can represent the company's views externally or when visiting units within their companies. Like chairmen they speak for the board on such occasions. In their senior independent director role, they are likely to chair the remuneration committee at least, and to take the lead over matters such as the chairman's succession. Hermes, an institutional investor which has been at the forefront of corporate governance developments and has always been distinguished by its readiness to discuss practical issues with the boards of companies in which they have invested, has published a job description for senior independent directors.[4] The first point which they make is that they support combining it with the deputy chairmanship.

They go on to suggest that outside directors should be able to discuss any concerns that they may have about the working of their boards with the senior independent director, who should have the authority to call meetings of all the outside directors, if necessary. They add that the senior independent director should complete a periodic performance appraisal of the company chairman. This looks straightforward on the job description, but how it is to be carried out will depend on relationships at board level. It will presumably be for the senior independent director to collect and collate the views of the other outside directors and then to discuss them with the chairman. It is clearly important for chairmen to have feedback on their chairmanship, as part of the board appraisal process already discussed.

I certainly benefited from the advice of my deputy chairmen, but this was given informally and personally, and so other board members would not necessarily have known what had transpired. It is, therefore, right that board members and shareholders should know that a formal appraisal process for chairmen is in place. Unless that is established, the appraisal is unlikely to be carried out at agreed intervals and is more likely to be left for a propitious moment, moments which have a habit of not arising. As with all appraisals, the aim is for the feedback to be constructive and based on observable instances, not perceptions.

The final element in the proposed job description is that the senior independent director should be available for consultation with major shareholders. The reason given is that: 'establishing direct channels of communication as a matter of routine should enable difficult issues to be aired before a crisis develops'.[5] The problem here is that the times when major shareholders feel that they cannot go to the chairman and must speak to the outside directors are fortunately rare. In such emergencies, senior independent directors are the right point of contact, but it hardly seems necessary to communicate with them routinely in order to be able to do so on those occasions. Major shareholders will be in touch with chief executives, finance directors, and chairmen as necessary and there is a danger of too many board members speaking for the company, if senior independent directors are to be added to that list, except in cases of last resort. Hermes, however, is notable for putting forward its proposals as guidance not as rigid rules, and is open to discussion about their application in individual companies.

The deputy chairman's post has the advantage of providing an opportunity to appoint someone to it who complements the abilities and experience of the chairman and the chief executive. I worked as chairman of Cadbury Schweppes with two different chief executives and, in each case, we were admirably supported by a wise and trusted deputy chairman. Both of these deputy chairmen brought additional attributes to the team at the head of the company, given that they had broad business experience and a professional knowledge of the law and of finance, respectively. They were both outside directors, whereas I and the two chief executives concerned had spent our working lives in the business; thus they added objectivity and independence of mind to our discussions. Both also undertook specific assignments on behalf of the board. They were in turn the most senior of the outside directors and would have filled the senior independent role established by the Combined Code, which is why I regard combining that role with that of deputy chairman as a natural and logical fit.

From a personal point of view, I found that there were definite advantages in having a team of three at the head of the business rather than simply myself and the chief executive. It made it easier to discuss and settle issues with the chief executive, which could have been potentially divisive. If a matter has to be resolved, two people can find themselves at odds and the only solution is for one to give way to the other. This is a normal feature of coming to decisions, but it puts a strain on the relationship between the two people involved. The win/lose situation can often be avoided if a third person, in whose impartial judgement the other two have confidence, is party to the discussions. In our case, we had the added advantage that both deputy chairmen, as outside directors, stood further back from the activities of the business than the two of us did.

The deputy chairman, therefore, shares the burdens of the chairman's office and, ideally, should complement the knowledge and experience of the chairman and the chief executive as well. If the senior independent director is the deputy chairman, the combined post thereby carries the authority of the outside directors and of the chairman. At the same time, it has to be accepted that the post of deputy chairman carries no pretensions to the chairmanship.

Triumvirates

I have referred to the advantages of having a triumvirate at the head of a company made up of the chairman, the chief executive, and the deputy chairman. A different set of three would be one made up of the chairman, the chief executive, and the finance director. It is not quite the triangle of equals that it is when the deputy chairman is the third member, because the finance director would normally report to the chief executive. Nevertheless, the finance director's relationship with the chairman and with the chief executive is not the same as that of the other executive directors. Finance directors have a certain independence of position on the board and a direct line, whatever the reporting arrangements, to the other two. In a number of companies this is the effective top team.

I should perhaps make it clear that, when I refer to a triumvirate, I have in mind three people each with their own clearly defined post, but working together as a team at the head of a company. A different approach is to form an 'office of the chairman', as one or two large companies have done, and to focus attention on the group at the top, rather than on the individuals concerned and the division of responsibilities between them. I have no personal experience of this method of heading a company and I can do no more than note its existence. It demonstrates that there is still enough dissatisfaction with traditional structures to encourage innovatory approaches to the task of company direction.

Clarity of purpose

In the end, those at the top of a company have certain duties to discharge and there are an endless number of ways in which those duties can be divided. The posts of chairman, deputy chairman, chief executive, and senior independent director can be held in different combinations by four, three or even two people. The objectives remain the same: to provide clear leadership, to ensure that the board is effective and the business well managed, and to represent the company to the outside world. The aim is to see that as many as possible of the qualities required for these different tasks are present among the members of the top team. How the tasks are allocated is less crucial than that there should be trust between the members of the team and no confusion about who does what.

The chairman's other board links

Clearly, chairmen need to have a wider range of contacts than solely with their chief executives or their deputy chairmen, if they are to be as in touch with the state of their companies as their responsibilities demand. For example, chairmen are concerned with the continuity of their companies and so with the resources of people in them. This gives them a link with human resources directors, who may well also provide professional advice on board salaries. There should be no objection to chairmen having direct contact with any executive director, provided that it is in furtherance of their board duties and provided that the lines of communication have been cleared with their chief executives. There are, however, two executives who would normally report to the chief executive, but who have particularly close ties with the chairman. They are the company or board secretary and the finance director.

The company secretary

At the chairman's right hand at board meetings is the company secretary. Company secretaries are responsible for board administration, whether or not they are full members of the board. Professional company secretaries who anticipate problems and who draft well make life a great deal easier for their chairmen. They prepare the board agenda with their chairmen, see that the right papers go out to board members on time and make certain that the necessary internal and external communications from the board are issued in the chairman's name—all other communications will be sent out under the authority of the chief executive.

It is standard practice for company secretaries to administer, attend, and prepare minutes of board proceedings—drafting minutes is an art in itself. They or their nominees will act as secretaries of board committees, in order to ensure that the work of those committees is coordinated with that of the board to which they report. In respect of their board secretary role, Sir Walter Puckey comments that, 'A board which arrives at the finishing post too late is a secretarial failure'.[6] I think that to hold board secretaries responsible for the length of either the meeting or the agenda is to load them with responsibilities which they do not have the authority to discharge. It is the chairman's fault if the meeting fails to reach the finishing post on time, and it is one which a competent board secretary will help chairmen to avoid.

The other main project on which the chairman and the company secretary are likely to work together is the company's annual report and accounts. This has become more onerous with the inclusion of corporate governance matters and environmental and social requirements; the company secretary is normally the authority on compliance in these areas. Preparation of the report has to begin well before the year has ended and the company secretary is the logical person to lead the team which, in a company of any size, is responsible for the production of this important document. In spite of the fact that so many copies of the report and accounts are scarcely glanced at, it is the one regular, direct communication from chairmen to their shareholders and it is kept by financial analysts and commentators as a source of information on the company. As a document of record, it is worth the effort that goes into its preparation, and the company secretary can take much of the work involved off the chairman's shoulders.

The company secretary has a key role to play in ensuring that board procedures are followed and regularly reviewed. Chairmen will look to company secretaries for guidance on their legal responsibilities and duties. The company secretary should be in a position to give objective professional advice to the chairman and to other members of the board. Arguably, company secretaries are better placed to give this kind of impartial guidance if they are not themselves board members. Chairmen will also be in close touch with their company secretaries over the range of regulations and official demands for information which apply, to a varying extent, to companies of all sizes. For quoted companies, there are stock exchange rules to be complied with and such matters as the rules governing notifications to shareholders and trans- actions in shares by directors. In addition to meeting the legal requirements of their home country, British companies have increasingly to be concerned with European regulations and with those of other countries in which they may have subsidiaries. In handling all the complex legal regulations which affect companies, board secretaries are the chairman's and the company's first line of defence. In drafting the board minutes, they ensure that they record the board's decisions, but offer no hostages to fortune should they be called in evidence by any of the regulatory authorities.

It follows on from the company secretary's responsibility for the report and accounts, that they would normally make the arrangements for the AGM. I always found it useful to go through with the company secretary all the eventualities which could arise at the AGM and to be briefed beforehand on possible shareholder questions which fell within the secretary's domain. The company secretary often acts as a link with shareholders and deals with shareholder correspondence which does not require the chairman's per- sonal attention. In an increasingly regulated and litigious world, a legal rather than an accountancy training, combined with professional corporate secretarial qualifications, has become the preferred background for a com- pany secretary.

One of the conclusions of the corporate governance committee which I chaired was how much effective boards owe to their company secretaries. In our report, we reminded directors that they have a duty under the Companies Act to appoint as secretary someone who is capable of carrying out the duties which the post entails. Equally, the board as a whole must be involved in any decision to remove the company secretary. One of the reasons why attempting to apply corporate codes of best practice to other types of organization is so often inappropriate is because these other bodies lack the post and the person of a competent company secretary.

A chairman is quoted in a recent research report as saying: 'The most underestimated people are the company secretaries.'[7] I agree.

The finance director

The finance director stands in a special relationship to the chairman and to the chief executive, which is why the three of them often form the top team in a company. The basis of this relationship is the finance director's professional independence. It is the duty of finance directors to give their chairmen, chief executives, and boards their own best judgement on the company's financial position. They are relied upon to present an unvarnished picture of the prospects for the company's half-year and full-year results, and where the risks to those prospects lie. Their relationship to their chief executives is more that of a professional adviser than that of an executive subordinate. They may well give their boards a more cautious view of the financial state of the business than their chief executives; what their chairmen and boards want to know is that they are capable of coming to their own informed judgement and sticking to it.

Chairmen are responsible for reporting their company's results publicly and so need to keep in close touch with their finance directors, and to have a feel for the way in which the figures are coming through. They have to know how to set their face in answer to questions from analysts, commentators, and shareholders and in doing so they rely on the finance director for guidance as to the financial state of the business. There are also decisions on matters like rights issues, borrowing limits, and dividend payments which involve chairmen, but on which they will look to their finance directors for a lead. They will turn to them, too, in defending their companies against unwanted approaches from outside. Most companies that consider that they could be under threat of a hostile bid have an internal group in readiness, which is responsible for updating their defence strategy. The finance director will probably chair this group and act as the link with the company's professional advisers.

Finance directors may, with chief executives, be the main points of contact with the financial world, but, in giving a company view, finance directors are representing their chairmen and boards and so they and their chairmen have to be in close touch and in complete agreement as to how the company's financial position should be presented externally. A majority of finance directors in a recent research considered that the onus was on them to ensure that their company was properly understood by the City.[8] A point, however, which chairmen need to watch is that too much of their finance directors' time may be taken up in administrative, compliance, and regulatory matters according to a 1997 report.[9] It may be necessary for some of this side of their work to be delegated, to ensure that chairmen continue to have the benefit of the strategic advice of their finance directors.

The auditors

The external auditors are not part of the company team, but chairmen have a direct interest in assuring themselves of the effectiveness of the audit approach within their companies. No chairman appreciates surprises, least of all in financial matters. Favourable surprises may be immediately welcome, but they raise doubts about the reliability of the information and control systems. Chairmen look first to their audit committees to ensure that the right relationship has been established between management and the external and internal auditors.

The auditors are formally appointed by the shareholders, although in practice selected by the company. It is the say in the choice of auditors which companies have in reality that makes the relationship between auditors and managers so crucial. The relationship should be one where the auditors work with the appropriate people in the company, but do so on a strictly objective and professional basis, never losing sight of the fact that they are there on the shareholders' behalf. Chairmen need auditors who will stand up to management when necessary and who will unhesitatingly raise any doubts about people or procedures with the audit committee or with themselves. Weak auditors expose chairmen to hazards.

A further reassurance for chairmen is for the external audit to be backed by an effective internal audit function. Internal auditors are in a position to monitor key controls and procedures regularly, to check on the efficiency with which they are being operated and to undertake investigations on behalf of the audit committee. Heads of internal audit should have unrestricted access to their audit committee chairmen to buttress the independence of their post.

The outside directors

The last set of relationships to consider are those between chairmen and the outside members of their boards. The chairman's position is an exposed and at times lonely one. Chairmen depend on their outside directors for advice, support, and criticism. It is a great help to chairmen to be able to meet with the outside directors from time to time, with or without the chief executive. These meetings may be informal, but they give the chairman the chance to try out ideas, to share concerns, and to discuss emerging issues before they have taken sufficient shape to be debated more widely.

Then there are matters concerning the top executives of the company, which chairmen can only discuss with their outside colleagues. It is because of the importance of this relationship between the chairman and the outside directors that such care has to be taken in adding to their number. The chairman has to be sure that any newcomers will strengthen the team of outside directors before their names are put forward.

The chairman has, of course, to avoid splitting the board between the outsiders and the insiders. However, the contributions of these two parts of the board are different, even though their board responsibilities are the same, and there is advantage in drawing on them separately at times. In the same way, chief executives usually meet with their executive directors in management committees which they chair. Chairmen need to make the most of all the counsel which their board colleagues have to offer, and there is no reason why the manner in which they consult them should impair the unity of the board.

The chairman's responsibility for strategy

Finally, there is the question of the chairman's responsibility for the strategy of the company. It is dealt with here, because it is an aspect of the division of duties between chairmen and their chief executives, and because the determination of a corporate strategy involves chairmen and all their board colleagues. As Michael Porter wrote: 'Corporate strategy is what makes the corporate whole add up to more than the sum of its business unit parts.'[10]

It is a key issue because, on the whole, successful strategies are those which are consistently pursued. The quality of a strategy is clearly important, but less so, in my view, than its continuity and the commitment with which it is driven home. All of which means that the chairman and the chief executive have to be at one over the course they set for the company.

Both the chairman and the chief executive have a responsibility to ensure that the company is working to a strategy which is understood inside the company and externally. Establishing a strategy is an issue over which they collaborate; it is not the separate responsibility of one or other of them. Strategy is a classic board responsibility and it is to that extent, therefore, in the chairman's field. Equally, the chairman is responsible for seeing that the company has an identifiable sense of purpose and that this purpose is regularly reviewed, in order to ensure the company's continuity in a turbulent competitive environment. In addition, the chairman is likely to have the task of putting across the company's aims to outside audiences. For all these reasons, chairmen need to be involved in the development of the strategy of their enterprises. Precisely how they do so will vary chairman by chairman and board by board.

Strategic options

Chief executives in their turn will be responsible for preparing the strategic options and for putting them to the board. Since they will be in charge of carrying out the agreed strategy, it has to be one to which, in its final shape, they are committed personally and absolutely. Hammering out a strategy is an iterative process in which ideas and plans move backwards and forwards between the board and the various levels of management. It is a process which has to be approached from the bottom up, as well as from the top down. The challenge lies in fitting these two approaches together coherently.

The board sets the boundaries within which operating units draw up their individual forward plans. In doing so, the operating units can be expected to put forward proposals which build on their existing activities. It is for the board, however, to take an overall view of the future shape of the company and to decide which of the existing activities should be developed and which should not. It is the synthesis of these two views of the company that the chief executive will put to the board—a synthesis which may only be arrived at after considerable internal discussion. What boards need to decide is which aspects of strategy are their responsibility and which can be delegated to operating units within a context set by the board. In a recent book on how directors view their roles and responsibilities, a chairman is quoted as saying: 'The first order strategy, deciding what areas of business to be in, what is the core business, what should be divested or bought, how resources are to be allocated around the organisation, is in the domain of the board. Specific strategies to do with subsidiaries or business units have to be delegated.'[11]

Strategic proposals

The strategic proposals which come to the board will represent the considered judgement of those within the company as to the direction which the business should be taking. These proposals then have to be reviewed by the board as a whole, where the outside directors will see them through different eyes, since they are outside the company looking in. In practice, it is far from easy to involve all board members usefully in a discussion of strategy and it may be best to do so aside from a regular board meeting. It requires imaginative effort, by both the chairman and the chief executive, to present strategic issues to board members early enough in the process for them to have real influence over the outcome, and in a form which encourages them to contribute positively to the development of the final strategy.

Strategic continuity

Chairmen have a particular part to play in stimulating their boards to reflect creatively on the company's strategy. They have largely handed over the responsibility for achieving the current year's results to their chief executives and so are free to concentrate their thinking on the years ahead. This is not meant to imply that the chief executive should be responsible for short-term results and the chairman for longer-term objectives. The development of a company is a continuous process and cannot be broken up into annual increments. The chairman and the chief executive have, therefore, to work together to make certain that the actions taken by the company today are in line with their vision of the company of tomorrow.

Notes

1. Clutterbuck, David and Waine, Peter (1994). *The Independent Board Director*, London: McGraw Hill, 77.
2. Gee Publishing Ltd (1998). *The Combined Code*, June (ISBN 1 86089 036 9), Provision A.2.1.
3. Gee Publishing Ltd (1992). *Report of the Committee on the Financial Aspects of Corporate Governance* (ISBN 0 85258 915 8), 58.
4. Hermes Investment Management (1998). *Statement on Corporate Governance and Voting Policy*, July, Appendix II.
5. Ibid., 5.
6. Puckey, Sir Walter (1969). *The Board Room* London: Hutchinson, 187.
7. Roberts, John (2000). *On Becoming Company Chairman: building the complementary board*, Saxton Bampfylde Hever, July, 19.
8. Barker, Richard G. (1996). *Financial Reporting and Share Prices*, Price Waterhouse, 5.
9. Nicholson and Cannon (1997). *The Chief Financial Officer in Top UK Companies*, Egon Zehnder International, 5.
10. Porter, Michael E. (1987) 'From competitive advantage to corporate strategy', *Harvard Business Review*, May–June, 43.
11. Stiles, Philip and Taylor, Bernard (2001) *Boards at Work*, Oxford: Oxford University Press, 39.

Representing the Company

Election of the chairman is the responsibility of the board; the whole tone of the company and its public image must be set by the board and, in particular, by positive leadership by the chairman. No company can be successful unless the chairman is of a calibre to provide this leadership and to represent the company properly to the outside world.

CBI Company Affairs Committee Report[1]

The chairman's representational role

The CBI Report

In 1973, the Confederation of British Industry's Company Affairs Committee under the chairmanship of Lord Watkinson published its report on the responsibilities of the British public company. Although addressed to public companies, its guidance was equally relevant to private companies. The report is an important document in its own right and has influenced the direction of company legislation since it was published. It was drawn up by business leaders and sets out their collective view of what was then expected of boards and of their chairmen. The report described for the first time what companies in practice saw as their obligations, beyond those which an out-of-date and out-of-touch legal framework prescribed.

One of the points which comes clearly through in the report is the significance of the chairman's role. As the extract from the report which heads this chapter emphasizes, it is the job of the chairman to provide leadership and to represent the company properly to the outside world. The board members share the responsibility for the public image of the company and for electing the chairman to represent them and their company. As always, the degree to which this responsibility for the company's external relations will be discharged by the chairman personally will vary between chairmen and between companies. The responsibility for ensuring that the company is properly represented, however, rests firmly with chairmen, irrespective of the size of the company and of the way in which they delegate their duties in this regard.

There have, however, been two major changes, since that CBI Report was published. They modify the part which the quotation at the head of this chapter envisages that chairmen should play in personally representing their companies. First, the representational role is now more widely shared between members of the top team and the focus has tended to shift from the chairman to the chief executive. One reason is that there are fewer chairmen whose main position is as chairman of a single company, with which as a result they become identified. Most chairmen spend only part of their time with one company and many are chairmen of more than one company. This means that it is normally the chief executive who personifies the company to the financial world and the media. Another reason is that the media's interest is usually in immediate issues of an operational or financial nature, which are clearly the province of the chief executive or the finance director.

Less specifically, there is an argument for chairmen keeping out of the limelight, which has been well expressed in a lecture given by Ian Hay Davison, an experienced director and chairman.[2] The point he makes is that in the event of a company crisis, it is not in the interests of the company for the chairman to be the target of the media and the market. The chairman needs to be somewhat above the battle in order to be able to pick up the pieces after whatever dismissals, resignations, and re-constructions are demanded in order to resolve the crisis. Chairmen are there to provide continuity, as well as to represent their companies. What has not changed, however, is that the ultimate responsibility for the standing of the company rests with the board, and therefore with its chairman.

Openness is the aim

The role of representing a company has become more onerous as the number of outside bodies with an interest in the activities of businesses has grown. The key question is to whom are those who represent their companies speaking on any given occasion? The more clearly the audience can be defined, the more certain they can be that their message to them will be relevant in its content and appropriate in its form. What is, of course, essential is that different messages to different audiences do not in any way conflict. This is why chairmen need to ensure that corporate policies and positions are agreed and understood by those who speak for their companies and that who says what is centrally coordinated. The overall aim of a company's public representations is to ensure that the outside world is as well informed as possible about the company and that it sees its activities in a positive light.

I believe that it is both right and sensible for chairmen and chief executives to be as open as they prudently can be about the affairs of their companies. Openness minimizes the risk of commentators being caught unawares by changes in the company's fortunes, which inevitably damages confidence in the competence of those running it. Openness also builds goodwill towards the company which can be drawn on in times of difficulty. Lastly, the more information which is openly available about a company, the less chance there is of anyone gaining a financial advantage through privileged knowledge.

The task of chairmen in relation to their representational role can be discussed under three main headings: their relationship with the shareholders, with the financial institutions, including the institutions as shareholders, and with the media.

Chairmen and shareholders

The shareholder audience

Representing the company to the shareholders is a good illustration of the need to define the audience. Shareholders can be divided into two distinct groups from the outset—private individuals and institutions. In 1988, 88 per cent of Cadbury Schweppes' shareholders were private persons; between them they held just over 15 per cent of the shares. This understates the number of individual shareholders, since some held their shares for convenience in nominee holdings, although as a result they did not receive communications direct from the company.

Banks, nominees, pension funds, and insurance and investment companies, on the other hand, held 81 per cent of the shares and accounted for 11 per cent of the shareholders. The information requirements of these two groups are clearly different, although there will be differences within those categories as well, between active and passive shareholders, for example, and between those who look principally to the company for information and those who rely more on outside advice.

There are two other shareholder audiences, which chairmen also need to keep in mind. Employee shareholders are one, and they are becoming an increasingly important group in most companies. They are interested along with the other shareholders in the profitability of the business as a whole, but they also have a particular interest in the activities of the part of the company to which they belong. In meeting their special interests, care has to be taken that they do not receive significantly more information internally, than is generally made available to shareholders externally.

The second audience is that of potential shareholders. Companies benefit from having as wide a spread of shareholders as possible, both geographically and as between types of shareholder. In framing their messages to present shareholders, chairmen will also be aiming to reach those institutions and individuals who might become shareholders in the future.

The chairman's main line of communication with the shareholders is the full or abridged report which is sent to them annually and the shorter interim report which goes out at the half-year.

The annual report

The annual report has to meet a number of needs and to address a number of audiences. The skill in preparing it lies in the degree to which these different aims can be reconciled, while still coming out with a document which is coherent and conveys some flavour of the company. In Britain, the annual report and the accounts which accompany it have to meet both legal and accounting requirements and those of the London Stock Exchange (if the company is listed) and of other regulatory bodies. From time to time further special charges are laid upon it, such as to report on the steps which the company is taking to encourage employee involvement, to comply with the Combined Code of corporate governance, and to care for the environment.

The Committee on the Financial Aspects of Corporate Governance specifically referred to the role of chairmen in reporting on their company's progress in the following terms: 'Research has shown that the most widely read part of company reports is the opening statement, normally by the chairman. It is therefore of special importance that it should provide a balanced and reasonable summary of the company's performance and prospects and that it should represent the collective view of the board.'[3] Evidence given to the Committee had suggested that, on occasions, chairmen had used their statement to express views which were more their own than those of their boards!

The balance of the full published annual report of companies has been dramatically altered by the demand for more detailed information in some fields and for the coverage of a wider range of items. The Cadbury Schweppes Annual Report for the year 2000 extends to 141 pages, of which the statements by the Chairman, the Chief Executive, and the Chief Operating Officer relating to the company's performance and prospects take up only ten pages. The notes to the financial statements, on the other hand, account for just over one-third of the document. An accounting firm once warned against the annual report becoming a bucket into which all manner of different types of information were being thrown. This is what has happened and into the bucket has to go everything the outside authorities demand and everything the company believes could be of importance to the shareholders, and to those who consult the annual report as a work of reference. What differentiates the annual report from other company communications is that it is of lasting value, and it will be kept by analysts and the media as a continuing source of information about the company. The report also has its place as a marketing document. Fortunately, the full, complicated, and costly printed report now need only have a limited circulation. Most individual shareholders prefer the alternative of a simplified version of the report and accounts, although the need to retain a balanced assessment of the company's performance and prospects becomes even more important in the shortened document. The fundamental change which is taking place in the field of reporting and which still has further to go is the growing use by companies of electronic means of communication. This advance and its implications will be picked up in a later chapter.

In the meantime, the general standard of published annual reports has undoubtedly improved, as more companies have employed professional design teams and as the techniques of printing and of presentation have advanced. There are also ways in which chairmen can make the best use of their annual reports and accounts from the reader's point of view, in spite of the financial and legal barnacles with which they are encrusted. The first is to arrange that a single hand edits the publication from start to finish, so that the report has coherence and continuity. This should ensure that the words and figures are consistent throughout and that they tell the same story. Lastly, the irrelevant parts of the report, from the point of view of the individual shareholder, can be separated from the relevant by the way in which the report is designed and laid out.

Information to employees

One of the fundamental rules governing the provision of information on a company's affairs, is that information should be made equally available to all those with a legitimate interest in the business. In this way no privileged groups are created, who might be able to gain financially through knowing more about some aspects of the company's affairs than the shareholders in general.

Against this background, companies are now taking more trouble to brief their employees (some of whom may also be shareholders) on the financial state of the business and especially on the financial state of their particular part of the business. The information, which is relevant to the employees on a given site, is not likely to be relevant to the shareholders in general. It may, nevertheless, be price-sensitive if, for example, it involves revealing plans for investment or divestment. The employees start from the position of being more knowledgeable about their side of the business than the shareholders and they are better placed to ask well-directed questions of the management in order to add to that knowledge.

Insider trading

Access to information about a company which is not generally known does not of itself create a problem. It is only when that information is used to deal in the company's shares that the issue of insider trading arises. To prevent insider trading, the London Stock Exchange sets out model rules for companies to adopt in respect of dealings by directors, and many companies restrict the period during which directors can buy and sell their company's shares, even further than is provided for under those rules. It is not only the directors, however, who know more than the shareholders in general about events within the company which may have a bearing on the value of its shares. To an extent, everyone who works in a company has access to more information than those outside it, and even a company's suppliers and customers could be in something of the same position. Thus, the definition of who might be considered to be an insider is a difficult one. Equal access to every kind of information about a company is an impossible aim, but the more widely such information can be made available, the less is the risk of inside knowledge being improperly used to gain a trading advantage.

Guidelines

Companies need to watch, therefore, that they do not inadvertently put some of their employees in a position to be accused of insider trading through their laudable efforts to keep them well briefed. This may become more of an issue in the European Union, if the Commission rules that the flow of information to employees should be augmented. In balancing the rights of employees to be kept informed on matters which directly affect them, against the rights of shareholders to parity of information, the guideline seems to me to be one of common sense.

It is in the interests of the company, and therefore of the shareholders, that employees should be aware of the true state of that part of the business in which they work. As a result, there may be differences between the information given generally to shareholders and to specific groups of employees. The requirements are that the information should be relevant to the needs of both categories and that information which could reasonably be expected to affect the share price should be made generally available.

The Annual General Meeting

Chairmen report to their shareholders in writing twice a year, but at the Annual General Meeting (AGM) they meet those who choose to attend face to face. The AGM is a formal occasion and it has essential business to conduct, such as the election of directors, the appointment of the auditors and the decision on the dividend. It also presents shareholders with an opportunity to question the way in which the business is being run and chairmen with an opportunity to bring shareholders up to date with the company's progress. Chairmen who pride themselves on the speed with which their AGMs are concluded are losing sight of the advantages to be won from encouraging shareholders to ask questions. Such questions give chairmen a feel for the issues which are on the minds of shareholders and in answering them they have the chance to put forward the company's point of view, persuasively and in a public forum.

Shareholders' questions

How shareholders' questions are answered at an AGM is a matter of individual choice for chairmen. I prefer to take them all myself and if I do not know the answer, I ask the questioner to talk to the appropriate board member after the meeting. It is less easy to keep the meeting under control if the board is turned into a panel and especially if the auditors are to be brought into the act as well, as some have suggested. The other advantage for chairmen of answering shareholders' questions personally is that it ensures thorough preparation for the meeting. This preparatory work gives chairmen a useful point of contact with a number of executives, and there is no more certain way of clearing your mind over the issues facing the company than to stand ready to answer questions on them. The publication of the Combined Code has, however, altered the position. Under its provisions 'The chairman of the board should arrange for the chairmen of the audit, remuneration and nomination committees to be available to answer questions at the AGM'.[4] It is still for chairmen to decide whether to refer a question to a board committee chairman; to that extent control remains in their hands, but the expectation now is that a question on directors' pay, for example, will be put by the chairman to the chairman of the remuneration committee.

The problem with the AGM as it stands is that institutional shareholders prefer to raise their points direct with board members outside the meeting and inevitably some of the questions from individual shareholders are trivial or not strictly relevant to the company's business. It has been suggested that shareholders should be able to send in written questions, in addition to being able to ask them at the meeting itself, and that all shareholders should receive a summary of questions asked and answers given after the meeting. This was given a trial but the idea did not catch on, presumably because the outcome was felt to be incommensurate with the effort involved. Nevertheless, from a shareholder point of view, the force of well-directed questions should not be underestimated and no chairman wishes to be in the position at an AGM of having to explain why they had not dealt with a matter, which a shareholder had raised at the previous year's meeting.

In addition to questions, shareholders are also entitled to put resolutions to the meeting, although the barriers to doing so are daunting. They include amassing sufficient shareholder support, a tight timetable, and possible costs. Shareholder resolutions have a longer history in the US than they have in Britain. The newly-privatized utilities were the first target for shareholder resolutions in this country. Shareholders of these companies were often customers as well, which assisted them to gain the necessary degree of support for resolutions on levels of service, directors' pay, and board membership. There is a lucid account of the mechanics and politics of shareholder resolutions in Jonathan Charkham and Anne Simpson's *Fair Shares*.[5] Shareholder resolutions are likely to become a more regular feature of AGMs in the UK and they provide an opportunity for the two sets of shareholders, individuals and institutions, to join forces.

The powers of the chairman

The course of a general meeting is not necessarily predictable; consequently, chairmen need to know just what their powers are and to have agreed with the company secretary how a demand for a poll or a serious interruption will be dealt with. It is also advisable to have outside legal advice on tap as well. This is because the powers of a chairman in general meeting are not all that clearly defined, as was apparent from the case of *Byng* v. *London Life Association Ltd.* (1988). There, the court found first in favour of the chairman of London Life—a decision which was then reversed in the Court of Appeal.

Byng v. *London Life Association Ltd*

The account of the case merits reading, since it covers a number of aspects of the powers of a chairman under the common law.[6] What happened, briefly, was that London Life had called a general meeting to pass a special resolution. The room in the Barbican, in which the meeting was to be held, proved to be too small for the numbers attending and the audio-visual links with the overflow rooms failed to work properly. The chairman, therefore, decided to adjourn the meeting until later in the day and to reconvene in a larger room at the Café Royal. He made this decision without taking a vote.

His action in adjourning was challenged on the grounds that he should have taken a vote on the adjournment, that by changing the meeting-place and time he was preventing a number of members from taking part in the debate and voting, and that he should have abandoned the meeting, reconvening it at a later date.

On the first point, the company's articles laid down that a meeting could be adjourned by a vote. The question was, therefore, whether the chairman's common law power to adjourn could override the company's articles. The Court of Appeal held:

That, although a motion to adjourn could not be put to the meeting as many entitled to vote would have been excluded, the common law permitted the chairman to adjourn the meeting and article 18 did not preclude the chairman from exercising the common law power to adjourn the meeting in circumstances where the views of the members could not be ascertained.[7]

On the central point, however, of whether the meeting should have been abandoned and a new one convened at a later date, the Court of Appeal found against the chairman of London Life. This was on the basis that the matter to be voted on was not so urgent that it justified effectively excluding a number of members from attending and voting. The Court of Appeal held that, 'Although the chairman acted in good faith, he was under a duty to act reasonably with a view to facilitate the limited purpose for which the power to adjourn the meeting existed'.[8]

Thus the chairman has powers, but they are restricted and can only be used to further the purpose for which they exist. In this case, the purpose was to enable more members to take part in the debate than had proved possible in the Barbican; in the court's view, that purpose was not adequately achieved by the chairman's decision. What is not referred to in any of the reports on the case is the relentless pressure which chairmen are under in these circumstances. They have to make the best decisions they can in the brief time they have for consultation and reflection, possibly in situations of considerable confusion.

Points of guidance

Nevertheless, there are useful points of guidance which arise from *Byng* v. *London Life Association Ltd*. In the first place, the case confirmed that chairmen have powers, under the common law, to take such steps as may be necessary to enable meetings to achieve their purpose. They can and should, for example, adjourn a meeting to prevent violence, although the definition of violence is itself a matter of judgement. A judge commented in an earlier case, Megarry J. in *John* v. *Rees* (1970) Ch. 345, 'Obviously there is no duty to adjourn if the violence consists of no more than a few technical assaults'. The same judge referred to the need for a chairman at an unruly meeting to have 'the voice of a good schoolmaster'. Second, the case has established that the members at a general meeting do not all have to be in the same room, provided that they are able to participate in the proceedings as if they were. This means that it has become possible to use forms of communication, such as teleconferencing, to allow members to take part in general meetings at a distance; always provided that they can participate as actively as if they were physically present.

Other practical points on holding AGMs include the advisability of having both room to spare and an efficient system of registration, the need to have the company secretary, legal adviser, and the articles of association all within easy reach—and the advantage of possessing a stentorian voice.

Correspondence with shareholders

While the AGM provides shareholders with the opportunity to put questions to their chairmen once a year, they can do so at any time by writing to them. Judging by the way in which some shareholders address their letters—'for the chairman's personal attention only' and so on—they expect them to be diverted down the line and doubt if they will reach their destination. In this, they underrate the importance which chairmen attach to the views of individual shareholders. Some of the points raised by shareholders with chairmen may best be answered by the appropriate executive; even so, in passing the matter on, chairmen will be aware of what caused the letter to be written in the first place and of the nature of the reply. Cranks apart, most shareholders only take up their pens when they feel strongly enough about something to overcome the inertia which normally precludes writing. Chairmen need to accord the same sense of priority to seeing that their letters are answered.

The chairman and the financial institutions

In relation to the financial institutions, chairmen have to ensure that good working links are maintained with three constituencies: financial analysts, institutional shareholders, and sources of finance. The importance of these links has grown in line with the greater interest now shown in the activities of companies and the increased incidence of bids and buy-outs. The responsibility for keeping these links in good working order is the chairman's, even though personal involvement in so doing will be limited, particularly in a company whose shares are widely traded. The need to keep in close touch with the financial institutions and with those who comment on the business scene has meant that more companies now have staff specifically assigned to investor relations and that they make greater use of outside specialists in this field.

Basic principles

The more the responsibility for contacts with the financial institutions is diffused within a company, the more important it becomes for chairmen to ensure that the principles which determine the nature of those contacts are upheld. I would put forward two basic principles governing the provision of information on the company and I have already referred to them. First, that the company should be as open as it sensibly can be about the financial and operational state of the business and, second, that it should treat equally all those whom it has a duty to keep informed. These two principles can only be put into practice if there is an efficient communication chain from the company to shareholders, commentators, and markets. Their application requires that the information provided by the company should be accurately interpreted and broadly disseminated. It is here that the financial analysts have come to play such a key role.

Financial analysts

The deregulation of markets has moved analysts, or the best of them, to the centre of the stage. Competition between those firms which offer a service in the buying and selling of shares has become severe. They compete on the basis of the judgement of their principals and the quality of the research which lies behind their judgement. It is the analysts who carry out research and who provide professional assessments of companies in a way which was rare in less competitive days. Financial analysts who become expert in particular companies or company sectors carry considerable influence, not only directly through their recommendations to buy, hold, or sell shares, but also as a source of information for the media.

As chairman, I met with financial analysts as a group on the announcement of the company's annual and half-yearly results. Originally, we met with the press first on these occasions and the analysts afterwards, leaving the more demanding meeting to the last. Then we changed the order round, recognizing that the press wanted to be able to consult selected analysts before going into print. All of which underlines the importance of a company's relationship with the analysts who follow its fortunes. This relationship raises a difficult and sensitive issue for boards.

Analysts' forecasts

Both the company and the analyst have a common interest in the relative accuracy of the latter's forecasts. It does the company and its shareholders no good if the expectations of analysts are unreasonably high, so that a respectable result from the company's viewpoint is greeted by the stock market as disappointing. On the other hand, if their expectations are too low, the company's shares will be undervalued, which will advantage buyers at the expense of sellers. Equally, analysts cannot afford to be too far out in their predictions, given that it is on this that their careers depend. The danger of this symbiotic relationship is that the dividing line between answering the analyst's legitimate questions and steering the analyst towards a particular conclusion will be crossed. The contacts which companies have with analysts are ultimately in the name of their chairmen, and so chairmen need to be able to reassure themselves that the line is being held and that an improper degree of guidance is not being given.

Analysts gain their competitive advantage by being better informed about a company than their rivals. Analysts, therefore, have an interest in acquiring information which is not generally available and will understandably seek to gain it. What matters to the company is that they should do so through their analytical skill, in deducing more than their competitors about the company's prospects from the way in which they piece the corporate jigsaw together from the same facts and figures, rather than from privileged information.

The other way in which they can gain a competitive edge is through their ability to assess the competence of the people running a company. What counts is the professionalism and the judgement of the analysts with whom the company deals; it is up to the board's top team to know what the standing of individual analysts is within their circle.

Analysts' skills

Analysts are important to companies and to their chairmen, because of their role in interpreting information about the company and in passing it on to other audiences. Professional analysts understand the structure of the businesses which they follow and so can assess what effect a particular event—a change in taxation, the loss of a market, the launch of a new product, and so on—is likely to have on a company's earnings in the short and long term. It was this more accurate assessment of cause and effect which was lacking before the rise of the professional analyst.

In addition, as communicators, analysts are the main link between the company as the source of information and those who have an interest in acting on that information, whether they are financial institutions, stockbrokers' clients, or the media. Their role is, therefore, central and deserves to be treated as such by their company contacts.

Institutional shareholders

The company's links with its institutional shareholders are sufficiently different from those with individual shareholders for them to be discussed under a separate heading. Institutional shareholders have a decisive voice in a company's affairs through their voting power. The relationship between chairmen and chief executives and their companies' largest shareholders is one which needs to be fostered on a continuing basis. Relationships cannot be established instantly, when the need arises from a company's point of view. The contacts between companies and their larger institutional investors will as far as possible be direct and personal, involving chairmen and their senior colleagues. The Combined Code sets out the principle on which relations with institutional investors should be based as follows: 'Companies should be ready, where practicable, to enter into a dialogue with institutional shareholders based on the mutual understanding of objectives.'[9]

In the past, there was understandable concern about select gatherings, usually over lunch, for a few institutional guests to meet the chairman, chief executive, or finance director of a particular company. The problem about such gatherings is that they came—in the words of an investment fund manager—'perilously close to passing price-sensitive information to a privileged group of investors who are given insights not available to the wider body of shareholders'.[10] The same fund manager went on to say that, to many investors, this would be the only point in attending meetings of this kind. Meetings of this kind, however, never seemed to be a particularly effective medium of communication, either for institutions or for companies. Now with the growing power of the investing institutions and the development of their own governance codes, contact is more direct and at a higher level in terms of representation from the institutions. In addition, there are two safeguards in relation to concerns about possibly putting institutional investors in a privileged position. In the first place, they are likely at their level to be more interested in longer-term issues of strategy and of board competence, than in information on current trading which might be price-sensitive in the short-term. Second, if the issues they wish to discuss are price-sensitive, they are normally willing to be made insiders, as the following extract from Hermes' *Code of Conduct in Support of Companies* makes clear: 'Hermes is always prepared to discuss companies' affairs with their boards and management. As this can, and on occasion does, make Hermes an insider, active fund management is foregone for the relevant period.'[11]

It is clearly important for companies, the majority of whose shares are held by institutions, to keep in close and regular touch with those shareholders who, between them, control the company. It is also important for wider reasons, because it is the institutions who are in a position to bring about change in the boardrooms of companies which are failing to meet their expectations.

Sources of finance

The relationship between companies and those who provide them with financial services of all kinds has altered dramatically in the last few years. This is as a result of deregulation, the merging of financial service companies into larger groupings, and the globalization of financial markets. The consequence is that the market for the provision of financial services has become more competitive and more specialized. At the same time, many of the larger companies have developed their own in-house treasury departments, which are often separate profit centres as well. There are, therefore, two pressures on company treasurers to treat each financial transaction on its own merits and to conclude it with whichever finance house can offer the best terms on the day. One is that each finance house will tend to have its own special area of expertise, which means going to different firms for different types of business. The other is that treasurers want to get the finest of possible rates from the point of view of attaining their own budget targets. Whereas, in the past, a company had a relationship with its main bankers which was built up over time, companies now may be dealing with a range of financial firms and have no long-standing links with any of them.

Chairmen are rightly concerned lest, in a predatory world, the bankers to whom they look for financial backing may be equally prepared to finance an unwanted bid for them. They are entitled to look for loyalty from their bankers, but their bankers are similarly entitled to look to them for loyalty in return. This presents chairmen with two options. They can establish long-term relationships with particular financial firms and those who manage them. Thereby, they will know that they can rely on the support of their bankers should they be in need of funds or under external attack. Alternatively, they can accept that their finance departments will shop around in order to get the keenest possible price for each transaction. Chairmen and their boards have to decide which of these two approaches best meets the needs of their companies.

Chairmen and the media

How far it is up to chairmen personally, 'to represent the company properly to the outside world', will depend on the way in which they and their companies divide the representational role. It is likely to involve being prepared to appear on television and to give interviews on the radio or to the press, as the occasion demands. The main point is that in doing so chairmen are representing their companies and not—deliberately anyway—promoting themselves. The decision, therefore, whether or not to take part in a programme has to be based on the benefit which taking part will bring to the company, or on the possible harm from turning the offer down. It is normally unlikely that anything will be lost by not taking part in a particular programme. It is better to decline to do so than to risk becoming involved in a feature which may have as its aim putting the company on the defensive and thus in a negative light.

The representational role is one in which chairmen will find professional help and advice invaluable. The back-up for chairmen in their public relations work may come from outside the company, from within it, or from a combination of the two. What chairmen need are competent practitioners in whom they have confidence and to whom they can turn for instant guidance. One of the characteristics of the representational role is that if chairmen are called upon to fulfil it, it is usually at short notice. Chairmen have to decide which aspects of the role they are good at, what training and experience they need and when they should leave the task to someone else.

Television

Television is the most exacting medium and the one where experience is the greatest help. When chairmen or chief executives appear on television they give a wide audience an impression of themselves as people and, thereby, an impression of the company they represent. There could even be rare occasions when the way they or their chief executives come across on television might prove to be crucial in commercial terms. If some disaster has struck the company, the chairman or chief executive in commenting on it has to convey that the company has matters under control and is taking every possible action to mitigate its consequences. Provided that impression is created, the company will win public support and sympathy and will be left to get on with managing the emergency. If the company's response appears to be uncertain, then the opposite will happen, making the task of recovery all the harder.

Such extreme situations aside, television appearances are more likely to affect the public image of the company than the share price. It is necessary, therefore, for companies to have a view as to the picture of themselves which they aim to present and to coordinate all the different aspects of their external relations to that end. Television, more than any other medium, tends to focus on personalities rather than events and institutions. To that extent, it is difficult for chairmen or chief executives to be certain that they are putting over the company rather than themselves. I used to encourage myself with the thought that my name was eponymous with one of our main brands and, in consequence, any appearance on television would, however modestly, reinforce the company's advertising.

It is also worth bearing in mind that employees and customers are more likely to see chairmen and chief executives on television than to read about them in the press, or to hear them on radio. It matters to employees that the company for which they work should be presented positively on their television screens; thus effective appearances by those representing the company are important to everyone associated with the enterprise.

Videos

A natural extension of appearing on television is for chairmen to make use of video programmes to reach specific audiences. The technical advances in the production of videos in the last few years have been impressive. It is a technique which is now widely employed for teaching and it opens up a range of new ways of putting over information about the company. Videos are mainly used for internal communications and offer particular advantages to international companies; but they can also be addressed to shareholders and customers or shown at investor presentations. The great plus of videos is that they enable chairmen or chief executives to be multiplied on the screen as many times as required and to appear at any number of sites simultaneously.

Another important advantage of the video, as a means of communication, is that those taking part can put across their messages in the form which suits them best. Chairmen and chief executives have little say over the nature of the television programmes in which they may appear; this is why it is essential to clear the ground rules with the producer before deciding whether to take part.

Radio

Radio programmes on company affairs usually provide their listeners with factual information, as they do when a company's results are announced, or they feature aspects of business life. Taking part in radio programmes is not, therefore, likely to have much commercial impact on the company. However, the way in which the chairman or chief executive comes across in them does give listeners an impression of what their company might be like. Some of the advantages of radio programmes are that their intent in discussing business affairs is normally serious rather than partisan and that, compared with television, they are in a better position to give time to an issue. Lastly, radio interviewers and producers are, in my experience, thoroughly professional in the way in which they present their programmes.

The press

Variations in professional standards are widest among the press. The reputations of the journals themselves vary, as do those of their contributors. At the top of the scale, there are experienced business journalists, writing in newspapers and magazines, whose articles on companies and on their management are well informed and authoritative. At the other end, there are reporters with no business grounding, whose comments are either unpredictable or slanted. Chairmen need to acquire a feel for the place on the scale of those journalists who approach them for interviews or who ring them up—usually when they are at home.

Press reporting does have an influence on the standing of a company, on the price of a company's shares, and on business issues. Although regular investors may rely on the research and recommendations of analysts, enough investors follow the financial advice columns in the press for them to be able to move share prices. Once that movement is established, it tends to go unjustifiably far before reality reasserts itself. In the same way, once a journal has formed a view for good or ill about the management of a company, it will be slow to change it.

On broader issues, such as those related to public health, social causes, and the environment, the press is in a position to mount campaigns which can directly affect companies and their markets. A further reason why the press has a lasting influence on businesses is that newspaper and magazine articles are kept on file and are referred back to, both by the media themselves and by financial commentators and analysts. This is why inaccurate or slanted articles are damaging; even if corrections are subsequently printed, they are rarely filed with the errors which gave rise to them.

The relationship between chairmen and chief executives and the press is, therefore, important and it helps if they get to know personally some of the leading figures among business journalists. It also assists in building the right relationship with the press if chairmen and chief executives are known to be reasonably accessible and straightforward in their response to questions.

Conclusions on the representational role

The importance of the role

It is essential that companies should present their past record and their future opportunities positively to the outside world. Markets, and those whose comments move markets, evaluate a company on the basis of what they believe it has achieved and will achieve. This evaluation is based on their necessarily limited knowledge of the business and of how it is run. It is the company's job to correct any misapprehensions in their assessments and to provide a rounded picture of the company and its prospects. The outside world judges companies by the kinds of business they are in, but above all by the competence and flair of the people who are running them. The chairman and the chief executive have the responsibility of conveying to the public the ambitions of the company and the abilities of its management.

The standing of a company and the way it is regarded externally are crucial for a number of reasons. In the first place, it is vital to shareholders that the market should appreciate, as nearly as possible, the true worth of their investment in the business. It is the job of the chairman and the board to see that the price at which the company's shares are traded is based on an adequate understanding of the company's potential.

The standing of the company

The standing of a company in the marketplace and the tone of the public comment about it are important not only in relation to the share price.

They have a bearing on the company's ability to recruit staff and on the quality of those who apply for jobs. They also matter to the employees, since the people who work in a company need to feel that their contribution to its progress is being properly recognized. It is natural for everyone to want to be part of a successful enterprise, and success in that sense is measured by the outside world.

Although it is usually chairmen or chief executives who take the lead in representing the company externally, it is a task in which they need to be backed by everyone in the business who is in a position to help. It is also an advantage if chairmen and chief executives can select professionals in the field of public relations, who think along the same lines as they do, and with whom they find it easy to work.

To the extent that chairmen and chief executives are responsible for representing their companies, they have to decide on the best means of communicating with a particular audience. The main distinction is between communications which originate from within the company, for which the company is solely responsible, and those which originate from outside the business, to which those representing the company respond. While the messages about a company conveyed, say, in answers to questions from an interviewer, are less under their control than a prepared pronouncement, they may, for that very reason, carry more weight with their audience.

Consistency and continuity

The central point is that it is for chairmen and their supporting staff to orchestrate the way in which the company presents itself, so that it takes advantage of all the opportunities which are open to it and, more importantly, that the responses to those opportunities are coordinated. The picture which the company presents through all its external communications has, above all, to be consistent, if it is to be persuasive.

Chairmen and their colleagues should acquire as much practical experience as possible in carrying out their representational role. This is in order not only to build on that experience, but also to find out where their particular strengths lie. At the same time, taking part in programmes of various kinds enables them to learn something about their presenters. When chairmen are seeking public support for their companies, it will help if they are respected by the media and can discuss the issues at stake with people whom they already know. A further point is that external contacts of all kinds, whether with the media or with shareholders, cannot be switched on or off to suit the company. The external relations programme has to be a continuing one, if it is to be effective.

Responsiveness

The focus in this chapter has been on what chairmen or chief executives say or write in their representational role. But the role also consists of listening to what it is that the outside world wants to know about the company and its activities. Communications should flow in both directions. Some companies go to considerable lengths to encourage questions by employees and share-holders and to have them answered authoritatively.

That approach makes it clear that the company is willing to explain its policies and actions; it also means that the concerns of individual question-ers are answered directly and precisely. The problem with general company pronouncements is that too much of their content may be irrelevant to indi-vidual members of the audience. The opportunity, particularly for employees, to question those with the power of decision in a company is important. Although the video is an effective means of presenting the company's point of view, its limitation is that it is a one-way transmission and it does not provide for questions and debate.

The rules

The primary rules for chairmen and chief executives, when they are in the position of representing their companies to the outside world are openness and even-handedness. The company should make available as much informa-tion as it reasonably can and this information should be provided equally to all those who have a claim to be kept informed. Since a number of people will be involved in representing the company, chairmen have to make certain that they are all playing to the same rules and presenting the same picture of the enterprise.

How much chairmen do publicly in representing their companies has to be their own decision and they have to do it in their own way. Coaching and advice are helpful, provided they encourage chairmen to develop their own natural style. What audiences are looking for is evidence that the company is competently run and that those at its head are both confident and in control.

Notes

1. Confederation of British Industry (1973). *The Responsibilities of the British Public Company*, 34.
2. Davison, Ian Hay (2001). 'Is Better Corporate Governance Working?', *P D Leake Lecture*, October.

3. Gee Publishing Ltd. (1992). *Report of the Committee on the Financial Aspects of Corporate Governance*, (ISBN 0 85258 915 8), para. 4.57.

4. Gee Publishing Ltd. (1998). *The Combined Code*, June (ISBN 1 86089 036 9), C.2.3.

5. Charkham, Jonathan and Simpson, Anne (1999). *Fair Shares*, Oxford: Oxford University Press, 67–74.

6. Weekly Law Reports, *Byng* v. *London Life Association Ltd.*, 28 April 1989.

7. Weekly Law Reports, *Byng* v. *London Life Association Ltd.*, 28 April 1989, 739.

8. Ibid., 739.

9. Gee Publishing Ltd. (1998). *The Combined Code*, June (ISBN 1 86089 036 9), C.1.

10. Skapinker, M. 'Free lunches and privileged information', *Financial Times*, 1 June 1987.

11. Hermes Investment Management (1998). *Statement on Corporate Governance and Voting Policy*, July.

IO

Corporate Social Responsibility

Few trends could so thoroughly undermine the very foundations of our free society as the acceptance by corporate officials of a social responsibility other than to make as much money for their stockholders as possible. This is a fundamentally subversive doctrine.

Milton Friedman[1]

Definitions of social responsibility

Chairmen and companies do not lack for advice on their responsibilities to society. Professor Milton Friedman measures social responsibility in earnings per share. The US Chamber of Commerce, on the other hand, has suggested that companies should consider restructuring their objectives, so that social goals are put on a par with economic goals. What these two divergent approaches to the question of social responsibility demonstrate is that the responsibilities of companies to society are difficult to define. In addition, they do not stand still; they are continually evolving.

It is precisely because social responsibility is a woolly term, that it is important for boards to decide what social policies their companies should follow—and companies have social policies, whether or not they are thought through deliberately. In the absence of a positive lead from the chairman and the board, the company's attitude towards its social responsibilities will appear confused to those inside and outside the company.

To put Professor Friedman's statement in context, his definition of social responsibility arises out of a discussion of the importance of maintaining political freedom. In pursuit of that aim, he would restrict companies to a narrowly defined commercial role, leaving the interaction between business and society to the political process. The difficulty about the Friedman approach in practice is its deceptive simplicity. It is not possible to isolate the economic elements of business decisions from their social consequences, because companies are part of the social system. Even the concept of making as much money for shareholders as possible begs the question—over what period of time?

The aim of maximizing profits next year, or the year after, is an objective which can be translated directly into management action. Once the time horizon is extended to five or ten years, as it has to be with a continuing business, the aim becomes of limited operational use. If the income of future shareholders is to be assured, resources will have to be invested, not just in machinery and buildings but in people and their training, and in maintaining or enhancing the company's reputation. Investing in people and in the standing of the company involves social as well as commercial judgements. The board has to hold the balance between profit now and profit in the future. The further a company looks ahead, the more difficult it becomes, in holding that balance, to maintain a simple separation between economic and social goals.

Shareholders' objectives differ

A further complication is that Professor Friedman assumes that shareholders share a common objective: that the company should make as much money as possible. In practice, as chairmen are well aware, shareholders have differing views on how companies should make their money and on how they should distribute it. Their objectives not only differ but they are not confined to furthering the strictly economic role of companies. Shareholders regularly question chairmen at annual general meetings about how far and in what ways their companies support charitable and community activities, and the space which companies give in their reports to their contribution in these fields reflects the value which companies and their shareholders place on it. Shareholder interest in the sense of social responsibility shown by companies is growing and the rise in the number of ethical and environmental unit trusts is evidence that shareholders wish to influence the degree to which companies take account of aims other than making as much money as possible. The implications of this growing interest in corporate social and environmental policies will figure later in the discussion of the future governance agenda.

The social dimension

It would simplify the position for companies if they could choose one of two ways of recognizing the social dimension in business decisions. The first, along Friedmanite lines, would be for them to concentrate on running their businesses efficiently. They would then, either allocate a proportion of their profits to some agency which would make the social judgements for them, or distribute as much as possible to the shareholders, who would make the social judgements for themselves. The alternative would be for the board to regard social aims as inseparable from business aims, as enlightened industrialists did in the nineteenth century. Most companies plan to steer a middle course between these two extremes, not keeping the social dimension completely at arm's length, but seeking ways of usefully combining their commercial and social goals. The aim of this chapter is to provide chairmen with some pointers to help them and their boards decide what course their company should follow in framing a social policy.

Why this interest in social responsibility?

Business success

There are a number of reasons why social responsibility has become such a live issue for boards. One is that business in the developed world has proved remarkably successful at meeting society's material needs. When economic growth and a higher standard of living were overriding aims, the contribution of companies to the attainment of those aims was well understood. Now, economic growth as an unqualified aim is increasingly being questioned, although the questioners often take the material benefits of growth for granted. At the same time, much more is now being learnt about the side-effects of economic growth and development on the environment. Just as companies have to balance the demands of the future against those of the present, so does society, and communities are becoming more conscious of their responsibilities to future generations.

Corporate power

Another reason is the apparent increase in the power of companies, particularly of large international companies, over recent years. They are seen as being capable of changing the societies in which they carry on their business, for better or worse. This view was expressed in a London Business School paper on corporate social responsibility in the following way: 'Corporate activity is seen as a major determinant of the shape of future society. There has been, it is felt, a quantum leap in the corporate power to create the social future. The company is a major initiator of change, and its power has exceeded the regulatory influence of current market or governmental forces.'[2]

What is self-evident is that there is now a greater degree of interdependence between business and governments, since governmental goals can often only be achieved through the cooperation of companies. Governments, for example, can only attain their aims in such fields as training and equal opportunities by working with and through companies.

On top of this, there has also been a general rise in the expectations of society, which has its roots in better communications, in a greater awareness of what is taking place in the wider world, and in a more questioning approach to previously accepted ideas. All of which challenge the traditional view of companies simply as providers of goods and services.

Company law and social responsibility

One of the problems during a period of rapid economic and social change is that the legal framework, within which companies operate, tends to become out of date and out of line with the ways in which boards act, let alone the ways in which society expects them to act. As the Final Report of the UK Company Law Review Steering Group put it:

Too much of British company law frustrates, inhibits, restricts, and undermines. It is over-cautious, placing too high a premium on regulation and avoidance of risk. The company remains the choice of corporate vehicle for over a million businesses, and the core principles established by company law have served our economy well for over 150 years. But significant parts are outmoded or have become redundant, and they are enshrined in law that is often unnecessarily complicated and inaccessible.[3]

The proposed reform of British company law has been widely welcomed by companies, since the law sets the framework within which boards have to strike a balance between the different sets of interests which they serve. Britain, for example, was behind the rest of Western Europe in accepting that companies had obligations to their employees as well as to their shareholders. It was not until section 309 of the Companies Act 1985 came into force, that British boards have been required, as part of the duty which they owe to the company, to have regard for the interests of the employees in general.

It is important that company law should be updated to reflect the changing pattern of responsibilities accepted by boards, in order to protect those companies who have moved in advance of the law and to raise corporate standards. Nevertheless, the law cannot be expected to give a lead over the social responsibilities of boards. The law consolidates changes in business conduct that have already occurred and represents enforceable standards rather than best practice. As the CBI report, referred to in the last chapter, stated: 'One cannot look to the Companies Acts to provide "a moral imperative". This must be one of the duties of companies and their boards.'[4]

In carrying out that duty, chairmen and their boards have to decide on their definition of social responsibility.

What is social responsibility?

A contract with society

The broadest way of defining social responsibility is to say that the continued existence of companies is based on an implied agreement between business and society. In effect, companies are licensed by society to provide the goods and services which society needs. The freedom of operation of companies is, therefore, dependent on their delivering whatever balance of economic and social benefits society currently expects of them. The problem for companies is that the balance of needs and benefits is continually changing and there is no generally accepted way of measuring those changes.

To start with, companies are expected to meet society's demands for goods and services, to provide employment, to contribute to the exchequer, and to operate efficiently at a profit. There is no conflict between social responsibility and the obligation on companies to use scarce resources efficiently and to be profitable—an unprofitable business is a drain on society. The essence of the contract between society and business is that companies shall not pursue their immediate profit objectives at the expense of the longer-term interests of the community.

Levels of corporate responsibility

In practice, it is possible to distinguish three levels of company responsibility. The primary level comprises the company's responsibilities to meet its material obligations to shareholders, employees, customers, suppliers, and creditors, to pay its taxes, and to fulfil its statutory duties. The sanctions against failure to match up to these relatively easily defined and measured responsibilities are provided by competition and by the law.

The next level of responsibility is concerned with the direct results of the actions of companies in carrying out their primary task and includes making the most of the community's human resources and avoiding damage to the environment. At this level, it is not enough to say that pollution or noise levels meet legal requirements. What is here required of companies is that they should be attempting to minimize any adverse effects of their actions, rather than adhering to the lowest acceptable standard.

At least at these two levels of responsibility, companies can define the issues in question and their boards can decide where to strike the balance between the different interests involved. It will also be possible to make estimates, however rough, of the costs which will be incurred and of the benefits which will accrue, since both costs and benefits will be largely internal to the firm.

Beyond these two levels, there is a much less well-defined area of responsibility, which takes in the interaction between business and society in a wider sense. How far has business a responsibility to maintain the framework of the society in which it operates and how far should business reflect society's priorities in addition to its own commercial priorities?

At this level, companies have to look outwards at the changing terms on which society will license them to carry on their activities, rather than inwards at their own performance, as is implied by the other two levels of responsibility. The definition of responsibility moves further out of the hands of companies at this stage, because business decisions are like stones thrown into a pool, which represents society, and companies are asked to take account of the ripples they cause as they move outwards to the shore. This requires companies to envisage the wider consequences of their decisions and to build that awareness into their decision-making processes.

Problems of definition

Who is 'society'?

I have used the word 'society' as if it were clear what it means, but this turns on how widely society is to be defined. If, for example, a factory is dirtying the neighbourhood washing by the discharge from its chimney, the local community is likely to press for the company to recognize its responsibilities to society, that is to say to them, by ceasing to pollute the neighbourhood.

One way of achieving this may be to erect a taller chimney on the boiler house, planners permitting, so as to throw the smuts into the upper atmosphere. This may meet the needs of 'society' locally, but 'society' as consumers of the products made by the factory will find themselves contributing to the cost of the chimney, and 'society' in some country outside Britain can now expect to receive the factory's imperfectly combusted discharge.

From the point of view of those living near to the factory the problem would be solved, because their washing would now be cleaner. But the board of the company concerned cannot take quite such a parochial view of its responsibilities. It will have to weigh up the consequences of its actions on the different sectors of society which will be affected by them, before it can decide on the best way of solving its pollution problem.

The concern expressed today about the worldwide consequences of damaging the environment is an example of the changing terms of the licence from society under which companies operate. In the past, that concern would have centred on the local effects of pollution; now companies are expected to answer for the international effects of any pollution they may cause. The key point is that boards, in framing their social policies, need to be clear who, in any particular instance, they mean by society.

Who are the employees?

The same kind of definitional problem arises when a company considers what its obligations are to its employees. To the representatives of the employees at the bargaining table, the definition of who is an employee is straightforward: employees are the people who chose them to represent their interests. To the board, the definition is less straightforward. The board may have to make investment decisions which will reduce employment in the short term, but will result in better value to customers, so making the jobs of the smaller work-force more secure, with the possibility of taking on more employees in the future.

In making such decisions, the board will be balancing its responsibilities to present employees against those to future employees, employees on pension, employees as consumers, and employees who are either directly or indirectly shareholders. At the bargaining table only the interests of present employees will be represented, but the board has to have some regard for the interests of these other categories of employee as well.

No universal guidelines

Because the factors which boards have to weigh in coming to their decisions are so complex, there can be no universal guidelines on how a company should take account of its social responsibilities. All that generalized definitions of social responsibility can achieve is to indicate the kind of considerations boards should have in mind in arriving at a social policy.

Chairmen and boards have to come to their individual conclusions on what constitutes social responsibility in the particular circumstances of their own companies. The priority for some will be to remain in business. Failing companies will rightly have a different set of social priorities from successful ones. Boards need to define how they currently see the social responsibilities of their companies, so that there should be no confusion down the line over aims and so that they can keep a check on their progress towards those aims.

The responsibility for defining the company's social policy and for supervising its implementation rests with the chairman and the board. It is easy, for example, for a board to agree on a policy of non-discrimination in recruitment, but their responsibilities do not end with passing an irreproachable board resolution to that effect. The place where discrimination is most likely to occur is not in the personnel department but at the factory gate, where would-be applicants first present themselves. It is the board's responsibility to initiate the company's policy on non-discrimination and it is equally the board's responsibility to see that it is followed through.

It is by its decisions and actions that a company's policy on social responsibility is ultimately defined. It is helpful to everyone concerned if the board agrees a written social policy, to which ready reference can be made. The test, however, which managers will apply to board statements on social responsibility is how far adherence to them is recognized in decisions on their pay and promotion.

The board has the task of balancing the different interests which companies have to take into account in arriving at such policy decisions as whether to enter a new line of business or to close an existing one. Managers in their turn have to balance the social objectives of their companies with meeting their budgets. The dilemma is the same at the policy level and at the level of implementation; that is, what weight should be given to which business and social pressures?

Interest groups

Here it is necessary to touch on the rise of organized interest groups, because of the part they can play in attempting to influence company decisions with consequences in the social or environmental field. The essential point about such pressure groups is that they are single-minded. They are formed to pursue a particular purpose, often a negative one—to campaign against the closure of a factory, for example. They carry no responsibility for finding a better solution to the problems which gave rise to the proposed closure; they are simply against it.

This narrow focus gives single-interest groups a debating advantage over company boards, which cannot evade the responsibility for taking decisions in the same way. In an authoritative book on business ethics, Mark Pastin has perceptively referred to 'the ethical superiority of the uninvolved'.[5] Chairmen will recognize that there is a good deal of it about. Pressure groups are skilled at seizing the moral high ground and arguing that the judgement of boards is at best biased and at worst influenced solely by private gain, because boards have a direct commercial interest in their decisions. But boards are also responsible for arriving at business decisions and for taking account of the various interests which will be affected by them; the uninvolved are not.

Public relations

Boards should consider doing more to explain the complexities which lie behind major business decisions. Single-interest groups aim to simplify and to distil all the arguments down to a question of right or wrong. If decisions were as straightforward as that, boards would be able to spend less time on them. The problem for an interest group is that once the wider implications of business decisions are brought into the discussion, the narrow preoccupation which gives the group its cohesion is weakened.

The uninvolved will also argue that information and comment from companies is just an exercise in public relations, using those words in a pejorative sense. Public relations, however, are an essential aspect of a company's links with society; what matters is the inspiration behind them which determines their trustworthiness. Soundly based public relations involve listening first and then responding to whatever points have been raised. Interest groups have their part to play in that process, by making companies aware of the concerns which brought their group into existence. Companies should listen to them and be prepared to debate their arguments openly.

Boards, however, have to assess the costs and consequences of their decisions for all concerned; they need to recognize that the views of interest groups are part of their input to those decisions, but only a part. Not all the interests involved will have organized groups to represent them. For a company to go along with the demands of the most vocal or best-organized pressure group on an issue could be the easy way out of resolving a difficult conflict of interest, rather than an expression of social responsibility.

Business and government

A different kind of pressure on companies is for them to become actively involved in social fields like education or urban renewal, which are basically the responsibility of local and national government. There has been a move in Britain to reduce the role of the state and to encourage individuals to take more responsibility for shaping their own futures. Companies are expected to play their part in enabling this shift of authority—from government at the centre to local groups in their own community—to take place. In addition, governments in many countries are unable to resolve on their own the overwhelming problems arising from the twin processes of economic growth and decay.

This presents companies with a dilemma, which Shell's report, *Profits and Principles—does there have to be a choice?* expresses well:

Clearly the forces of globalisation, rapid improvements in technology and dramatic changes in world order have caused considerable confusion over what is—and is not—expected of business. Should it play a bigger role in society by providing infrastructure and social services where government does not, and then face accusations that it is interfering or buying influence? Or should it concentrate on what it does best: serving its customers and getting the best return for shareholders?

Answers are not always easy to find, but managers who run a business in this uncertain world have no choice but to make difficult decisions in the face of complex dilemmas.[6]

There is no doubt that in many parts of the world, governments are encouraging businesses to become involved, either in partnership or on their own, in fields which were once solely the responsibility of central or local authorities. In part this reflects an acceptance by politicians of the limits to their ability to bring about social improvements without the benefit of business support and expertise. In coming to some of the difficult decisions to which the Shell report refers, what are the kind of issues which chairmen and their boards might have in mind in deciding how to respond to requests for them to take on responsibilities which were once those of government? The key point is that companies need to be clear about the terms on which they are being asked to become involved.

First, the choice of social goals has to be a political decision, which should not be delegated to business. Second, companies should not undertake governmental obligations for which they do not have matching authority. Lastly, the state should not be attempting to transfer its responsibilities to companies. What it can sensibly do is to look to companies for help in carrying out some of its responsibilities, where companies have the capacity to do so.

There are government-backed social initiatives, such as vocational training for young people and the encouragement of new enterprises, which can only succeed with the active support and involvement of companies. They are examples of the interdependence of government and business, which in turn is the reason why companies cannot be neatly detached from the communities of which they are a part, as Professor Friedman's approach to social responsibility would require.

Company social policies

Because each company will approach its social responsibilities in its own way, discussion of these responsibilities has been in general terms. Boards will come to their own decisions on what the social policies of their companies should be and on the principles on which they should be based. Nevertheless, it may be helpful to be rather more precise about how boards might set about defining their policies in this imprecise field.

Internal responsibilities

I drew a distinction earlier between three different levels of responsibility against which society could measure the actions of companies. The first was their responsibility to meet their material obligations and the second went beyond adherence to acceptable standards, in order to meet those set by best practice. A company's policy towards its responsibilities at these two levels is largely an internal matter. It is directed at making the most of the company's resources, along with providing for their renewal, and at minimizing any negative effects of the company's actions on the community. This reflects the board's responsibility for the continuing health of the business, rather than its external involvement in the community.

There clearly is a social element in a company's policies at these levels. Behaving responsibly towards customers and suppliers makes business sense to any company thinking beyond the short term, but it is also one of the ways in which a company fulfils its obligations to the community. Involving employees in the decisions which directly affect them is an issue on which the European Social Charter places considerable importance, as I would. Nevertheless, it is more of a business responsibility than a social one. A company needs to have established a sense of common purpose among all those who make up the enterprise, if it is to carry out its primary task efficiently.

A company's responsibilities for matters affecting health, safety, and the environment are another example of what is primarily a business responsibility, but one which entails particular duties to the community as well. The reason why companies have a special responsibility in these fields is that they know more about their products and processes than anyone else. They should, therefore, be the first to be aware of any hazards which could be attached to them.

If companies do have any doubts about the effects of their products on people or on the environment, they have a duty to share their concerns with the appropriate authorities as soon as they become aware of them. In consumer goods companies, this may result in expensive recalls of goods which are already in the shops, when the chances of a serious problem arising from their sale are minimal. The evidence is that companies which accept the costs of working to high standards of care benefit from the loyalty of their customers. A company's policies in respect of the first two levels of responsibility will reflect the views of its board on how they believe the business should be run. The board will arrive at them after weighing the interests of all those who have a stake in the continued success of the enterprise. It is when we move to the third level of responsibility—how far a company has a responsibility to maintain the structure of the society in which it operates—that the decisions for the chairman and the board become more difficult.

External responsibilities

The argument for companies to take on the responsibilities which society expects of them is largely one of self-interest. If a company invests in training its own employees, the costs are known and the return is direct to the company. If, however, a company gives managerial time to an educational partnership with the local schools from which it recruits, the returns are indirect and do not accrue solely to the company. This means that the board's decision on the amount of effort to put behind community initiatives has to be more a matter of judgement than of calculation.

First, the board needs to decide what resources of time and money it is prepared to put into meeting its external social responsibilities—those which are not an integral part of the business. Once that overall budgetary decision has been made, the board has to make choices and set priorities with the aim of concentrating the company's efforts where they can achieve the best results.

Choices and priorities

Boards have to choose from a formidable list of worthwhile social causes, all of which are looking for the backing of companies. Links with schools have already been mentioned. That is a straightforward way for companies to involve themselves in their local communities, and both companies and schools have a common interest in enabling school pupils to make the most of their abilities. But staying within the educational field, companies in Britain are also being asked to find appropriate work experience places for pupils and their teachers, to provide teaching materials and equipment, to fund specialist colleges, to back enterprise schemes in schools, and to sponsor students. All of these initiatives depend for their success on the active support of companies.

Education is not, however, the only claimant; there are a number of other causes, such as the regeneration of inner-city areas, the encouragement of new enterprises and the raising of standards of training, which are seeking company involvement under the banner of social responsibility.

Reference to the range of demands which are being made on companies in the social field could give the impression that the issue of how best to respond to them mainly faces larger companies. In fact, companies of any size can make a useful contribution to the community; thus businesses big and small need to decide what their policies are in this regard.

Some of the most effective education/business partnerships have been between small shops and businesses and their local schools. A small business can often give children a better insight into the world of work than a large company, because its activities are on a more human scale. The cost of this kind of social initiative to a one-man or one-woman business is the time of its owner/manager, which is its main resource. The balance between the interests of the business and the interests of society has, therefore, to be as carefully struck by an owner/manager as by the board of a large corporation.

Need for structure

Large companies in their turn, particularly those with locations right across the country, are already involved to a greater or lesser extent in most of the social initiatives which have been mentioned. They have a particular need to establish clear social priorities, because the execution of those policies will be local and therefore the responsibility of a site or branch manager. For companies to obtain the best value for their efforts on behalf of the community, it is essential that local management decisions should be made within the context of a well-defined company policy.

The lead, however, has to come from the top and it is for the chairman and the board to draw up the company's community affairs policy and to communicate it throughout the enterprise. They also have to ensure that there is an organizational structure in place for putting the policy into effect. Unless this is done, the response to the policy will depend on the public-spiritedness of individual managers and there will be no reliable means of monitoring its progress or of modifying it in the light of experience.

Guidelines

What criteria might boards use to decide on the level of support to put behind their company's social objectives? The main resources which companies have to offer to the community are people and money; on the whole, management skills are in even shorter supply in the social field than funds. Loaning experienced and committed managers to the community can achieve what donations of cash on their own cannot. There are, however, strict limits to the extent to which companies can second active and capable managers at a time when organizations have all become leaner. What they may be able to do is to arrange for members of their staff, who are prepared to undertake community activities in their own time, to have some company time off as well for the same purpose. In addition, there may well be recently retired employees who are willing to lend their skills and experience to socially worthwhile projects at home or abroad.

When it comes to companies providing funds for investment in the community, the way in which boards allocate their community affairs budget is a matter of individual choice. In my former company, Cadbury Schweppes, the board began by defining the kinds of community activity which it thought the company should support. The first test was that the organizations concerned should be working in fields which were relevant to the company's long-term strategic objectives. Within that category, a further test was the degree of common interest between the aims of the organization and those of the company. In addition to common aims, the board was also looking for shared values, for bodies which had the same kind of outlook as the company on people and on priorities. Two further points to be taken into account were the capacity of the organizations concerned to become self-sustaining and the closeness of their links with any of the company's sites.

The company also gave its support to Business in the Community, an organization set up and funded by companies to put new heart into Britain's older industrial areas. They did this on the basis that many community problems were best tackled by companies working together in a coordinated way, rather than on their own. By working through a collective body, like Business in the Community, companies encourage others to join it. One of the ways in which established companies can help new local initiatives is by backing them at a formative stage and thereby giving them their seal of approval.

The main point is that by having clear guidelines, the difficult task of discriminating between the many worthy causes which come across the chairman's desk is made manageable. A clear policy focus means that the company's support is targeted and therefore more effective than if it were spread more thinly and more widely. It also enables a brief statement of the company's policy to be sent to those whose appeals fall outside the guidelines.

Two further points concern the support which companies give to the community in terms of the time of their employees and the backing which companies can give to the voluntary efforts of employees.

Backing employees

The sheer scale of the part-time help which people from business give to the community is impressive. Some of it is in working hours, most of it is not. By sitting on a school governing body, by being a committee member of a voluntary organization or by belonging to one, employees are putting business experience to work in the community. Most of this volunteer help will be the result of individual initiative, rather than being organized through the company. Where the company can play its part is by letting employees know what kind of help is needed by local organizations and by making it as easy as possible for employees to serve the community in this way.

On the second point, there are two useful means of backing the voluntary efforts of employees. One is to regard the active involvement of employees in a cause as a strong argument for giving it company support. The other is for the company to match charitable donations made by its employees. This ensures that the company's contributions go to causes which the workforce has identified as worthwhile; it also helps to raise the level of charitable giving in general.

Jobs

Decisions on which community activities a company should support and the extent to which it should support them are not the sum of a company's social policy. It also has judgements to make in the middle ground between its inward responsibilities to the business and its outward responsibilities to society. The decisions which face a company when it introduces new technology or concentrates its production facilities, are examples of this kind of issue. They are business decisions with social implications. The immediate effect of investing in automation or of closing a factory will be to reduce employment. What responsibilities do companies, taking such actions, have to the community over the provision of jobs?

The primary aim

The starting-point has to be the primary aim of companies, which is to meet the needs of their customers for goods and services and to do so profitably. Everyone is a consumer; some consumers are employees. Satisfying customers requires companies to compete in the market-place; they cannot, therefore, opt out of introducing new technology in order to preserve jobs. To do so would be to deny consumers the benefits of technical progress, to short-change the shareholders and, in the longer run, to put the jobs of everyone in the company at risk. What destroys jobs certainly and permanently is the failure to be competitive.

The record of experience is that technological progress creates more jobs than it eliminates, in ways which cannot be forecast. It may do so, however, only after a time-lag and those displaced may not, through lack of skills, be able to take advantage of the new opportunities when they arise. Nevertheless, the company's prime responsibility to everyone who has a stake in it is to retain its competitive edge, even if this means a reduction in jobs in the short run.

Management of change

Where the company does have a responsibility to society is in the manner in which it manages change. This includes the need to foresee and plan the introduction of new technology, at the same time involving those who will be affected by it in the way in which it is to be introduced. The longer the notice of changes resulting in a loss of jobs, the better the chances of using natural wastage or early retirement to close the gap, and the greater the likelihood of those who will lose out being able to find alternative employment. If the reduction by one company in its workforce hits a particular area, then the company can take steps to encourage new businesses to start up in the locality; the steel and coal industries have demonstrated in Britain what it is possible to do through successful initiatives of this kind.

Companies also possess a vital resource, from the community's point of view, which is their capacity to provide training. The provision of appropriate training enables continuing employees to take advantage of change and those who lose their jobs as a result of it to find new ones more readily.

Companies cannot set out to create jobs as a goal. Their task is to meet the needs of their customers; if they do that successfully, the jobs will follow. What they can do, however, is to support organizations like Business in the Community and local enterprise agencies, which have been set up to encourage the formation of new enterprises. In this way, companies are able to create employment collectively, even if they are unable to do so individually.

Benefits of change

It is easier for boards to see the need for change and its ultimate benefits, than it is for most other groups in society, including politicians, administrators, and those belonging to the professions. Companies earn their living in markets which are forever changing. Their continued existence depends on their ability to read the signs of change correctly and to make the most of the opportunities that change presents. Society, on the other hand, has a literally vested interest in preserving the present structure, whether it be of industry or of jobs. This is why the balance on this issue of jobs now, versus jobs in the future, is difficult to strike in a way which society in general will see as socially responsible.

Decisions not drift

The last point which needs to be made on the issue of jobs is to draw attention to the pressures on boards not to put through programmes of change which will have repercussions on the community. It is the job of chairmen and their boards to see that companies face up to the difficult choices which confront them and to implement such changes as are necessary promptly and efficiently, and with due regard to their consequences for people. What is a matter for concern is when public pressure—usually well-intentioned—is brought to bear on companies in the name of social responsibility to put off such disagreeable decisions as the closure of an uneconomic plant.

The board which takes drastic action in order that its company should survive is more likely to be criticised publicly, than the board which fails to grasp the nettle and whose business gradually, but inexorably, declines. There is always a temptation in business to postpone difficult decisions, but it is not in society's interests that hard choices should be evaded because of public clamour. True social responsibility requires that chairmen and boards should be encouraged to take the decisions facing their companies, however thorny. The responsibility for providing that encouragement rests with society as a whole.

The business record on social responsibility

By way of conclusion, what has been the record of British companies to date in carrying out their responsibilities to the community? I would suggest that the main failure of business has been its slowness to pick up society's signals and to see the direction in which companies were bound to move. Over such issues as pollution or consumerism, the first reaction of business has been one of opposition. As a consequence of taking up this position, later attempts to modify proposals for controls in a practical way have been seen as a change of tactics, not of heart. In other instances, companies have lain low and hoped that the pressures for action would prove ephemeral. The lesson is that companies should pay attention to forecasting social changes in the same way as they do changes in their markets. This will guide them as to which social trends are relevant to their type of business and help them to identify appropriate social objectives; these may well be different from the ones which are being pressed on them most stridently.

Openness

Companies have to pick up the signals as to the pace and direction of society's expectations of business, so that they can play an active part in shaping the new rules, whether statutory or voluntary, within which they will have to work. A readiness by companies to provide more information about their policies and actions in fields of social concern is an important element in encouraging this dialogue. Disclosure is not in itself a panacea for improving the relationship between business and society, but it represents a willingness to operate an open system which is the foundation of that relationship. Companies need to be open to the views of society and open in return about their own activities. This is a necessary condition for the establishment of trust and for the sensible resolution of conflicts of interest.

Involvement

Next, companies have to be prepared to become more involved in the political process through which governments respond to social pressures, so that they can play their part in that process more effectively. Companies have to learn how to combine serving their customers in the marketplace and the social interest in the political forum. One way of doing so is to encourage employees at all levels to play their full part in social and political affairs. Not only will they have a valuable contribution to make, based on practical experience, but they will also become more aware of the trend of social aims and more alert to society's expectations of business.

The involvement of company employees in helping to achieve community goals brings benefits all round, to the giving and receiving institutions, and to the individuals concerned. It is a working example of the way in which business and society interact. Companies are part of society and their ability to achieve their business aims depends on the health of the society in which they operate. By contributing to the solution of some of society's most pressing problems, companies improve their own environment and therefore their own chances of success.

The defensive argument to the same end is that failure by business to keep in touch with and respond to society's views of its responsibilities will lead to increasing regulation, with all its attendant inefficiencies. Alternatively, society will attempt to reduce the power of business, if it thinks that power is being used to the detriment of the community. What was referred to in an article in the American journal *Business Horizons* as, 'the Iron Law of Responsibility' states: 'In the long run those who do not use power in a manner which society considers responsible will tend to lose it.'[7]

Finally, an important positive reason for companies to be seen to be meeting society's expectations of them is the vital need to attract able young people into industry and commerce. This is essential for companies and for society, if scarce resources are to be used effectively and the social aims of the community and of business are to be realized. Companies will win the commitment of people of the calibre they need, only if they are seen to be making a worthwhile contribution to society.

Notes

1. Friedman, Milton (1982). *Capitalism and Freedom*, Chicago: University of Chicago Press, 133.
2. Beesley, M. E. and Evans, T. C. (1973). *The Meaning of Social Responsibility*, London Business School, December, 3.
3. Department of Trade and Industry (2001). Company Law Review Steering Group, *Modern Company Law: Final Report*, 1: ix.
4. Confederation of British Industry (1973). *The Responsibilities of the British Public Company*, 9.
5. Pastin, Mark (1986). *The Hard Problems of Management*, San Francisco: Jossey-Bass, 72.
6. Shell International (1998). *Profits and Principles—does there have to be a choice?* 2.
7. Davis, Keith (1975). 'Five propositions for social responsibility', *Business Horizons*, June, 20.

11

Issues for Chairmen

Given the importance of a candidate's motivation—particularly their attitude to executive power—as well as the knowledge required, one of the surprises of the research was the lack of rigour that often seemed to characterise the appointment process.

On Becoming Company Chairman[1]

Appointing a chairman

In Chapter 7 the division of responsibilities between chairmen and chief executives and the question of finding and appointing a new chairman were considered in that context, but they need to be more fully explored. On the assumption that the two top jobs were divided, two options were discussed, both of which involved appointing from within. One was to choose an existing outside member of the board and the other was to appoint the chief executive and search for a new chief executive.

The chief executive as candidate

The latter course demands a great deal of the chief executive who takes the chair and of the incoming chief executive. The majority of the executive team will owe their positions to their former CEO and the new chief executive will have to win their loyalty and support. New chairmen will as chief executives have set a style and pattern of working which their successors will need to adapt in order to match their methods and approach. Equally, new chairmen will have left strategies, projects, and policies in place, which are their creation and which they will understandably want to see furthered. To allow successors to put their own stamp on the way in which their companies are to be run, with the implication that what had gone before could be improved on requires restraint of a high order.

The chief executive to chairman option is workable and is helped if there is an age gap and if, on becoming chairman, the new incumbent takes up outside posts or activities which will assist in restraining any temptation to cross the boundary into the chief executive's domain. It is equally important for there to be an opportunity for the relationship to develop, with new chief executives taking time over making changes in policies and people, and in accepting guidance in so doing, thus making the most of their chairman's knowledge and experience. New chief executives can then expand their role as they in turn acquire knowledge and confidence. Once again, the acceptance of a transfer of power and authority of this kind depends on the willingness of their new chairmen to enable a shift in relative responsibilities to take place through time. Everything can and should fall into place, provided that erstwhile chief executives fully absorb the nature of their new role and appreciate its importance to their successors and to their companies. The message for boards is that the key to choosing this option is their assessment of the personality and motivation of the chief executive who is to take the chair. They need, so to speak, to be convinced that the leopard can change his spots and intends to do so. (Curiously and irrelevantly, leopards do not strictly speaking have spots).

An outside director

The other course, choosing one of the outside directors who is already on the board, offers a number of advantages. They will be known to their fellow board members and to some of the executives and they will have acquired a degree of knowledge of the company and its markets. In addition, it is a form of selection for which preparation can be made in advance. Nomination committees will have potential chairmen in mind when selecting outside directors. Quite apart from providing an opportunity for planned succession, there may be a need to fill the chairman's post unexpectedly. Thus, to have a deputy chairman, and perhaps one other outside director, who could take the chair at short notice seems a sound precaution.

However, there is a significant difference between being a good team player and leading the team. It is also important to recognize that an outside board member's knowledge of a company's business is likely to be fairly superficial. Even after nearly twenty years as a director of IBM (UK), I appreciated how limited was my understanding of where the real risks and opportunities for the company lay in a fast-changing environment. The need for existing board members, and all the more so for external candidates for the chairmanship, to apply themselves to gaining the necessary understanding of the business should not be underestimated.

Equally, it may be hard to foresee how someone whom board members have known as a colleague will act if they take the chair. As a chief executive explained in the research report from which the chapter heading is taken: 'You're always taking a chance because a person in a non-executive role won't necessarily behave the same way as chairman. You haven't seen them managing a meeting, for example, you haven't seen how they operate in a crisis, or how they function at a personal level when the going gets tough.'[2]

Even if there are appointable outside directors on the board, the nomination committee may well feel that they should cast their net wider. The arguments for looking outside the company, as well as within it, and for enlisting the help of professional agencies in the search, is that this is a crucially important decision for a board. The board should not simply be concerned to find a chairman, but to find the best chairman that it can. The only way in which the board can assess the calibre of the inside candidates is by comparing them with those who might be brought in from outside the company. If the decision is to appoint from outside the company, then the board must appreciate how much their new chairman will need to learn about the company and its people, even if they already have experience as chairmen elsewhere. During that learning period, they will be dependent on their chief executives who will be their main source of information and advice.

Considerations to take into account

Whether the board intends to appoint one of its members, or someone not currently on the board or in the company, there are a number of issues to consider in coming to a decision. First, does the selected candidate seem to have the qualities which make for a good chairman? These include the ability to listen, to lead, and to weld the board into an effective team. It includes having the commitment to learn what needs to be learnt about the enterprise and those who make it up. Above all, it involves accepting that the post is that of chairman, not that of chief executive, and the willingness to establish a relationship with the chief executive which will foster unity of purpose throughout the organization. The advantage of choosing someone who is already chairman of a company elsewhere is that this provides evidence of their capacity to take the chair and of their having turned their back on an executive role.

Perhaps the key quality which chairmen need to have or to acquire in their relationship with their chief executives is that required of a good coach. Sporting coaches are not looking to win medals for themselves, though they have probably done so on their way up. Their satisfaction derives from the achievements of those they coach. Chief executives are responsible for achieving results and should receive the credit for them. The role of chairmen is to support their chief executives, and to enjoy their success and whatever reflected glory goes with it. A recent survey by Russell Reynolds of chairmen of leading companies elicited this comment, which admirably sums up the relationship I have in mind: 'The main objective of the Chairman is to help the CEO to be successful.'[3]

Both jobs are in their own way lonely. The time which chairmen can spend with their outside directors is limited although, as has been said, a trusted deputy chairman is a great asset as a confidant. Similarly, there are issues which chief executives cannot discuss with their executive colleagues and their chairmen are the only people in whom they can confide. This is why the ability of chairmen and chief executives to build a relationship of mutual trust and confidence is so essential to board and corporate effectiveness. Their relationship sets the pattern for the way in which outside and executive directors work with each other on the board.

All of this is in the context of the separation of the posts of chairman and chief executive. If boards are appointing, for whatever reason, a chairman/chief executive, then the choice is likely to be based on their managerial skills rather than their chairmanly qualities. The role of the deputy chairman/senior independent director will be to ensure that an appropriate division of responsibilities is established between the chairman/chief executive and the board and that the chairman/chief executive's accountability to the board is maintained.

Board support

When a new chairman is appointed whether from within the board or from outside it, they inherit their board. The board may not have the balance of membership which incoming chairmen feel is necessary for the challenges facing the company and so they may want to bring about changes in the composition and methods of working of the board. It is important for boards to have considered what manner of chairman they believe that their company needs, before making an appointment. In the same way, prospective chairmen need to know what it is that their boards are going to expect of them. An example of the problems which can arise, if expectations on either side have not been made clear, occurred when a UK clearing bank announced the name of its forthcoming chairman. The chairman-elect then explained that on taking up the post, he proposed to slim the board down to a manageable size. When the board rejected this proposal, the chairman-elect, in my view rightly on all counts, refused to take on the chairmanship. Quite apart from the board being remiss in not having discussed the basis on which the prospective chairman was to take up the post, the composition and nature of a board have to be a prime responsibility of its chairman.

As well as sorting out the relative expectations of boards of their chairmen and chairmen of their boards, it is the responsibility of current chairmen to be able to assure prospective chairmen that they will have the support of the whole board on taking the chair. The outside directors, usually as a nomination committee, will have an agreed selection procedure in place and will have carried it out, in conjunction with the chief executive. Chairmen will probably have sounded out their executive directors individually, to ensure that they are of the same mind and have no alternatives to put forward. Chairmen can then give their successors the assurance, which they must have, that they will have the full backing of the board, from which their authority derives.

What manner of chairman?

The underlying issue for a board, in coming to a conclusion about the chairmanship, is what kind of chairman will best meet the board's needs? One element of choice is between a chairman who will broadly maintain the company on its existing course and one who is likely to feel that a change, either of direction or of pace, is needed. The labels 'conservative' and 'radical' have perhaps too many political overtones to describe at all accurately the choices a board has in this matter; they may unintentionally belittle the importance, at certain stages in a company's development, of consolidating what has gone before. Conservation does not mean inaction, since it requires the organization to maintain its capacity to progress through investing in its human and physical resources. Nevertheless, the first divide is between a conservative chairman, who will aim to keep the company on its present lines, and a radical chairman, whose instinct will be to bring about change.

The other divide is one of style—and styles of leadership vary considerably from the authoritative to the participative. The personal styles of chairmen also vary. There are those who lead from the front by force of personality and there are those who fit the classical description of leadership with which the book began—'He that governs sits quietly at the stern and scarce is seen to stir.' Individuals have to discover for themselves their natural style of leadership and then develop it. The straightforward point is that a particular kind of chairman will suit a particular board at a particular time. Boards, therefore, need to decide what it is that they are looking for in their chairmen and what type of chairman would best fit their needs. The clearer the picture that they have of their prospective chairman, the more likely it is that they will make a successful appointment. I feel it is also helpful for chairmen either to have terms of office or some understanding with their boards over the age at which they expect to retire. As with outside directors, the end of one term of office provides an opportunity for boards and their chairmen to review the position and then to proceed to reappointment, provided that meets the aims and needs of both parties. The advantage of agreeing an expected retirement date is that it sets a timetable for planning for succession.

In drawing up their specification for a chairman, boards will have two points in mind. One is the likely span of the chairman's appointment. The board has to assess not only what manner of chairman their situation demands today, but what it is likely to demand during the chairman's tenure of office. The second point is that chairmen are entitled to assume that their appointment was made after due analysis and that it was a deliberate decision whose consequences were anticipated. That was my view on being first appointed as chairman of a board of a public company. As the youngest member of the board, I had never expected to be appointed and I took the decision as a vote in favour of breaking with the past.

Dropping the pilot

So much for the appointment of the chairman; but there will also be occasions for parting, when the board decides either that their vision of the future of the company has diverged from that of their chairman, or that their chairman's style no longer meets the needs of the situation. When, for whatever reason, chairmen have lost the confidence of their boards, they have to give way to someone in whom the board can place its confidence. Their authority is dependent on their enjoying the confidence of their boards and if that confidence is withdrawn, their position falls and their authority with it. In the past, the problem has been that it was not always clear whose job it was to take the initiative if a chairman seemed no longer to command the respect of the board. Whose duty was it to assess the views of board members and then to speak on their behalf to the chairman? This is now firmly the responsibility of the deputy chairman or senior independent director, and it is simplest, as before, to take them as being the same person.

Change from within

What is likely to happen, when the move for change comes from within the company, is that concerned board members would, in the first instance, approach the deputy chairman, or possibly the chief executive, and ask them to sound out other board members. If a clear view emerges, as a result of discussions with directors individually that the chairman should be replaced, then it would be for deputy chairmen to tell their chairmen that the board no longer had confidence in their leadership. Faced with this situation, chairmen have no alternative but to resign and the board meeting, chaired by the deputy chairman, to appoint another chairman would be to that extent uncontentious.

The objective is to avoid an atmosphere of conspiracy and period of uncertainty while board members are making up their minds whether or not to act. This would inevitably become a source of rumour which would be damaging to the company. The fact that boards might possibly face the need to replace their chairmen reinforces the argument for terms of office and once the issue has arisen the sooner it is resolved the better. Even when the resignation and replacement of the chairman of a company has been resolved internally and straightforwardly, the necessary formalities and announcements have to be made. A change of chairmanship is not solely a domestic issue for the board and company concerned.

Change from without

It may be, however, that the pressure to replace the chairman comes not from within the board, but externally from the shareholders. This pressure may be applied privately or publicly. A private approach could be made by one or more major institutional shareholders to influential members of the board, in order to persuade them that change was needed. Again, under the Combined Code it would be the deputy chairman/senior independent director to whom they would address their concerns.

Assuming that their arguments were accepted, the main body of board members would arrange for the resignation or retirement of the chairman and for the appointment of someone in their place, who better met the needs of the board and of the shareholders. Bringing about change at the top in this way seems to me to be an unimpeachable example of the institutions using their power in the interests of all the shareholders and of the company. The acceptance by the institutions of that degree of responsibility for the governance of the companies in which they have invested, is to be encouraged.

A more contentious means to the same end comes about when the pressure for the chairman to stand down is brought to bear publicly. A press report describing just such a situation ran as follows: 'Institutional shareholders are sounding out those who support the move and are confident that they can muster the numbers. They will shortly present the chairman with a *fait accompli*—that he either resigns or they will call an extraordinary general meeting and vote that he be removed from the board.'

That describes a method by which shareholders can bring about change through a general meeting. But it is change in response to a crisis and it risks forcing the resignation issue through, without proper time for reflection or for a thorough search for the best available successor. Private pressure is likely to lead to a better outcome in the longer term than public clamour. If there was more of the former, there would be less cause for the latter.

Be that as it may, chairmen presented with this kind of ultimatum, backed by the shareholders, have little option but to resign. While this may be in line with their duty to the company, they will also have regard to their duty not to leave the board in disarray at a time of difficulty. This may involve riding out the storm, until a suitable replacement can be found who commands the confidence of the shareholders and the board.

The Guinness approach

Guinness plc is an example of a company which, unusually, has included in its Articles of Association formal arrangements for the election and removal of their chairman. The Guinness board is required, under its Articles, to establish a Non-Executive Committee made up of all board members save those appointed as executive directors. The relevant Article sets out the Committee's remit as follows:

The Non-Executive Committee shall have the sole power to elect the chairman and any vice-chairman or vice-chairmen and any deputy chairman or deputy chairmen of the Board with the power to remove any person so appointed, the power to determine the period for which and the basis on which any chairman, vice-chairman or vice-chairmen or deputy chairman or deputy chairmen holds office.[4]

As a result, the Guinness board has an overt and orderly process for appointing or removing its chairman; an example which deserves consideration. In more general terms, the appointment of the Non-Executive Committee was part of the board's system of checks and balances. Guinness had, at the time, a chairman who effectively combined the posts of chairman and chief executive. The basis for this arrangement was that the chairman had two managing directors, each in charge of one of the company's two core businesses, reporting to him. There was, therefore, a division of responsibilities at the head of the company. The chairman was, nevertheless, in a powerful position, being responsible both for the board and for the management of the enterprise. This made it prudent for the board to build appropriate checks and balances into its governance structure.

Thus the Non-Executive Committee was formed to strengthen the position of the outside directors, and thereby of the board, in relation to the chairman. It acknowledged the role of the outside directors in the election and dismissal of the chairman and made clear how, and by whom, these crucial decisions were to be made. The Guinness example also illustrates that companies have to shape their own patterns of governance, in the light of the particular needs of their boards and shareholders.

Replacing the chief executive

While dealing with the manner in which changes at the head of a company may be brought about, it is relevant to touch on the issue for chairmen if board members approach them over whether their chief executive should be replaced. Chairmen would be likely to begin by sounding out their outside directors to see how widely and firmly this view was held and on what basis they had come to their judgement. Assuming that there is agreement among the outside directors over the need to ask the chief executive to resign and to appoint a new one, chairmen have to consider the position of the executive directors, whom they will no doubt consult individually. If they do not stand in the way of the move, the chairman will put the board's position to the chief executive. Should the chief executive accept the position and resign, then the board discussion and decision becomes a formality. If, however, the chief executive contests the request to resign and takes the fight to the board, the executive directors may be faced with a conflict of interest. In the event of the board being divided and the decision depending on a vote, the executive directors will have to vote for or against the person to whom they report, or abstain.

Abstention may be the politic course, but the executive directors are as responsible for any decision over the chief executive as other board members and their attitude to the question of whether or not the chief executive should be replaced is crucial to the future management of the company. Given that the appointment or replacement of the chief executive is a central decision for boards to make, it is unsatisfactory that one set of members of a unitary board could find themselves on the sidelines. Chairmen will have ascertained the views of their executive directors outside the board meeting and so they will to that extent have played a part in the decision as individual board members. The position of executive directors over the replacement of their chief could be made even more complicated, if the chairman was also the chief executive, or if the chairman were to disagree with the outside directors and support the chief executive.

Principles

Because it is possible to think up any number of hypothetical situations of this kind, it makes sense to try and draw some principles out of this discussion of replacing chairmen or chief executives. First, it is the cardinal duty of boards to ensure that their companies have effective leadership. Therefore, the choice of their chairmen and of their chief executives is usually the most important decision which they have to make. Second, the lead in bringing about change has to come from the outside directors. It is for them, not for the executive directors, to form a view on the quality of the board and company leadership. That is what the shareholders elected them to do. Provided that the outside directors are united in whatever view they come to, an issue over the chairman or the chief executive can be resolved. If the outside directors are divided, the situation will drift and deteriorate until the membership of the board is changed.

A good example, both of the process by which decisions on corporate leadership are taken and of their complexity because of the relationship between chairmen and chief executives, came with the decision by the Standard Chartered Bank board, whose chairman is Sir Patrick Gillam, to replace their chief executive Rana Talwar. The manner in which this was brought about was reported in a newspaper as follows:

While Talwar supped a cocktail, the bank's non-executive directors met at Standard Chartered's head office in Aldermanbury Square to decide whether Gillam or Talwar should go. Gillam told them he wanted Talwar out, but then left them to conduct their own meeting. After 90 heated minutes the decision to axe Talwar was made. On Wednesday, Talwar heard the news from Cob Stenham, a leading non-executive director, and Lord Stewartby, the deputy chairman.[5]

This account underlines the reliance which the governance process places on outside directors to resolve problems which may arise over the conduct of chairmen or chief executives. Their central responsibility is not sitting on audit committees or acting as monitors, it is taking the necessary decisions to ensure that the leadership of their company is in the right hands.

Bids and mergers

Chairmen have a central role to play when their companies either make a bid for another business or receive one. The issue of bids and mergers follows on from the previous discussion, because the lead players are the same— chairmen and outside directors. The advantages of having disinterested, independent directors on either side in a bid have been cogently argued by Lord Rees-Mogg in an article in *The Independent*. The article was entitled: 'The value of an outside voice in the drama of a takeover bid' and was based on his experience as an outside director of both bidding and defending companies.[6] The reason why making or defending a contested bid lays such a burden on chairmen is because of the conflicts of interest which a bid can generate. Oversimplifying the situation considerably, the key interests to be taken into account are those of the shareholders and those of the employees, which may in turn subdivide into the interests of the executive directors and senior managers and the interests of the employees in general.

Since the executive members of the board have a career interest in the outcome of bids, whether making them or defending against them, chair- men have to be especially vigilant in ensuring that the board holds a proper balance between the interests of the shareholders and those of the rest of the employees. This is likely to be a demanding test of chairmanship. Difficult matters of business judgement are involved, to which are added strong emo- tions, extreme pressures of time, and perhaps the glare of publicity as well. The responsibilities of chairmen are to hold the board team together, while ensuring that in coming to its decisions the board strikes the right balance between the different interests involved.

A basic cause of conflict in a bid situation is the poor record of mergers and takeovers in living up to the claims made by those who promote and pursue them. 'According to a study of the US based consulting corporation Mercer Management Consulting two-thirds of all mergers result in a debacle for shareholders. According to consultants McKinsey only one fourth of all analysed firms have recouped their cost of mergers.'[7]

The general picture is similar in the UK where the outcome of bids is that in aggregate the shareholders of the bidding company lose and the share- holders of the target company gain. Shareholder value overall is lost since the losses tend to outweigh the gains.[8] The question which then arises, given that efficiency gains from mergers tend to be low, is who pays the bill? Too often it is the work force, because factories and offices are closed and emp- loyees laid off in an attempt to make the savings on which the bid was predi- cated. There are a number of reasons why the shareholders of the bidding company are likely to lose out. The most common are paying over the odds in an auction and failing to achieve the benefits on which the bid was justified.

Role of board members

If a company's executive team aims to make an acquisition, they will present their case to the board. The task of the board is to test the assumptions on which the acquisition case has been made and its fit with the company's strategy. The board, led by the chairman and the outside directors, will then set the negotiating limits. If the target company rebuffs the approach, the acquiring company may decide to go ahead with a bid. This is the point at which it is the job of the chairman and the outside directors to keep the interests of their shareholders firmly in mind. The executives have an understandable interest in enlarging their company and their prospects with it, as well as an equally understandable interest in winning the battle, if that is what it turns out to be. The only interest of the raft of professional advisers involved is to encourage all concerned to proceed regardless. It is solely the chairman and the outside directors who are in a position to judge when it may be in the best interests of the shareholders to call a halt. If outside directors do nothing more than prevent shareholder value being destroyed by paying too much for acquisitions, they will have earned their fees many times over.

The role of chairmen and outside directors is equally crucial if they are defending against a bid rather than making one. The board will, almost by definition, reject the first approach by an acquiring company, in order to raise the offer and because it would be hard to justify to shareholders accepting an offer without testing the market. If a bid is then launched, it is for the chairman to ensure that an effective defence is mounted and to obtain the support of shareholders. That support needs to be retained as well as obtained and turns on the relationship which the chairman and the chief executive have built up over time with their shareholders. If boards are looking to the loyalty of their investors when a bid comes, they need to have earned it by having established open channels of communication with them beforehand. At this stage, chairmen and boards are likely to be on safe ground in believing that the interests both of shareholders and of employees will be best served by rejecting the bid and perhaps exploring other options.

Need for independent judgement

It is when the bidding company either stands firm on its initial offer, or raises it, that chairmen along with their outside directors have to exercise their independent judgement. In terms of the value which the bid places on the company, the board has to weigh the bid offer against what it can realistically expect to achieve for the shareholders itself. This requires considerable judgement, given that the offer price will be firm, while the board's forecast of the future earning power of the company has to be estimated. In pursuing this course, they will be aiming to do their best to serve the interests of their shareholders.

Where the interests of the employees lie will depend on the intentions of both the bidders and the defenders. By which I mean that the figures put forward by either side will be justified on the grounds of the actions to be taken to live up to them—selling parts of the business, closing factories, reducing labour, and so on. The higher the price, the more drastic the action which may have to be taken by whoever ultimately controls the company. The board, therefore, needs to take account of the implications for the employees of their defensive tactics.

A further area of responsibility for chairmen and boards is to safeguard, as far as possible, the executives of their company against retribution for the vigour of their defence, if the bid succeeds. This is where it is advantageous, should the bid be hotly contested, for the defence to be clearly seen to have been led by the chairman and the board. It is then they who have forced the price up against the bidder, rather than the executives, whose careers may well be at stake if their company is taken over.

Conclusions

There are two final points to be made in the context of bids and mergers. The first is the advantage of having both a chairman and a chief executive when a company is making or faced with a bid. The person who is both chairman and chief executive is more likely to feel vulnerable to the charge of favouring the interests of management as against those of the shareholders; equally, their position is not as objectively independent as that of a chairman in resolving conflicts of interest. In defence, the plus of having two people at the helm is that the chairman can take on some at least of the tasks of dealing with the external work involved with the bid, allowing the chief executive to concentrate as far as possible on the continued running of the business.

The second point is that bidding companies normally give assurances over the way in which the company they aim to acquire will be run if their bid succeeds. Too often, those assurances are disregarded when the takeover has happened. The market in the control of corporate assets would be less imperfect, if the appropriate authorities, say the Monopolies and Mergers

Commission in the case of the UK, had the power to hold companies to the commitments which they had made over their intentions in relation to people and activities in the companies they had taken over. While they might not be able to hold them to specific assurances about conditions of employment or job security, they should be able to require them to pay for their failure to do so. This would encourage a more realistic approach to the making and honouring of pre-takeover commitments. A levy of this kind would also help to offset society's share of any loss of value arising from takeovers.

Chairmen's interests and activities

An issue which has caused boards to part with their chairmen is whether they are giving enough time to their responsibilities as chairmen. Now that chairmen are more often chairmen of more than one company, they have to strike a balance in terms of the time which they spend on each of their business interests and between those interests and other types of activity. Having a spread of interests and activities is an asset to chairmen in maintaining their focus on the work of their boards, rather than on the cut and thrust of operations, and in keeping strategy and the future of their businesses in the forefront of their minds.

Such an approach does not imply any lack of commitment to the enterprise, but it enables chairmen to review the business scene as a whole and to do so reasonably objectively. It means that chairmen can come to a judgement on issues facing the company, without being unduly constrained by the received wisdom with which most businesses are well endowed. A certain independence of thought is a valuable attribute for a chairman, but how can that independence best be developed?

Transfer of experience

When chairmen are involved in activities outside their businesses, they are engaged in transferring what they have learnt from their own enterprises into those outside activities and vice versa. They can check that the decisions being made in both spheres reflect a common view of the way in which the world is moving and of the way in which people behave. If they do not, chairmen will analyse why the discrepancy has occurred and question which of their sources of experience seems to be out of line.

Because the problems and choices confronting their companies are in chairmen's minds, they file away information which they pick up elsewhere and which could have a bearing on their main businesses. In the same way, they will be exchanging ideas between their different interests and activities. As Alfred Sloan wrote in *My Years with General Motors*, the best of books on organizing a company: 'There is a logical way of doing business in accordance with the facts and circumstances of an industry, if you can figure it out.'[9]

It is the figuring out that is the challenge and the more contact chairmen have with the world outside their companies, the better their figuring is likely to be. What does this suggest in terms of the relationship between the job of chairmen as chairmen and any other interests which they may wish to pursue? We are back to balance again, and the first factor to be considered is how much time the chairmanship demands. Clearly the chairman's job as chairman has first call not only on their time, but on how it is distributed.

There are, perhaps, four main fields of activity open to chairmen, in addition to their task as chairmen. They are other chairmanships or directorships, serving on bodies which are associated with business, public service in various forms, and the whole range of other activities, from charitable work to how they use their spare time. All four can have a part to play as sources for ideas, which either are directly relevant to their companies or which help chairmen to see business problems in a new light. They also have a part to play in keeping chairmen sound of body and mind. Although the four headings are listed in order of the closeness of their relationship to the business world, this does not imply that holding an outside directorship is necessarily of greater value than any other kind of external involvement.

Outside activities

I felt that, as chairman of Cadbury Schweppes, I gained most benefit from being a member of the boards of two other enterprises in entirely different fields. I was clear, however, in terms of the balance of time, that I could not sit on more than two outside boards if I was to be able to give the necessary attention to their affairs and to those of the company of which I was chairman for the greater part of my time. The practical advantage of being on boards other than your own is that you learn directly from them, largely to the extent to which you contribute to them.

The second category of business-related bodies covers a number of different types of organization. To start with, there are industry and trade associations. I have been involved with such industry-wide associations as the Confederation of British Industry and the Chambers of Industry and Commerce and also with the associations representing the interests of the food industry in Britain, in the European Union and in the US.

Organizations such as the CBI offer the opportunity to become involved in the ways in which business policy is formed and in which business influences political opinion. It has to be useful to chairmen to have some understanding of how to translate corporate aims into political action. Another advantage of taking part in an organization which represents business on national and international issues is that it opens up new networks of contacts. It provides a structure within which personal links can be formed through working with individuals, as opposed simply to meeting them. Industry-wide bodies can, therefore, provide an insight into the political process, an opportunity to have a hand in formulating policies, and the chance to work with a cross-section of people in the public and private sectors.

Representing the company's interests on a trade or professional association offers more limited openings into the wider world. The argument for spending time on this kind of work is based on ensuring that the company's interests are effectively represented, rather than their being represented by those whose time the company can most easily spare. Trade association representation is an investment by the company, and by the individual concerned, in safeguarding the interests of the company, and it is an expression of the company's duty to its industry.

Duty to the industry leads on to public duty and to service on government commissions, local authority bodies, and so on. Again, there is much to be gained from a first-hand understanding of the workings of institutions outside the private sector. The experience of serving on an official commission of inquiry will have something of value to offer to chairmen in their work and will put them in touch with people whom they would be unlikely to come across in the world of business. Nevertheless, a sense of duty will be the main reason for chairmen undertaking public work.

The final heading covers everything else, such as charitable, political, or educational activities. All are ways of putting business experience to social use and will not be without benefit to the company.

Benefits from outside interests and activities

There are a number of general points to be made about the advantages of chairmen undertaking activities removed from the company. One is that it prevents chairmen becoming too inward-looking. Their positions outside the company give them an external standpoint from which to judge the issues arising within their businesses. Outside posts confer on them a degree of independence, in the literal sense, because they are not then wholly dependent on the ways of thinking of the companies whose boards they chair. The independence of outlook required of a chairman is not a passive quality derived from not being wholly involved in the company's affairs. Effective independence is established through knowledge and experience acquired in other companies and other fields. They give chairmen confidence in their own judgement through knowing that their standards and their approach to their tasks are broadly based.

The second point is that the chairman's role as initiator is greatly assisted by having access to sources of innovative thinking, not just outside the company, but possibly quite unrelated to business at all. In theory, there are unlimited opportunities to pick up ideas on direction and management through reading books and articles. Interestingly, most people in business fall into two distinct groups over management literature: some can never bring themselves to open a book on business, others read them avidly—especially on flights. That aside, having responsibilities unconnected with the company provides chairmen with first-hand experience of the way in which ideas are applied in other contexts. This is of much greater practical value than simply culling ideas from a variety of sources. What is useful to chairmen is to see new concepts put into practice in other organizations, and this can only come from being directly involved in their activities.

Finally, any of these external activities, from serving on the board of another company to assisting in some charitable endeavour, may provide the opportunity to take the chair, or indeed may provide no escape from so doing. Wider experience of chairmanship can only be of value to chairmen and their boards. In the same way, serving on other bodies may offer the opportunity, as it did for me, of learning from their chairmen.

As a last word on this subject, the relationship between a chairman's task as chairman and everything else that they may undertake comes back to questions of balance and of individual inclination. The position in the company for which I believe it is especially important to have outside points of reference to work to, is that of chairman. Every chairman will have their own view on how such points of reference can most appropriately be established.

Subsidiary boards

Further issues for chairmen are the roles and structures of subsidiary and advisory boards within their companies. I served as a member of a UK subsidiary board of an American company and when I was chairman of Cadbury Schweppes, I worked closely with the chairmen of companies within our group in which the parent company held all, a majority, or a minority of the shares. On the basis of that experience, I believe that there are issues of relevance to chairmen over the way in which the boards of subsidiary companies are made up and over their relationship with their parent company.

Wholly owned subsidiaries

The first category are wholly owned subsidiaries. It is for their parent companies to decide how such boards should be made up and what their functions should be. They can simply be management boards composed of executive directors and chaired by their executive heads, with or without directors from the parent company in addition. The chairman's role in their case is effectively exercised by the parent company. If the subsidiary is in a foreign country, it may be considered helpful to have nationals of the country concerned as outside directors on such boards. Their role would be to advise on the subsidiary's external relations and its policies towards the host government and community. They might well be the subsidiary's financial and legal advisers, rather than being independent outside directors. In effect, a board of that kind remains a management board with the parent company in a supervisory role, retaining strategic and financial control.

Local shareholders

Into the next category come foreign subsidiaries where there are local shareholders, whether or not their companies are publicly quoted and whether the parent company owns a majority or a minority of the shares. There are a number of reasons why a foreign subsidiary may have local shareholders. It could, for example, be as part of a deal to acquire a business, or because it was a legal requirement, or because local involvement was thought to further the subsidiary's commercial prospects. The problem for boards of subsidiary companies which are partially owned by a parent company is that the interests of the local shareholders and those of the parent are sure at times to diverge. Assuming that an outside director is chairman and that there are other outside directors on the board, the parent company will wish to avoid using its voting strength to overrule local board members, if it can help it. Yet when the interests of the parent company differ from those of the subsidiary board, the voices of managers and shareholders on the spot sound more loudly and more immediately in the ears of board members than those of the distant parent. The role here of chairmen of subsidiary boards is crucial in holding the balance between these two forces. They have the task of reconciling the interests of the parent company and those of the company they chair.

There are all manner of conflicts of interest which can arise between parent and subsidiary. It may be over dividend policy, or the payment by the subsidiary of royalties or fees for services to the parent. It may be that the subsidiary is generating cash which the parent wishes to invest elsewhere, or that the host government is bringing pressure to bear on the subsidiary to undertake a diversification in an untried field. It is the chairmen of subsidiary companies who have to resolve these different pressures. They have to carry local shareholders, local sources of finance, and the authorities with them in the decisions of their boards. This puts them in a strong position to persuade the parent company to accept the judgement of the local board.

Role of chairman

It all turns on chairmen of subsidiary boards being able to retain the confidence both of their own boards and those of their parent companies. It is a fine balance. There are hazards in having a subsidiary board which fails to make the local case as forcefully as it should and does not fulfil its role to act as an effective and independent source of advice to the parent board. The likely outcome would be an unnecessary degree of involvement by the parent company in the subsidiary's affairs. Yet the more the subsidiary board acts as a true, independent board, the greater the chances of a clash of views. This is why so much depends on their chairmen. It is only by building up good personal contacts with the appropriate people in the parent company that chairmen of subsidiaries can earn their trust and enable them to appreciate the local point of view. It is the responsibility of parent companies to find subsidiary company chairmen who understand and accept their role, and then to keep in touch with them and give them the backing they need in a difficult task.

The same applies to outside members of subsidiary boards. There is a need for caution in appointing local directors who are figures of influence in their own country. The more influential they are, the more they will be seen locally as being in charge of the operations of the company and the more they may be tempted to follow plans and projects which they consider to be in the interests of their country and compatriots, regardless of the interests of the parent. Having been involved in a situation where a subsidiary board took it upon itself to compete at a loss with its majority shareholder in a third market, I am conscious of the absolute necessity of ensuring that chairmen and outside directors of subsidiary boards agree their role with their parent boards and accept it.

Chief executives of subsidiary companies with a local shareholding have two masters, their local board and chairman, and the chief executive of the parent company. This dual structure will work satisfactorily only if local chief executives resist the temptation to play one off against the other, and if their chairmen frustrate any attempt to do so. What has to be settled are the respective responsibilities of subsidiary and parent company boards to avoid ambiguity and uncertainty. Agreeing these provides the framework within which the legitimate aspirations of the local board, management, and shareholders can be accommodated, while leaving the parent board with an appropriate degree of control. In addition to responsibility for strategy and overall financial control, I would expect the parent company to control trademarks and intellectual property and to set quality and ethical standards. But most importantly, arising from all that has been said, the parent company should have the final say over board and senior executive appointments in their subsidiaries.

Advisory councils

One way for companies to keep in touch with opinion in countries in which they do business is to assemble an advisory board or council, whether for a country or a region. The advantage of such a body is that those who make it up do not take on the responsibilities of a director and they are clear that it is not their job to be involved in the management of the business. Equally, the time commitment, perhaps meeting twice a year, is more limited than that required by membership of a subsidiary board. This should enable companies to attract as councillors people of standing in their own communities, whose knowledge and experience would be of value. The role of advisory councils is to contribute to the strategic thinking of companies and to give them an insight into the direction which political, financial, and commercial movements are taking in the countries they represent. They are there to provide the kind of guidance which boards might expect from independent outside directors, but from a broader and less directly business-based standpoint.

Because such councils are advisory, they are not usually responsible for decisions and thus have little control over whether their advice is taken or not. As a result, they stand some way back from the action and it may be difficult to continue to hold the interest of councillors of the quality which boards are looking for, if they can act only in an advisory capacity. Keeping advisory councils lively and effective will turn on the inherent interest of the subjects of their meetings and on how well they engage with their fellow councillors. It may even be possible to involve councils over specific issues, where their advice will be sought with the expectation of it being put into effect. To recruit a good advisory council and retain its commitment, requires careful selection of its membership in the first place and then a well-planned programme for keeping the members in touch between meetings, and all the while making clear the value which is attached to their contribution.

A company's values

The final aspect of the chairman's role which I want to pick up in this chapter, is that of guardian of the company's values. This is likely to be shared with the chief executive, but the ultimate responsibility for actions carried out in the name of the company rests with the chairman. Chairmen, therefore, need to be aware of what the people who make up their companies believe is expected of them. They will also be concerned to ensure that the values for which their companies stand are maintained.

A good deal has been written about the so-called 'cultures' of companies. I welcome the recognition which has thus been given to an important element of company life, although I do not think that the word 'culture' is particularly appropriate. The basic meaning of culture as defined in the dictionary is: 'the training and refinement of mind, tastes and manners'. If that definition is applied to companies it carries with it the suggestion that culture is a result of training and that, therefore, it can be changed in a desired direction through the refining process.

The character of a company

This is altogether too superficial a view of what I prefer to call the character of a company. All groups evolve an identity over time and develop their own codes of conduct and systems of values. That identity and the unwritten rules which summarize the way in which things are done in a company add up to its character. Every company has its own character, some more distinctive than others. The reason why I doubt if the character of a company can be changed at will is that it is an amalgam of the beliefs and attitudes of everyone who is part of the enterprise.

If the company's character is formed from within, then this limits the ability of chairmen to bring about changes in it—except for the worse, if they were to set a bad example from the top. While the chairman's influence may be limited, it is nevertheless important. In the first place, aspects of a company's character can be changed, provided all concerned can be brought to see the need for change. It is possible, for example, for the chairman and the board to encourage a shift from a conformist attitude to a questioning one. A shift of that kind does not alter the basic values of the company, but it will change behaviour. Similarly, concern for quality or for customer service can be heightened. The stronger the degree of trust in the leadership, the more possible it is to bring about changes of that kind.

Establishment of values

A further compelling reason why the character of their companies should be a matter of concern for chairmen is that, without a clear lead from them and their boards, there may be confusion down the line as to what their real values are. One source of confusion can be doubts over whether value statements by the board are exhortatory or for real. In *Strategies and Styles*, a US manager is quoted as saying: 'All the words sound great—entrepreneurship, ownership, risk-taking—but at my level it's still making the budget that counts.'[10] If the leader's trumpet gives an uncertain sound, it will not be clear what the relative priorities are between meeting profit targets and the way in which they are met. Chairmen and boards not only have to establish their company's standards of behaviour, but they have to ensure that they are communicated throughout the organization and above all that the company's reward system reinforces them.

Jack Welch, CEO of General Electric, is an excellent example of a leader who makes it clear that his company's values count. In an interview his approach was described as follows:

GE managers are judged on two things, whether they can 'make the numbers'—do the technical side of their jobs—and whether they 'live' the company's values. Managers who don't make the numbers or live the values are out. Those who live the values but don't make the numbers are given chances to improve. Those who make the numbers and don't live the values are the worst, he says. 'These are the people that too many companies keep, because they kiss the boss's ass. Unless you get these people out you get your values wrong.'[11]

No one in GE can be in any doubt over what is expected of them nor where their priorities should lie.

Company principles

In my judgement, it is helpful for chairmen to commit to writing what they believe their companies stand for. This is hard to do, because such statements are apt to seem platitudinous to their authors, but that is not how they will seem to others in the company, especially those who are furthest from headquarters. I have included as an Appendix a statement, which I wrote as chairman of Cadbury Schweppes, called *The Character of the Company*. It represented my view at the time of the kind of company we were and of the kind of company we should aim to become. The point about time is important, because any such statement should be open to rewriting, in whole or in part, as circumstances change. Its purpose is not to act as a brake on change, but to encourage change in the right direction.

There is value in chairmen setting down some guiding principles when their companies reach such a size that they are no longer in regular personal contact with senior people throughout the enterprise. Such principles are particularly useful to those working in an international business. To compete in the markets of the world, managers on the spot have to be given as much operating freedom as possible. As companies extend geographically and as they devolve more responsibility from the centre to the operating units, there needs to be some means of holding the enterprise together in the face of these forces for fragmentation. I believe that the glue which holds a company together is its beliefs and values, more than its structures and systems.

Notes

1. Roberts, John (2000). *On Becoming Company Chairman: building the complementary board*, Saxton Bampfylde Hever, July, 8.
2. Ibid., 7.
3. Russell Reynolds Associates (2002). *Effective Boards*, 13.
4. Guinness plc, *Powers of Non-executive Committee*, Articles of Association, article 89.1.
5. Ringshaw, Grant, 'Interview with Mervyn Davies', *Sunday Telegraph*, 2 December 2001.
6. Rees-Mogg, Lord, 'The value of an outside voice in the drama of a takeover bid', *The Independent*, 12 September 1989.
7. Gugler, Klaus, (ed.) (2001). *Corporate Governance and Economic Performance*, Oxford: Oxford University Press, 32.
8. Davis, Evan and Kay, John (1990). 'Corporate governance, takeovers and the role of the non-executive director', *Business Strategy Review*, Autumn.
9. Sloan, Alfred P. (1965). *My Years with General Motors*. London: Sidgwick and Jackson, 58.
10. Goold, Michael and Campbell, Andrew (1989). *Strategies and Styles*, Oxford: Basil Blackwell, 276.
11. Pickard, Jane, 'Electric General', *People Management*, 22 November 2001.

12

The Governance Agenda

The governance of business, in other words, is likely to become an issue throughout the developed world.

Peter Drucker[1]

Identifying the issues

This chapter considers some of the issues which are likely to engage the attention of chairmen over the next few years. Peter Drucker, with his customary perception, identified corporate governance as an issue for the future, when writing in *The Economist* in 1989. The widespread nature of the governance debate since then has decisively confirmed his conclusion and it is on governance-related matters that I intend to focus. There are other agents of change which are more all-pervasive, since they help to determine the competitive environment within which companies carry on their business. They include advances in technology, the emergence of the newly industrialized countries, the dismantling of state controls, the internationalization of markets and, most recently, increased risk through political instability. Combined, they will make competition more global, more intense, and more uncertain. They will also have their effect on governance: as companies and markets become more international, those investing in them will look for common standards of corporate direction and control. Their influence will, for all that, be primarily on the marketplace and on the relationship between companies, their customers, and their sources of finance.

Background

The pace of change in the field of corporate governance has been, as we have seen, astonishingly rapid over the last ten years. There is a need now to pause, in order to allow time for the whole range of initiatives that have been put in place, nationally and internationally, to be put to the test of experience. How well do they interact, what works and what does not, what can be done away with because the benefits do not outweigh the costs, and so on? An advantage of the code approach to governance—'comply or explain'—is that through time the relevance of recommendations to board effectiveness and accountability become clear. If a recommendation is widely not complied with for good reason, it can be dropped. If a recommendation emerges as too crucial to be left to voluntary compliance, then it may be right to put statutory weight behind it, but that can then be done in the light of operating experience. The higher standards of disclosure, and I believe of board effectiveness, to which codes of best practice have contributed have come about because in the aggregate they were seen by companies to be of value and to be needed. That willingness to make the best of governance recommendations and to accept the judgement of the market over compliance is at the heart of the matter. Willingness, however, cannot be stretched too far, which is why a period of consolidation is now called for. The process of change in governance practices and standards will continue, but it should be driven more by competition and the market than by external intervention. The aim of this chapter is to focus on some of the consequences of change which are likely to feature on the agendas of chairmen.

Forces for change

There are two main sets of forces which will continue to bring about change in the field of corporate governance worldwide. They are first market forces, primarily driven by investors and the providers of corporate funds, but also by the ever-rising expectations of society. Then there are regulatory forces of one kind or another pursued by national and international authorities. It is these whose impact is easiest to discern, because their form is precise and they are the product of a predictable procedure. I start with them because of the importance to UK companies of the proposals which have been tabled to reform corporate law in this country. Although the proposed reforms may appear to be a domestic matter, of interest primarily to UK companies, their significance is wider. As the Company Law Review Steering Group's Final Report says: 'Our aim has been that British company law should once more be world class, setting the example that others will wish to follow.'[2] The European Union looks to Britain to give the lead in the field of corporate governance and so the Steering Group's proposals are certainly relevant to boards in other European Community countries.

Company law reform

What the Steering Group have published are their proposals, but these have been put forward after extensive consultation to ensure that they have a strong basis of support among practitioners. They are likely, therefore, to be adopted; what remains uncertain is when Parliamentary time will be found to turn the proposals into law. The scale of what is proposed is impressive and as the Foreword to the Final Report says, it is the first fundamental review of company law for at least forty and arguably one hundred and fifty years. It goes on to say: 'All agree on the objective—we need to turn our Victorian infrastructure into a modern framework designed for the 21st century.'[3] I will focus on those proposals which most directly affect boards of directors. They are all aimed at improving governance and fall under three headings: directors' duties, transparency and accountability, and empowering shareholders.

Improving governance: directors' duties

The recommendation here is that there should be a legislative statement which would set out what is expected of directors and provide guidance on such issues as, for whose benefit directors should run their companies, the appropriate time horizons for decision-making, the nature of the standards of care and skill demanded of directors, and the position of stakeholders other than shareholders. This would be the first time that the legal duties of directors have been brought together in a single document and would resolve many of the misunderstandings and uncertainties which have long perplexed directors over precisely what was expected of them in law. The Final Report includes a draft clause and Schedule setting out the principles governing directors' duties.[4] Directors would then have clear, accessible, and authoritative guidance on which they could safely rely, because it would be binding on the courts and thus could be expected to be consistently applied.

The proposed legislative restatement would settle a number of controversial issues. It resolves the shareholder/stakeholder debate by making it clear that the duty of loyalty would require directors to serve the purposes of the company, as laid down in its constitution, and as set for it by its members collectively. Thus, the basic goal for directors would be the success of the company in the collective best interests of shareholders. At the same time, directors would be required to recognize the company's need to foster relationships with its employees, customers and suppliers, its need to maintain its business reputation, and its need to consider the company's impact on the community and the working environment. In effect, accountability would remain to shareholders, but directors would have a legal duty to take account of all the other constituencies which could have a part to play in the company's continuing success. The argument against widening the accountability of directors beyond shareholders was that a wider accountability would be a weaker one. By including in the draft Schedule that a director must 'take account in good faith of all the material factors that it is practicable in the circumstances for him to identify'[5] in promoting the success of the company, the claim on companies of any constituency coming under that heading is strengthened. It would be up to the courts to determine what failure to take account of a material factor amounted to and how it should be redressed.

The Schedule also sets out the duty of obedience—to obey the constitution and to exercise powers for their proper purpose: the duty of loyalty, already discussed, including the need to act fairly as between shareholders: the duty to exercise independence of judgement, and to exercise care, skill, and diligence. Where the proposals break new ground is over directors' duties in relation to conflicts of interest and the risk of insolvency. The issue over conflicts of interest is who, for example, should be able to authorize directors to exploit for their own benefit business opportunities arising from their position as directors. The balance is between making the process so burdensome that opportunities may be lost and protecting against abuse. The proposed solution is that independent directors should be responsible for authorization, which would be specific and disclosed in the report and accounts.

On the duty to creditors, the key issue as the Report points out is: 'when should the normal rule, that a company is to be run in the interests of its members, or shareholders, be modified by an obligation to have regard also to the interests of creditors, or in an extreme case, by an obligation to override the interests of members entirely, to the extent necessary to ensure creditors have the best protection?'[6] Section 214 of the Insolvency Act 1986 makes directors liable if they fail to take all reasonable steps to minimize the loss to creditors after they should have recognized that the company had no reasonable prospect of avoiding insolvent liquidation. The further issue is whether directors should have a duty to recognize, at an earlier stage in the slide towards insolvency, that they should consider the interests of members and creditors together, rather than make an abrupt and complete switch from one set of interests to the other when the prospect of insolvency was judged inevitable. This issue is unresolved and has been left to the Department of Trade and Industry to pursue.

Improving governance: transparency and accountability

The proposals which come under this heading are aimed at providing share-holders with the information which they need in order for them to be able to hold directors to account. The sting in the tail, so to speak, is the onus this places on shareholders to make accountability effective. Shareholders are to have the information which they need in order to assess the performance of the company and the directors' stewardship of their assets. The Report emphasizes that timely access to high quality information is fundamental to the proposals for effective governance being put forward, but that this needs to be matched by mechanisms which enable shareholders to respond appro-priately to that information. The Report makes the further point that it is not only shareholders who have a legitimate interest in the activities of compan-ies, but also, for example, employees, trading partners, and the wider com-munity. The proposals, therefore, aim to meet the needs of these other constituencies for corporate accountability. An issue here is that the Report refers to the interest of these constituencies in the activities of companies, 'particularly in the case of companies which exercise significant economic power'.[7] This is an important principle which runs through the Report; it no longer classifies companies solely by structure, public or private for example, but by their perceived economic power.

The object of the proposals in this section is to improve the quality, use-fulness, and relevance of information, to provide more timely information, to offer better access to information—particularly by use of electronic communication—and to facilitate a responsible shareholder response to that information. The Report accepts that there is already a well-developed system of financial reporting in place in this country and so it should, given the gulf between reporting standards in the UK and those in many other European countries. However, the new objective is to move beyond reporting on a historic and quantitative basis, in order to include qualitative as well as financial information, and intangible as well as tangible assets. It is pro-posed that this should be achieved through the addition to the report of an Operating and Financial Review, to be known as the OFR.

The OFR

The proposed OFR is described in the Report as having a pivotal role in improving standards of corporate governance. It is, therefore, worth quoting section 3.34 of the Report which summarizes its nature and purpose:

We therefore propose that all companies of significant economic size should be required to produce, as part of their annual report and accounts, an OFR. This would provide a review of the business, its performance, plans and prospects. It would include information on direction, performance and dynamics (capital projects, risks, etc.) and on all other aspects which the directors judge necessary to an understanding of the business, such as key business relationships and environmental and social impacts. The requirement to produce an OFR would improve the quality, usefulness, and relevance of information available to the markets and to everyone with an interest in the company. As such, we expect it to lead to improved understanding of business performance and prospects, as well as promoting accountability and encouraging responsiveness and high standards of business practice.[8]

All companies preparing an OFR would be required to report on three mandatory items: the company's business, strategy, and principal drivers of performance; a review of the development of the company's business over the year; and the dynamics of the business, including events, trends, and other factors which may substantially affect future performance. What is included in addition would be for directors to decide on the grounds of relevance and materiality. The prescribed contents of the OFR, indicating which headings always have to be addressed and which are required where directors in good faith judge them to be material, are set out in tabular form on pages 183 and 184 of the Report. The report on corporate governance required under the Combined Code would be covered under the heading of 'Corporate governance—values and structures' to the extent that it was material. The OFR would be reviewed by the auditors for consistency and for the process by which it was prepared.

The central role which the Steering Group accord to the OFR and the breadth of its coverage raise questions about the burden that it will place on boards in meeting its demands. There is already a voluntary OFR in place and there is a risk that a mandatory OFR will be seen as an uncalled-for addition which will temper the willingness of boards to cooperate in freely providing further information on the scale proposed. There are, however, the safeguards that, other than the matters always to be covered, it is for directors to judge what should be included and to decide what information not to publish, in case it might prejudice the company's competitive position. A trial was also carried out by five companies, all of whom were said to be positive about the proposed OFR and its value to them. The Report includes possible criteria for determining which companies, public and private, might be considered to fall within the ambit of this proposal on grounds of being of sufficient economic size.

Timeliness and access

The proposals under this heading address the timing of company announcements and the way in which they can be accessed. It is proposed that preliminary announcements should be published on a web site, as soon as they have been released to the market, and notified electronically to those shareholders who ask for them in this form. Equally, reports and accounts should be available on a web site within four months of the year-end. After publication on the web site, companies would have to wait a minimum of fifteen days before circulating the report and accounts and AGM notice to shareholders. This would give time for shareholders to assimilate the information and to submit resolutions, which met the requirements of the Act; such resolutions could then be circulated with the meeting notice free of charge.

The recognition in the Report of the possibilities opened up by electronic communication is an important issue. In the reporting field, it puts those individuals who wish to be informed in this way on a par with the market in terms of timing. Publication on the web also places corporate information in the public domain. Thus, these proposals would have far-reaching consequences, in enabling individual shareholders to be informed at the same time as the market, and in greatly extending the audience for company reports, which in turn would cover more ground if the OFR proposals are adopted. It is encouraging that the fact that not everyone will be able to access information electronically has not inhibited these suggestions.

Improving governance: empowering shareholders

The aim of improving the timing and accessibility of information to shareholders is to enable them to exercise their powers at company meetings. To do so, they need to have the appropriate information. The Steering Group has, rightly in my view, rejected the suggestion that there should be rules over age limits, and directors' qualifications and roles. It is for shareholders to judge the qualities of directors up for election, but in order to come to a considered judgement they need the relevant information and it is proposed that this should be included in the notice calling the meeting. In addition, the Report has addressed the issue of investors who hold their shares through nominees. This is to be left to the market, to find a means of enabling those who have an interest in shares, but not the legal title to them, to influence the way they are voted. The more fundamental issue is the way in which the investing institutions use their voting power in the cause of good governance.

Institutional investors

The proposals to provide more timely and easily accessible information to shareholders is in order that they can play their full part in the governance process. Given that the majority of shares in UK companies are held by investing institutions, effective governance is dependent in the words of the Report, 'on the responsible, diligent and active exercise of their powers by these fiduciary investors'.[9] These investors may however face conflicts of interest, where they are fund managers, which deter them from the active exercise of their voting power. The Report lists four possible reasons why institutional investors may not be using their influence with companies and their boards, when there was cause for them to do so. They can be summarized as companies threatening to take business away from them: their perception that being active would be bad for business, failure in the governance process such as votes not being correctly communicated or executed, and finally what the report refers to as 'slacking'. That final point is expressed more fully, as investors not taking their fiduciary responsibilities to their beneficiaries sufficiently seriously, for them to intervene to protect and enhance the value of their investment where companies are being incompetently or dishonestly run.

As the Report says, failure by institutional investors to use their voting power to promote good governance is a matter of major public interest and at the heart of the purposes for which the reform of company law has been instituted. It links to the findings and recommendations of the Myners Report[10] which will be referred to later. The proposals for encouraging effective monitoring by investors are based on the need for transparency. They are, that major relationships between companies and financial institutions should be disclosed in annual reports, that institutions managing funds on behalf of others should disclose how they have exercised their powers, that the process of executing votes on key company resolutions should be audited, and that companies should report on votes recorded on all resolutions put to the poll. The central issue of how to ensure that fiduciary investors act in the best interests of their beneficiaries falls more within the remit of the Myners Committee than that of the Steering Group, since the legal position appears to be clear. The question is how to make it effective.

The institutional framework

To give effect to their proposals, the Steering Group would look to secondary legislative powers which would be used to keep the legislation up to date. The devolved powers of the existing corporate governance bodies, the Financial Reporting Council (FRC), the Accounting Standards Board (ASB), and the Financial Reporting Review Panel would be extended to include the broader range of matters covered by the Steering Group's proposals. In recognition of the wider role suggested for them, they would be renamed and become respectively, the Company Law and Reporting Commission (CLRC), the Standards Board and the Reporting Review Panel. Such a structure would build on the present framework, where the FRC sponsors the Combined Code and the ASB advises on the OFR. It is suggested that a new Private Companies Committee should be formed which the CLRC and the Standards Board would be obliged to consult to ensure that the needs of small and private companies were taken properly into account. The Standards Board would be responsible for keeping the Combined Code under review.

The danger of over-regulation and excessive intervention is recognized by the Steering Group and their aim is that the proposed institutions should be 'consultative and close to market conditions, responsive to changing needs, as light in terms of intervention as possible and based on generally accepted perceptions of best practice'.[11] The progress in corporate governance which has been made to date has turned on the acceptance by boards of directors of the need for change and of the benefits to board effectiveness of the 'comply or explain' approach to market regulation. It will be essential for future progress for that goodwill to be retained and not jeopardized through intervention which goes against the grain of markets.

It is useful to turn to the OECD report, *Corporate Governance*, in this context. Its advice was to limit regulatory intervention to ensuring fairness, transparency, accountability, and responsibility, with the aim of encouraging 'the development of improved governance practices, with strong emphasis on government enabling voluntary private sector development rather than attempting to regulate it . . . '.[12]

Market forces

It follows from the previous section that institutional investors are the main force responsible for market-driven change. What is it that they look for from boards of directors and how do they aim to effect changes in ways which they perceive as advantageous? Increasingly, leading institutional investors are publishing their own corporate governance codes, which set out what they expect of the boards of the companies in which they invest. One of the largest institutions, TIAA-CREF, has for example brought out its *Policy Statement on Corporate Governance* which 'is offered as a basis for dialogue with senior corporate management and boards of directors with the objective of improving corporate governance practices'.[13] Similarly, Hermes in the UK has published its *Statement on Corporate Governance and Voting Policy*, to which reference has already been made.[14]

What these leading institutions are doing is to set out an agenda for their dialogues with boards, alerting them to the issues which they see as significant in terms of board effectiveness. Taking Hermes' code as an example, Hermes expects the company to be run in the long-term interests of the shareholders and goes on to say that 'A company run in the long-term interests of its shareholders will need to manage effectively relationships with its employees, suppliers and customers and with regard to the common weal'.[15] Hermes looks for a balanced board with a strong core of independent outside directors. It proposes its own criteria for defining independence and favours the separation of the posts of chairman and chief executive. It suggests that one new independent outside director should join the board every three years and that outside directors should not normally serve more than ten years. It advocates an annual appraisal of the performance of the outside directors and the chairman, and of the effectiveness of the board as a whole. Hermes also recommends that boards should encourage their outside directors to participate in seminars and workshops concerning their board role.

By setting out their stall in this way, Hermes targets the aspects of board structure and board composition which it regards as relevant. It is then for boards to decide how far they agree with Hermes' governance principles and to convince them where they take a different view. The essential point is that a basis for purposeful dialogue has been established. Looking ahead, some of the issues which are likely to feature in the dialogues between investors and boards have already been referred to in the Hermes code.

It is clear that the demands made on boards have become greater and that directors are being expected to take a professional approach to their duties, hence the Hermes code recommendations in relation to performance appraisal and to outside directors, attending appropriate seminars and workshops. I would expect the whole question of how directors can best prepare themselves for their increasingly demanding role to feature in the dialogue between investors and boards. As Reuters' company secretary has said on the question of training for directors 'In terms of the corporate governance movement's general thrust, the more there is emphasis on the value of training and the value of explaining the role of non-executive directors, the better'.[16]

What corpus of knowledge should directors have mastered before being nominated for a board seat? What experience will enable them best to contribute to the work of the board? What forms of continuing study to keep up with developments in the directorial field might be relevant? The pitfalls are obvious; investors are looking for directors who will take intelligent risks and grow their businesses, not for successful exam takers. Entrepreneurial flair has to be recognized and cannot be examined for. Nevertheless, the professions no longer accept that an initial qualification will see their members through to retirement, to the relief of their clients!

Clearly, the issue for investors is what value will directors who are up for election add to their respective boards. An imaginative answer to this question has been put forward by an American businessman, in the form of two proposals to the US Securities and Exchange Commission:

Require by SEC rule that proxy statements contain a 300–500 word essay from each board candidate explaining why he adds value to, and would be a good director for, that particular board. No 'mission' or 'vision' statements. No windbaggery. The candidate should tell us about his personal and professional competencies. Should his essay be less than coherent or suffused with platitudes, the electorate can weigh that in casting its vote.

Require by SEC rule that prior to each annual meeting, companies host a conference call at which all board candidates are available for questions from their electorate. The session should be recorded to afford subsequent access to it.[17]

While these self-styled 'modest proposals' may as yet seem out of reach, they are directed at an issue of direct concern to investors—the effectiveness of the directors who are up for election. Following the same line, there is likely to be pressure from shareholders to add their candidates to the electoral slate, rather than being limited to registering protest at board nominations to which they object. Shareholders may well feel that their greater involvement in the selection of board members will lead to the appointment of more effective directors. The fundamental issue, however, is how well their chairmen weld them together into an effective board. This is why all investor codes and some national governance codes stress the importance of boards appraising their own performance as boards. This point has already been discussed and it is an aspect of governance where governance practice has yet to match investor expectations. Investors will increasingly want to know how boards have assessed their collective performance and what they have learned from the process.

Another aspect of the composition of boards, which features in the Hermes' code and on which investors require to be reassured, is that there should be a strong independent element among the directors, capable of taking an informed but objective view of matters that come before the board, and whose contribution to decisions will carry weight. Hermes refers to boards having at least three 'vigorously independent' directors on whom shareholders can rely for their independence of judgement and, interestingly, for their ability to act as agents of change should that be called for. Although investors use their own criteria to determine which directors they regard as independent, the heart of the matter is the quality of their independence and the ability of this vigorous minority to carry the board with them when necessary. They have to rely on their powers of argument and persuasion and on the respect in which their judgement is held by their fellow board members and the investors who elect them. It is because technical independence has to be combined with character and personality that investors can be expected to take an increasing interest in the process by which directors are selected, as well as in their selection itself.

Myners Report

In March 2001, Paul Myners presented the Chancellor of the Exchequer with his report on the process by which institutional investors make their investment decisions. The recommendations for reform which he advocates are on the basis of 'comply or explain', with statutory regulation as a fall-back if voluntarism fails. Because, like the Combined Code, this is essentially market-regulation, it follows on from consideration of the influence of the market on governance processes. The Report explains why the decisions of institutional investors and the means by which they arrive at them are of such economic and social importance. It is a masterly analysis of the complex mechanisms through which the savings of the public become invested productively. I believe that the impact of the Myners Report will prove as significant in its field, as the governance codes which preceded it have proved to be in theirs. The Chancellor has already declared the government's broad support for Myners' proposals and its intention to act on them.

The whole Report deserves study, but the part which is especially relevant to chairmen and boards concerns the duty of investors to take active steps to intervene where such intervention could protect the value of the assets which they hold on behalf of beneficiaries. The proposals in this part of the Report cut through the conflicts of interest, identified by the Company Law Review Steering Group, which were thought to contribute to holding institutions back from using their votes and influence as effectively in governance matters as their beneficiaries had a right to expect. Under the heading of pension funds, the Report makes proposals in relation to trustee expertise and surpluses, before going on to a key proposal under the heading of *activism*, which reads as follows:

Third, the review is particularly concerned by the value lost to institutional investors through the reluctance of fund managers to actively engage with companies in which they have holdings, even where they have strong reservations about strategy, personnel or other potential causes of corporate underperformance. It therefore recommends that the US Department of Labor Interpretative Bulletin on Employment Retirement

Income Security Act (ERISA) 1974 which deals with this issue be included in fund management mandates, and incorporated in law. The guidance clearly articulates the duties of managers to intervene in companies—by voting or otherwise—where there is a reasonable expectation that doing so might raise the value of the investment.[18]

Myners bases his case for action, not on arguments of public interest and shareholder responsibility, but on the fundamental duty of managers to do their best for their clients, a duty which overrides any other interests which might conflict with its exercise. Funds specifically set up to take holdings in underperforming companies, like Hermes Lens Asset Management, have shown that active investment of this kind pays. A move to mandate fund managers to follow suit would have far-reaching implications for the relationship between investors and boards, and for investors who would thenceforth have to equip themselves to carry out their duty to intervene, where this could reasonably be expected to benefit their clients. Investors would not only have to acquire the expertise and experience necessary for constructive intervention, but also the ability to persuade boards to adopt their proposals. As Myners recognizes it will demand a difference in approach: 'As those managers who do engage with investee companies make clear, intervention requires persistence and a thick skin, perhaps raising issues repeatedly over a period of time with firmness until concerns are addressed. Merely meeting senior management and expressing polite reservations about strategy is not sufficient, if it is not effective.'[19]

As the Company Law Review Steering Group pointed out, the duty of fiduciary investors to their beneficiaries is already established under Trust law, the issue is how far that duty can be promoted in practical terms. The consequences of putting Myners into effect will go wider than altering the terms of engagement between investors and boards, it is also likely to encourage beneficiaries to intervene more actively with those investing on their behalf. Clearly the Myners' proposals will be high on the agendas of chairmen and their boards.

Social forces

Expectations

The chapter on social responsibility discussed how a much broader range of questions were now being raised by investors at annual meetings and that these included social issues such as human rights, child labour, and fair trading. I believe that attention will increasingly be paid to the record of companies in the social and environmental fields and that the way in which their record is perceived will have consequences for their revenues, their reputation, and shareholder value. Companies will be expected to report, as with the proposed UK OFR, on the social and environmental impact of their policies and actions, which in turn will promote further interest in, and enquiry into, these aspects of business. The appetite for information feeds on itself. This growing concern with basically non-financial measures of performance raises a number of questions. Has there been a change in society's expectations of companies, what are the issues that are now being raised with boards, how are social and environmental performance to be measured and reported and how can and should boards respond to the expectations of society?

Have expectations changed?

There is no doubt about the increased pressures on companies to take social and environmental issues into account, but do these reflect the views of society on a broad front or are they the well-orchestrated views of special interest groups, which are neither accountable nor widely representative? There are pressure groups whose demands are both extreme and run counter to extending the benefits of economic progress internationally, like those whose aim is to disrupt World Trade Organisation conferences. They represent political movements rather than the expectations of society. There are, however, good reasons to think that in a more general sense society, as consumers and citizens, is now expecting more of companies than it did. It has to do with the power of an all-pervasive international communications network, with less willingness to accept things as they are and have been, and with a sharper focus on social and environmental concerns. As the Institute of Business Ethics puts it in a publication on managing reputation risk:

Today's investors, consumers and employees are better informed and more discerning. They are sophisticated, challenging and demanding and are equipped with detailed information provided by the media, pressure groups and the Internet. They expect transparency, accountability and consistently responsible and ethical behaviour from the organisations they invest in, buy from and work for. They are now prepared to vote with their feet if their expectations are not met.[20]

The argument is not whether the changes in attitude to the problems facing society, and the role which companies might play in resolving them, are well-founded or not; it is that expectations are changing and that companies need to take account of these changes. A straightforward measure of these changes lies in the responses to a UK consumer survey question which is asked monthly: 'How important is the social responsibility of a business to you when you are purchasing a product?' In 1998, 28 per cent answered 'very important'; by 2001 that figure had risen to 46 per cent. In *The New Rules of Corporate Conduct*, Ian Wilson writes: 'The spirit of the times is changing and with it the model of desired corporate behaviour.'[21]

I believe that this view is correct and that boards will have to devote increasing attention to social and environmental issues and to understanding the directions in which expectations of corporate behaviour are moving. A good example of the changing spirit of the times is the clear evidence that individuals are becoming more concerned about the way in which the money they invest is used. Ethical investment funds have been around for some time, but their limitation was that they narrowed their choice of investments to avoid companies of which they disapproved, focusing on the three 'Bs', Baccy, Bombs, and Booze. Socially responsible investors, on the other hand, are ready to engage with the companies in which they invest, where they consider that this would be to the benefit of the aims which they have determined to pursue. They are now a mainstream form of investment and, according to the European Commission, socially responsible investing accounts for 5 per cent of all funds invested in the UK.[22] The members of the Socially Responsible Investment Forum, established by leading UK fund managers, companies, and pension fund trustees, are responsible between them for one trillion pounds sterling of assets.[23] The UK Forum has in its turn joined Eurosif which describes itself as, 'the pan-European stakeholder network for promoting and developing sustainable and responsible investment'.[24]

Under the Pensions Act Regulations, which took effect from 3 July 2000, trustees of UK occupational pension funds have to disclose in their Statement of Investment Principles, 'the extent (if at all) to which social, environmental and ethical considerations are taken into account in the selection, retention and realisation of investments'.[25] As a result, the Association of British Insurers have published disclosure guidelines for their members. The guidelines open with this statement: 'Public interest in corporate social responsibility has grown to the point where it seems helpful for institutional shareholders to set out basic disclosure principles, which will guide them in seeking to engage with companies in which they invest.'[26]

The guidelines themselves begin by saying that listed companies should state in their annual reports, whether their boards take regular account of the significance of social, environmental, and ethical (SEE) matters in their business decisions, and whether they have identified and assessed the significant risks which they involve. The ABI goes on to say that institutional shareholders consider that adherence to the guidelines which they have proposed will help companies to develop appropriate policies on corporate social responsibility. There can be any amount of theorizing about how wide the public support is for companies to take social responsibility into account, but the reality is that an authoritative group of institutional investors regard it as an issue which boards should address, and the market is the ultimate judge of relevance.

There is also evidence at the local level that individuals and companies are sufficiently concerned by the growing gap between those who have benefited from the progress of the economy and those who have not, to see the need for action. I chair a small community finance initiative in inner-city Birmingham which depends for funds on investors who are prepared to forego a normal dividend in order to support a project whose purpose is both economic and social. We have been backed by mainstream banks, who see our initiative as a practical way of tackling inner-city financial exclusion. Their contribution to resolving the problem has been to make it possible for us to fill a gap in the existing network of financial services. The emergence of such partnerships reflects corporate concerns for the divides in our society and a willingness to look for business like ways of, at the very least, preventing them from widening.

What issues are being raised?

An example of the kind of issue which is coming increasingly to the fore is that of companies in developed countries manufacturing abroad to reduce their costs. This is a complex issue, which single-interest groups aim to simplify to make their case over one particular aspect of the transfer, such as the difference in the level of wages paid in the two countries concerned. There are advantages to the receiving country of these transfers in terms of jobs, management and skills training, and the introduction of new technology, but there are also questions over wage levels, standards of health and safety, and minimum ages of employment. Companies have to meet the expectations of both the receiving country and their home country. Failure to do so can have serious consequences, as Nike found when under attack from a San Francisco-based interest group, Global Exchange, over conditions in plants manufacturing for them abroad. Eventually, to resolve matters, Nike's CEO raised the minimum worker age, upped wage levels, and agreed to use US health and safety standards, as well as allowing human rights groups to monitor its overseas plants. Until this settlement was reached, Nike's sales and the reputation of their brand had suffered worldwide.

The companies most exposed to controversy over social and environmental issues are energy, mining, and pharmaceutical enterprises, as well as those who transfer their production to countries where costs are lower in order to meet competition. The former group of industries are, in addition, dominated by large multinational companies which brings politics into the debate about their policies and actions. It is these companies which have published the most detailed and comprehensive statements of their position on social responsibility, of which Shell's *Profits and Principles—does there have to be a choice?* is a good example. It is, therefore, for individual boards and their chairmen to decide what balance to strike between the competitive pressures with which they are faced on all aspects of their activities— economic, social, and environmental—in the long-term interests of their shareholders.

Misguided virtue?

A recent book by David Henderson, entitled *Misguided Virtue,* presents a well-argued case against a too-ready and uncritical acceptance of all that is being demanded of companies under the banner of social responsibility. His particular target is an extreme version of social responsibility, which he distinguishes by gracing it with capital letters, as Corporate Social Responsibility or CSR. He writes: 'CSR assigns to business a new role and purpose. They are to embrace "corporate citizenship", and run their affairs, in close conjunction with an array of different "stakeholders", so as to promote the goal of "sustainable development"'.[27]

His arguments against CSR, in the terms in which he defines it, carry weight and contribute usefully to the debate about where the responsibilities of companies lie in the social and economic field. The CSR against which he argues seems to be aimed at creating a new world order in which interest groups, or non-governmental organizations, would be given a degree of authority to which only effective accountability should entitle them. He accepts that corporate social responsibility (lower case) has its place, although he assigns it a narrow role. He claims, for example, that companies should take, 'profitability as a guide, subject always to acting within the law, and that they should not go out of their way to define and promote wider self-chosen objectives'.[28]

This strictly economic definition of corporate purpose would outlaw companies like Body Shop, which have defined and promoted self-chosen, social objectives. It assumes that the sole concern of all shareholders is maximizing profits. The fact that companies can be launched to pursue wider objectives demonstrates that this assumption is false. Indeed that kind of limitation on purpose runs counter to the concept of a free market economy, which should enable as broad a variety of corporate objectives to be promoted as shareholders are willing to support. The one absolute constraint on self-chosen objectives is that they should be unambiguously disclosed. Shareholders must know precisely how their money is to be used before they subscribe.

Where Henderson's analysis is helpful is in pointing to the need to look at the costs, alongside the benefits, of corporate social and environmental policies. The case for involvement in these fields is that it will be to the advantage of the companies which do so, in terms of shareholder and public support and enhanced reputation. He instances, however, the possibility that the costs of reducing a company's impact on the environment, in answer to pressure, may be out of proportion to the value of the outcome. Clearly, companies should not go along with uneconomic demands and should be prepared publicly to explain their reasons for not doing so. Wasteful use of scarce resources is not in society's interests.

Measures of social responsibility

If companies are to report on their social and environmental policies, as they are being recommended to do, what form should that take? On the environmental front, a body of institutional investors, environmental groups, and companies have formed CERES—Coalition for Environmentally Responsible Economies. Around sixty companies have joined and have endorsed a set of Principles, which cover such areas as reducing waste, conserving energy, and minimizing health and safety risks to employees and the community. They agree to report publicly on their progress in these areas and they would presumably need the same information from their own management point of view, in order to measure costs, benefits, and progress. Their approach to disclosure is included in the CERES Principles under the heading of 'Audits and Reports': 'We will conduct an annual self-evaluation of our progress in implementing these Principles. We will support the timely creation of generally accepted environmental audit procedures. We will annually complete the CERES Report, which will be made available to the public.'[29]

One of the CERES Principles is that the board of directors and the CEO should be fully informed about relevant environmental issues and fully responsible for environmental policy. It continues by saying that 'demonstrated environmental commitment' should be a factor in selecting board members. Fortunately, that is not too precise and it is an improvement on the equivalent Valdez Principle, (the Valdez Principles were the forerunners to CERES) which stated that at least one board member was to be 'qualified' to represent environmental interests. Boards today need to have independent outside directors who are in touch with external opinion, but the essential test remains the value which they will add to the board as a collective body. Equally, no director should be representing an interest.

Out of the CERES Principles has come the Global Reporting Initiative or GRI. This aims to design a reporting system under three headings, economic, social, and environmental. Its objectives are admirably described in Robert Monks' *The New Global Investors*. He provides, as well, useful evidence of the value which the market now attaches to environmentally sensitive policies.[30] The GRI has made more progress with its environmental than with its social and economic indicators. One of the problems on the economic side is how to express concepts like human and intellectual capital in a world where fixed assets are diminishing in importance and human assets are the opposite of fixed.

Another model which moves beyond traditional financial and historic reporting has been developed by the Centre for Tomorrow's Company under the energetic leadership of Mark Goyder. *Prototype plc, an imaginary Annual Report*,[31] is a reporting model which requires companies to analyse the factors and relationships on which their success depends and then to devise appropriate forms of measurement to test their performance against them. The Centre emphasises that profit and the creation of long-term value for investors remains crucial, but goes on to say that profit can only be sustained, provided that companies respond to the changing world around them.

The best example of the GRI approach in practice, which I have had the chance to see, is The Novo Group's Environmental and Social Report 2000. The Novo Group is a Danish company which has recently split itself into two, Novozymes, an industrial enzyme company and Novo Nordisk which is a pharmaceutical company. They introduce their Report as follows: 'This Novo Group Environmental and Social Report 2000 accounts for the way values are put into practice in Novozymes and Novo Nordisk. It presents overall objectives and targets, and documents our environmental, social and economic performance.'[32]

It is very well presented and gives a rounded picture of what the Group stands for and how, to use Jack Welch's phrase, it lives its values. There are two points worthy of particular note. The first is the emphasis in the Report on constructive dialogue with all of the Group's constituencies. The Group works in areas which could bring them into conflict with frontline single-interest groups. Their response is to engage in dialogue with such groups, to develop relationships with them, and to be entirely open about the nature of their work, thereby building trust. The second is that, even from reading the Report, but far more so by meeting some of those who work for the

Group, you can sense the enthusiasm which finding ways to husband scarce resources and contributing to the local community generates. Appropriate social and environmental aims are powerful motivators.

Conclusions

My conclusions are, first, that society's expectations of the role of companies in the community are changing and that individual enterprises need to be alert to the way in which these expectations affect their ability to create value for their shareholders. Society's expectations are not necessarily based on scientific reason and economic logic, but we have to take the world as it is, not as it rationally might be. Second, single-interest groups will apply pressure over a variety of issues and cannot be ignored. Companies need to engage with those groups which can affect their ability to conduct their businesses and to do so, if possible, before issues have hit the headlines and attitudes towards them have hardened. Companies should stand their ground for what they believe to be in their and society's interests, even if this may lead at times to confrontation.

The aim of dialogue is to understand as clearly as possible the reasoning on which the positions of both sides are based. This should lead on to what practical proposals pressure groups are putting forward to resolve the issues at stake, in order to move the debate from negative onto positive grounds. At the same time, a constructive and public debate will bring out the complexities attendant on action on social or environmental issues. Resolving such issues is a matter of balance, weighing benefits against adverse consequences. In doing so, boards have to take account of all relevant interests, not simply the one which is being pressed on them. Boards also have to come to decisions leading to action, a responsibility from which the promoters of specific interests are largely spared.

It is for every board to decide for itself what social and environmental policy is appropriate for their company. These can range from a single-minded focus on financial survival to the comprehensive array of initiatives which leading companies in the energy and extractive industries are undertaking. The common thread is the need for disclosure. Boards have to make it clear where they stand on these matters. The same kind of logic applies to the manner in which companies report on their social and environmental policies. Whatever the level and extent of these policies, boards will need to know whether they are fulfilling their purpose and whether they are justifying the resources involved. Boards, therefore, require measures of their policy aims and achievement, and it is these internal management measures, which should form the basis of their reporting.

Finally, while *Misguided Virtue* makes the case against too ready an acceptance of what Henderson refers to as the doctrine of 'global salvationism', there is one aspect of corporate involvement in social and environmental initiatives which he disregards. This is the enthusiasm which a well-defined and constructive approach to these matters can generate in everyone in a company. Companies need to capture that enthusiasm. Employees at every level can see that in these areas their efforts count and they want to belong to enterprises which are both successful as businesses and contribute to their communities. In the competition for recruiting and retaining committed and talented people, an appropriate social and environmental policy has its place.

Institutional accountability

An issue which will surely feature on the governance agenda, as we look ahead, is the accountability of the investing institutions. The landmark Myners Report has put forward a package of measures aimed at encouraging investors to be the active ingredient in governance, which it is their job to be, if a market-regulated system is to function for the benefit of shareholders and society. Reference has already been made to the recommendation that UK fund managers should have a clear legal duty to intervene—by voting or otherwise—where this might reasonably be expected to raise investment values. The institutions will, in consequence, increasingly be using their voting power to influence companies over issues like board composition and board strategy. A single institution may even be in a position to determine whether a takeover bid succeeds or not. Such decisions can have considerable economic and social consequences. Ought they not to be taken in the light of the views of those whose money the institutions are investing, for that is what has given them their power and influence?

The question of how the institutions decide what is in the best interests of the spread of clients whom they serve is, therefore, becoming more crucial. Members of pension funds will be mainly concerned about the level of their pensions, but they will also be concerned about the nature of the society into which they will be retiring. In the past, it would not have been practical to canvass the opinions of fund members, given the layers of authority between members and those voting on their behalf, and the problems of communication. Now, with advances in information technology, it has become feasible for individuals, who wish to have a voice in the governance decisions of those investing their money, to do so. It is another example of the manner in which an increasingly 'wired' world enables individuals to participate in the governance process.

Once again, this raises the way in which the balance of power within the corporate system is changing. We saw that the power of the executives to control how enterprises were run was checked by a freer market in the control of assets and the beginnings of investor pressure on outside directors to require higher levels of performance in the interests of shareholders. This, in turn, increased the influence of outside directors on boards and strengthened the hand of boards in relation to executive management. As a result, boards have become more accountable to shareholders, mainly the investing institutions. Now investors are being pressed to play a more active part in improving corporate performance on behalf of their beneficiaries. But the chain of accountability cannot end with the accountability of boards to investors. The investing institutions, in their turn, have to become more accountable to those on whose behalf they are investing.

The consequences of a move in this direction could be far-reaching. It would entail a shift of power from the top to the base of the corporate system, from institutions to individuals. More significantly still, given the dominance of pension funds among UK investing institutions, the views of pension fund members could be said to represent a reasonable approximation of the views of society. The legitimacy of any form of intervention by institutional investors would be enhanced to the extent that they took the views of their beneficiaries into account. Equally, the issue of what constituted corporate social responsibility might become less contentious, if institutional investors were able to inform boards what their clients, representing society, thought their position on this issue should be. Such direct accountability would also strengthen the position of boards in standing up to pressures for action in the social or environmental fields, which seemed to reflect sectional rather than societal interests.

Further agenda issues

Risk management

The loose end which was left after the Committee of the Financial Aspects of Corporate Governance published its Code of Best Practice was the recommendation in respect of internal control. The proposal that boards should report on the effectiveness of their system of internal control was not acceptable (see page 23) and the matter was only finally laid to rest with the Report of the Turnbull Committee, *Internal Control: Guidance for Directors on the Combined Code*, which was published in September 1999.[33]

When the Combined Code came out in June 1998, the Institute of Chartered Accountants agreed to provide guidance to companies listed on the London Stock Exchange over how to implement the Code's requirements in respect of internal control. *Internal Control* is a commendably clear and succinct account of what is entailed in maintaining a sound system of internal control. It begins by emphasizing that the responsibility for a company's system of internal control rests squarely with its board of directors. It goes on to define the ground which internal controls should cover, and how boards should assess the effectiveness of their systems and report on them. A key point is that companies are continually having to adjust their plans and strategies in the light of a changing competitive environment and thus the risks they face, and the priorities to be assigned to them, are continually changing as well. The Report emphasizes that the taking of risks is what business is all about and is indeed a justification for profit, therefore its guidance is aimed at identifying and assessing risks so that they are adequately taken into account in coming to decisions. 'Since profits are, in part, the reward for successful risk-taking in business, the purpose of internal control is to help manage and control risk appropriately rather than to eliminate it.'[34]

It is also important to accept that risk is not only about threats to the business which have to be managed, it is equally about the failure to seize opportunities. Risk management and internal control are linked to the ability of companies to fulfil their business objectives and that is how they should be seen at all levels. This is why it is helpful to work risk management into existing procedures, rather than appearing to bring in yet another new initiative thus adding to bureaucracy. *Implementing Turnbull: A Boardroom Briefing* is a useful guide on how to ensure that putting an internal control system in place can add value and afford a competitive advantage.[35] *Implementing Turnbull* stresses that boards should not expect their audit committees to identify and manage risks, because this is a management responsibility. It is for boards to set internal control policies and to assure themselves that they are working as they should. It is the job of management to put those policies into effect. There are likely to be lessons to be learnt in this whole field from the Enron affair.

Risk management has moved up the board agenda for a number of reasons. A wider range of constituencies are now taking an interest in the activities of companies and there are more sources of information on which they can draw to satisfy that interest. Global competition and a rapidly changing environment have enhanced the degree of risk which companies face and the speed at which they need to respond to threats and opportunities. Organizations are subject to detailed scrutiny and to an invasive media on an international basis and on a greater scale than ever before. Reputational risk has therefore become, as has already been discussed, more significant to companies, investors, and consumers than would have been true in the past. The decision by the UK government to put Railtrack into administration in October 2001 was a reminder to investors that no country is entirely free of political risk. The media focus on corporate affairs means that the impact of poor risk management on shareholder value is likely to be severe and swift.

I leave the last word with *Implementing Turnbull*:

Effective risk management and internal control can be used to manage change, to involve all levels of people in the company in meeting its business objectives, and to improve a company's credit rating and ability to raise funds in the future, not to mention its share price over the longer term. Therefore, the proper focus on risk management and internal control can result in considerable benefits being gained by a company.[36]

Remuneration

Executive pay remains on the agenda, because it continues to excite public and political criticism. Much of the criticism is directed at settlements which some departing executives have received to speed them on their way after failing to meet expectations. The main defences against unwarranted pay-offs are mitigation and shorter contracts. Boards cannot, however, evade their legal liabilities. They accepted these liabilities, when they agreed the remuneration package which they judged necessary to attract the candidate of their choice. Criticism of the outcome should be more properly directed at the board's selection process, than at what may well have been their reluctant but enforced generosity.

There is, in addition, widespread disapprobation over the remuneration of a minority of directors, both on grounds of its quantum and the absence of clear links with results. As a consequence, the UK Trade and Industry Secretary announced, in October 2001, that she would be requiring quoted companies to report annually on directors' remuneration and to put the report as a resolution to shareholders. This would provide shareholders with the opportunity to express a view specifically on pay policy and on the totality of directors' pay. At present all they can do, if dissatisfied over remuneration, is to vote against the annual report or against the election of directors. There have, in the past, been suggestions that shareholders should be able to vote on the remuneration of individual directors, but this is impracticable. If, for example, a company's finance director leaves, it is essential to find a replacement without delay and no one worth their salt would take the job without a sufficiently attractive and firm contract. This could not be left dependent on a shareholder vote at a subsequent AGM.

The issues which need to be addressed under this agenda heading include, how should top pay be set, what should be disclosed to shareholders, to whom is executive pay a matter of concern and why should it appear to have risen to the degree that it has?

Remuneration committees

Directors' pay can only be set by boards themselves, by shareholders, or by regulation. Shareholders should have the opportunity to express their views on the matter and the proposal put forward by the Trade and Industry Secretary formalizes what the Combined Code recommends that boards should consider doing voluntarily, a recommendation that a number of boards have put into effect. The problems with attempting to regulate directors' pay are obvious and executives always have the option of declining to become directors. The role of government is to use taxation to trim what they regard as excessive rewards. It is not their role to become involved in settling the pay of individuals. Remuneration committees made up of independent outside directors remain the least unsatisfactory means of dealing with an intractable problem.

Being a member of a remuneration committee is exacting and unrewarding. In the first place, there is little firm ground on which to stand when attempting to arrive at a 'market rate'. Pay differences between industries, and between companies within industries vary and remuneration packages include incentive schemes, both short and long term, which make comparative calculations uncertain. Consultants are unlikely to win business by encouraging the committees they advise to take too stern a line and committee members have to live with their executive colleagues. Shareholder criticism for allowing key directors to be poached will be far sharper than their grumbles over generosity. Altogether a remuneration committee member's lot is not a happy one, so what can be done to improve it?

One answer, which has already been referred to, is for remuneration committees and their boards to consider the pay structure for the company as a whole, in coming to their decisions about the pay of the executive directors. There are a number of reasons why this is a logical approach. In the first place, the results which a company achieves are those of their workforce as a whole; no one should be employed who is not contributing to the outcome. What, therefore, matters in terms of equity and of employee morale is that the relationships within the overall reward structure should reflect the relative contribution of everyone involved. Second, shareholders and the media should be concerned about the pay scene in total, not simply what is earned by a few at the top. This, in turn, would suggest the form which corporate reporting on pay might take. The whole pay picture could be presented in the form of a pyramid with pay brackets as the vertical measure and numbers employed in each bracket forming the horizontal scale. This could be shown for the company as a whole, and by units within the company. Comparing the shape of the pyramid year by year would provide information which would surely be more relevant to understanding a company's pay policy and its consequences, than focusing on the complex packages of a few executive directors?

A well-designed remuneration system should present a coherent whole from the top to the bottom of a company. At each level within the structure, pay should be such as to attract and retain people of the calibre that the company needs. Equally, the structure should provide a measured progression from the lowest to the highest paid, with relationships between the various levels which are explicable and therefore justifiable. The logic in setting directors' pay in relation to the structure of pay throughout a company is that it puts it in the correct context. Executives capable of achieving outstanding results should be able to earn outstanding rewards, but they achieve those results through everyone else in their companies and so there needs to be an appropriate relationship between their earnings and those of their supporting staff. This is where the analogy between highly paid executives and, for example, highly paid entertainers breaks down. The latter earn their rewards largely through their own efforts as individuals, not as part, even if a crucial part, of a team. The danger of the pay of the few at the head of a company seeming to become detached from the pay of those in the enterprise as a whole is the effect that would have on the motivation and morale of everyone else in the company. A sense of equity in the way in which all the individuals who make up a company are treated is one of the factors which holds an enterprise together. Acceptable differentials in rewards are disregarded at a cost.

There is, however, no doubt that there has been a step change in the differential between the highest paid and those on the average level of pay in business, most notably in the US. According to *The New Global Investors*, the average CEO makes about 475 times what a full-time factory employee does.[37] The difference in pay relativities between countries was highlighted by the Daimler–Chrysler merger where, in 1997, Robert Eaton, CEO and chairman of Chrysler, earned more than the whole management board of Daimler–Benz.[38] The problems of agreeing a common corporate pay policy in cross-border mergers are clear. It is not only in business that what seemed once to be stable pay differentials have altered recently and markedly. There seems to be a growing divide between the rewards of 'stars' and the rest, whether in sport, in entertainment, in the media, in financial services and to an extent in the professions. This may be a combination of media exposure and media concentration on personalities, of instant and universal communications, and of living increasingly in one world. It certainly owes something to the relentless public focus on what people earn. Although reporting the earnings of directors was a necessary element in corporate transparency, it has played its part in fuelling the upward movement. The former benchmarks in relation to differentials are no longer there, but it remains important to look, in a company context, at the coherence of an enterprise's pay structure as a whole.

Stock options

There is another item of unfinished business in relation to remuneration which chairmen and boards need to keep on their agendas. This is the matter of stock options. There are two issues here. One is that, at some point, they are going to have to be accounted for. The other is the consequences in the longer term of the transfer of corporate ownership which they represent. The case for accounting for stock options was made most cogently by Warren Buffett in a masterly letter to the Chairman of the Securities Subcommittee of the Senate Committee on Banking: 'It seems to me that the realities of stock options can be summarised quite simply; If options aren't a form of compensation, what are they? If compensation isn't an expense, what is it? And if expenses shouldn't go into the calculation of earnings, where in the world should they go?'[39]

Accounting standards for options have been prepared and although there are inevitable differences of view over valuation methods, the argument is not about valuation. It is about the impact that accounting for options would have on corporate profits, and especially on start-up businesses in the technological field. These reservations are understandable from the point of view of the companies concerned, but they are self-serving and fly in the face of the whole movement towards disclosure and transparency. There is a further reason why refusing to recognize the cost of options is unlikely to continue. The national income figures in the US now, in the words of *The Economist*, 'take account of the true cost of stock options'.[40] The result has been to show that profits have been falling as a share of US national income since 1997, whereas the figures without taking stock options into account showed them as rising. Now that statisticians are having to take account of stock options because of their impact on the national income, the pressure will be on companies to follow.

The second point concerns the transfer of ownership which is coming about through stock options. Again this is most marked in the US, where the average company in the S&P 500 now has options outstanding equivalent to 15 per cent of its share capital, and 2 per cent of its equity is being transferred each year through options.[41] Once more, the issue is one of disclosure and of enabling shareholders to assess the potential dilution which the exercise of outstanding options would create. The fact that many options will currently be worth less than before the economic downturn alters the figures but not the argument. Options do not put the executives who receive them on a par with shareholders. Executives gain with rising stock markets and all they lose when markets fall is the chance to gain. Theirs is a one-way bet, with the possibility of other forms of remuneration taking the place of options should they become valueless.

What would resolve both the question of valuation and of dilution would be for boards as far as possible to award shares bought in the market to their employees rather than options. This would put employees and shareholders genuinely on a par, support the share price, and avoid distorting national income statistics.

Are dotcoms different?

A final item on the governance agenda relates to differences between the boards of what might be called 'New Economy' and 'Old Economy' companies. How far are these a function of a particular type of company, and how far do they raise governance issues, which the boards of new economy companies should keep in mind, and of which potential investors should be aware? I am indebted to two researchers, with whom I have been in correspondence, for information in this field. In the UK, Hewitt Roberts of Lancaster University Management School has written an MBA dissertation on *Corporate Governance in Smaller Technology Firms: Is There a Better Way?* In the US, Andargachew S. Zelleke has studied the position of internet companies which have come to the market for funds in that country and he co-authored an article in the *Harvard Business Review* with Jay W. Lorsch and Katharina Pick, entitled 'Unbalanced Boards'.[42] The significant finding from their studies is the similarities between the boards of these companies in both countries. This suggests that the technical nature of new economy businesses, and the way they are financed, have a strong influence on the make-up of their boards. This in turn results in forms of governance which may prove to be less than appropriate, once these companies have gone beyond the start-up stage and wish to attract and hold investors.

Typically, these companies have small boards, they combine the roles of chairman and CEO, directors are chosen primarily for their technical skills, their boards are less diverse than those of companies in general, with a minority of outside directors and few women directors. As a consequence, boards of this kind concentrate mainly on managing their businesses rather than on governing them. All of this derives understandably from the background and commitment of their founders and from the way in which their starting up has been financed. The review on which the findings of 'Unbalanced Boards' is based was of fifty of the largest internet Initial Public Offerings in the US in 1999. It found that the typical board was made up of two members of management, two venture capitalists, one other significant shareholder, and two independent outside directors. This led to two of the article's conclusions. First, the need for independent outside directors to make up half the board and second for the potential conflict of interest between venture capitalists and investors in general to be made explicit. Venture capitalists can be expected to be looking to maximize profits in the short term in order to sell out and make a capital gain, while other investors are investing for continuing profitable growth. A board which lacks a strong independent element is not well placed to hold the balance between these two objectives.

Hewitt Roberts' research reaches the same conclusion about the need for independent outside directors, especially in the context of being able to provide advice based on sound business experience. Another feature of new economy businesses is that their founders and the executives who are on their boards are usually young and, until recently, had not been through the inevitable downs as well as ups of the economy. In *De Senectute*, from which the quotation on the opening page was taken, Cicero explains that reflection, leadership, and judgement are attributes of age and play an important part in the achievement of aims.[43] Experience and wider business knowledge, perhaps especially in the field of finance, are aspects of the balance which is needed on the boards of new economy enterprises. Hewitt Roberts rightly points out that these kinds of boards have to be ready to adapt to the changing circumstances of their businesses. They need to evolve from management boards to governing boards, if investors are to have confidence that their interests are going to be properly looked after. To split the top posts and to have an independent outside director in the chair would assist technology companies to make that transition.

In sum, the boards of technologically based, new economy companies are different and this may be no disadvantage in the early stages of their growth. As they develop, however, they should consider strengthening the independent, outside element on their boards and give thought to the merits of balancing technical expertise and drive with age and experience.

Convergence?

The broadest issue on the governance agenda is how far the ways in which companies are directed and controlled in different countries are likely to converge and what forces will be driving any such convergence. Both political and market forces have a part to play in determining the direction which corporate governance will take both nationally and internationally. For UK companies, the political force for change in the country's governance regime has been expressed in the proposals for the reform of company law, which have already been discussed. Political forces could, however, have their impact on British companies through the UK's membership of the European Union.

The European dimension

The European Commission has published proposals for a European Company Statute in the form of a draft Regulation, which deals with company law and taxation, and a draft Directive covering employee participation. The object of the Statute is to enable companies to be set up which can operate across the Union, governed by European rather than national regulations. The formation of European companies under this Statute is open to businesses which wish to take advantage of its provisions, although it has not as yet made much progress. Interestingly, the European Court of Justice has recently ruled in the *Centros* judgment that a British incorporated company, which carried out all its activities in Denmark, cannot be compelled to register there, even though it admits that it registered in Britain to avoid Danish minimum capital requirements. This implies that companies can operate throughout the European Union without creating separate subsidiaries in each country and can choose where they incorporate.[44]

Even though companies already doing business within Europe may not be intending to set up companies under the European Company Statute, it could be a useful pointer to the future. Its proposals are complex, because they include a number of options to cover the different board models that have evolved in the countries within the Union. The key proposals in the Statute relate to board structure and to employee involvement.

Board structure

On board structure, the Statute offers a choice between a two-tier or single-tier board. Under the two-tier option, there is a supervisory board which appoints and monitors the management board. At least one-third and not more than one-half of the members of the supervisory board have to be appointed by the employees. The supervisory board must receive quarterly reports on the progress of the business and can call for additional information on company matters at any time (this represents a strengthening of the existing rights of a supervisory board).

The single-tier option consists of an administrative board, on which non-executive members must be in the majority. All members of the administrative board are now to have the same rights and obligations—a concession to Britain—but the Statute still lays down that the main function of the non-executive members is to supervise the executive members. Its form is, therefore, that of a unitary board, but the executive and non-executive directors do not have precisely the same functions. Employees may be represented on the administrative board along the lines of their representation on the supervisory board in the two-tier option; they may also be represented through separate bodies by collective agreement. The Statute prescribes minimum requirements for informing and consulting employees.

There are likely to be tax incentives to encourage businesses to form European companies and, in time, their structure could become mandatory rather than optional. The thinking behind the European Company Statute is, therefore, of practical relevance to companies within the Union. It also indicates the direction which the drive to reform and to harmonize the structure of European enterprises is likely to take.

Employee involvement

The emphasis which the European Company Statute puts on employee involvement at board level raises an issue for the future, which is rarely debated. This is that employee representation on boards is feasible for a national company, but impractical for an international enterprise.

The descriptions of co-determination in Germany, for example, refer to half the members of the supervisory boards of companies, employing more than two thousand people, being representatives of the employees. A more accurate statement would be that half the seats on the upper boards of these companies are filled by representatives of the German employees. So long as the main centres of employment of these companies were in their home territory, this system met the aim of ensuring that the views of employees were taken into account at the highest level of governance, and the distinction between nationals and others was unimportant. Now that so many of these companies have operations outside Germany, confining employee representation on the supervisory board to Germans looks increasingly anomalous. Volkswagen, for example, has around 85 per cent of its assets, 61 per cent of its sales, and 44 per cent of its employees outside Germany, but all the employees on its supervisory board are drawn from its domestic operations.

The historical and practical reasons for this are obvious enough, but it raises two governance problems. One is the possibility of conflicts of interest. The employee members of the supervisory board of a German company considering transferring production overseas are in a difficult position. They are there to represent the interests of those who elected them, not the interests of all employees, including those abroad who might benefit from the transfer. The second problem is constitutional. The two halves of the supervisory board of a German company which operates internationally represent different constituencies. The employee members represent a domestic interest, while the other members have to have regard to the company's interests worldwide.

The question of how employees should be involved in the enterprises in which they work is of concern to chairmen and boards, inside and outside the European Union. The parochial nature of the German co-determination model looks increasingly out of place in a world where companies operate and compete globally. The logical way forward in Europe is to pay more attention to methods of involving employees, other than through board representation. The aim of involvement is to give employees a genuine say in the decisions which touch them most directly, and to which they can contribute most effectively, before those decisions are taken. The majority of such decisions never reach the board. This suggests that involvement is more relevant at the workplace than at the board and is better built from the bottom up than from the top down.

Code convergence

Given the spread of governance codes across the European Union, it is always possible that the European Commission will attempt to achieve a greater degree of coordination between them, for the sake of bureaucratic tidiness. A Centre for European Studies Report has recommended the drawing up of a set of guidelines in order to promote convergence, on the following basis:

Considering the specificity of national corporate governance systems and the sensitivity to centralising legislation, the Working Party proposes a set of Guidelines for the operation and control of a corporation in the European Union. These Guidelines should function as a minimum framework for corporate governance standards in the EU. It is suggested that all listed corporations should comply with these Guidelines; other companies, especially those in which there is a high degree of public interest, should attempt to meet the requirements to the extent possible.[45]

The Centre's proposal has not been implemented and I believe it to be wrongly directed, as well as otiose. National codes have had an important part to play in raising governance standards. They can take account of the considerable differences between countries within the EU in terms of patterns of ownership, corporate structures, and legal and regulatory frameworks. The risk of attempting to amalgamate them into a European Code would be that they would lose their cutting edge in the interests of uniformity and, as a result, would add nothing of value. The logical approach, when looking beyond national codes, is the one taken by the OECD, when it published its *Principles of Corporate Governance* in 1999.[46] The OECD publication sets out five basic principles of corporate governance which are internationally valid and which can be drawn on by member countries in setting their own governance frameworks.

Convergence on governance principles makes sense, because it goes to the heart of the matter. There is no virtue in trying to harmonize governance structures, because the structural design of boards is not ultimately decisive. Structure is important; its precise form is less so. The effectiveness of governance systems depends primarily on the clarity with which responsibilities are assigned within them and the quality of the people who undertake those responsibilities. As Demb and Neubauer's researches have shown, the ways in which boards in practice are involved in matters of governance vary considerably, even within the same national setting.[47] What matters is that the principles of sound governance should be observed, within whatever structure boards and their shareholders choose to adopt.

Market-led convergence

The fundamental reason why there is no call for aiming to achieve conformity between the governance systems of different countries by means of supranational codes is that the market is already bringing about a greater degree of conformity, precisely where it is needed. There are two forces driving governance standards internationally towards convergence, both of which were mentioned earlier. First, there are the institutional investors. In the UK, the dominance of institutional investment, and especially of investment by pension funds, was referred to on page 9. While pension funds of this kind, which are significant investors, are found only in a limited number of countries as yet, there is a growing need to provide for ageing populations throughout most of the world. The rise in the number of pensioners will put limits on the ability of states to provide adequate pensions and thus will encourage individuals to provide increasingly for their own retirement. In any case, although institutional investment is at present centred in a few countries, it is those countries which are the main providers of international capital. They are having to invest outside their domestic markets, in the search for higher returns and in order to spread their risks. In doing so, they require the countries and the companies in which they invest to conform to accepted corporate governance standards. The standards they are looking for are based on the OECD Principles of Corporate Governance, which cover shareholders' rights, the equitable treatment of shareholders, the role of stakeholders in corporate governance, disclosure and transparency, and the responsibilities of boards. Companies which wish to attract investment have to meet the standards which the international investing institutions demand.

The capital markets of the world are the second force for convergence. Expanding companies, wherever they are situated, are likely to need to tap international capital markets, either because they have outgrown their domestic sources of capital, or in order to raise their funds on better terms. They will only be able to access international capital on favourable terms, provided that they meet the disciplines of the market in respect of the accuracy and transparency of their financial reporting and the adequacy of their systems of financial control.

Thus institutional investors and capital markets are bringing about a degree of governance convergence worldwide. It is, however, a convergence of standards not of structures. There is no call for companies all to adopt the same governance forms, provided that they achieve the same governance aims. Interestingly, market forces have played their part in bridging what earlier seemed to be a fundamental divide over the nature and purpose of companies, a divide which had corporate governance consequences.

Company purpose

The difference of view over the place of companies in society is brilliantly and clearly expressed in a book written by Michel Albert of the Banque de France, entitled in its English translation, *Capitalism vs. Capitalism*.[48] Over-simplifying the debate, the divide is between the Anglo-American concept of capitalism and what might be termed the Rhenish or Continental European model. In America and Britain, companies are seen as enterprises based on the capital invested in them by their shareholders. The key relationship in a capitalistic enterprise of this kind is between owners and managers, hence the emphasis in Britain on the rights and responsibilities of shareholders.

In countries that follow the Rhenish model, like France, Germany, and the Netherlands, the accent is more on companies being basically partnerships between capital and labour. Companies are seen as coalitions of interests and as serving a wider social and economic purpose than providing a return to shareholders. Emphasis is therefore placed on the relationships with employees, on the place of companies in the community and on their contribution to the cohesion of society. This is in contrast to the rights of shareholders, especially minority shareholders, which have traditionally received scant consideration.

Now, within Europe at least, economic and social pressures have narrowed the differences between these two concepts of company purpose. The strength of international competition has forced Continental European companies to focus more sharply on their financial objectives and rates of return on capital. In the same way, their need for funds has led them to give greater consideration to providing value to their shareholders. Shareholder groups have sprung up in Continental countries, where previously investors had no collective voice, and they are beginning to exert an influence on corporate policies. Companies have even been forced to back down on deals which overrode the rights of minorities. The importance of the role of companies in society continues to be recognized, but it is tempered by giving greater recognition to the place of shareholders in the corporate framework.

In the same kind of way, what appeared in the UK to be an exclusive focus on returns to shareholders has broadened to take account of the corporate responsibilities to society which were discussed earlier. This is as true of investors as it is of companies. It is summed up in the extract from Hermes' *Statement of General Principles*, already quoted: 'A company run in the long-term interests of its shareholders will need to manage effectively relationships with its employees, suppliers, and customers and with regard to the common weal.'[49]

The need to run companies in the long-term interests of their shareholders, while having regard to the common weal, represents a notable degree of convergence between what, at the time of Michel Albert's book, were two opposing theories of capitalism. Further evidence of common ground is the acceptance that boards are accountable to shareholders, while recognizing their responsibilities to their other constituencies. The relevant passage in the OECD's Principles of Corporate Governance refers to the corporate governance framework recognizing 'the rights of stakeholders as established by law'. This wording aims to meet the views of both camps in relation to the duties of boards beyond their obligations to shareholders.

The next, and necessary, step in international convergence is to move to a single and universally accepted set of accounting standards. Markets are bringing about greater consistency in financial reporting, but two primary sets of accounting standards remain—the US Generally Accepted Accounting Principles and those of the International Accounting Standards Committee. The EU is moving towards convergence with the proposal that International

Accounting Standards should be compulsory for all listed companies in Europe by 2005. An agreed set of international accounting standards would improve financial transparency and lead globally to a more efficient allocation of funds. Once again, the Enron affair emphasizes the need, not simply for agreement on common standards, but agreement on highest common standards.

Daimler–Chrysler

A practical example of convergence between the two contrasting approaches to corporate governance and purpose, which have just been described, came with the announcement in May 1998 of the merger between Daimler–Benz AG and Chrysler Corporation. A fascinating account of the way in which the boards of the two companies put the merger together appeared in the journal *Corporate Governance*.[50] Drawing on that account, it was notable that when the merger was announced it was described as a merger of growth with no lay-offs, while at the same time one which would increase shareholder value to the tune of $1.4 billion in the first year. This neatly combined German social aims with American financial ones.

From a governance perspective, the way in which a US unitary board and a German two-tier board handled the negotiations over a massive merger is instructive. Discussions between Jürgen Schrempp, as head of the Daimler–Benz management board, and Robert Eaton, CEO and chairman of Chrysler, opened in January 1998. On February 5, Eaton informed his board of the proposal. Thereafter, his board met roughly fortnightly to keep track of the negotiations, with the board approving the merger on May 6 and announcing it the next day. On the German side, Schrempp did not tell his management board what was proposed until April 7, and the head of the supervisory board nine days later. The supervisory board itself was not officially informed until May 6, the day before the merger was announced. The contrast between the working of the two board systems could not be clearer. The US board with only two executives on it was closely involved from the outset, whereas it was Schrempp with one executive colleague who negotiated for Daimler–Benz, bringing the rest of the management board in a month before the announcement. The Daimler–Benz supervisory board effectively had no role, (although the head of the works council was put in the picture on May 5), since it could do nothing but approve a proposal which had already been taken so far.

Another board issue, given that Daimler–Chrysler was incorporated in Germany, was the make-up of the new supervisory board. I wrote earlier that the representation only of German employees on supervisory boards was anomalous for international companies. Daimler–Chrysler are the exception, since the German metal workers union, IG Metall, gave up one of its seats to allow a representative of the United Auto Workers Union of America to join the supervisory board. The way in which that compromise works in practice will be closely followed by the trade union movement and by all those with an interest in governance structures. The merger raises questions about the limitations of board structures whose membership is laid down by law, and about the effectiveness of the supervision which can be exercised under the two-tier system in cross-border mergers. Nevertheless, mergers between companies with different board structures and across national boundaries will, without doubt, further the convergence process.

Notes

1. Drucker, Peter. 'The futures that have already happened', *The Economist*, 21 October, 1989.
2. Department of Trade and Industry: Company Law Review Steering Group, (2001) *Modern Company Law: Final Report*, Vol. 1, 11.
3. Ibid.
4. Ibid., 345.
5. Ibid.
6. Ibid., 43.
7. Ibid., 48.
8. Ibid., 49.
9. Ibid., 58.
10. Myners, Paul, (2001). *Institutional Investment in the UK: a review*, HM Treasury, March.
11. Department of Trade and Industry (2001). Company Law Review Steering Group, *Modern Company Law: Final Report*, Vol. 1, 62.
12. OECD (1998). *Corporate Governance*, Paris, (ISBN 92-64-16056-6), 18.
13. TIAA-CREF (1997). *Policy Statement on Corporate Governance*, October, 1.
14. Hermes Investment Management (1998). *Statement on Corporate Governance and Voting Policy*, July.
15. Ibid., 1.
16. Martin, Rosemary (2001). Quoted in *Governance*, May, 10.
17. Kaback, Hoffer (1998). 'Two Modest Proposals', *Directors & Boards*, Winter, 10.
18. Myners, Paul (2001). *Institutional Investment in the UK: a review*, HM Treasury, March, 14.
19. Ibid., 90.
20. Rainer, Jenny (2001). *Risky Business*, Institute of Business Ethics, June, 9.
21. Wilson, Ian (2001). *The New Rules of Corporate Conduct*, Westport CT: Quorum Books, 83.

22. European Commission (2001). *Promoting a European Framework for Corporate Social Responsibility*, July, 20.
23. Rainer, Jenny (2001). *Risky Business*, Institute of Business Ethics, June, 13.
24. *Governance* (2001). December, 5.
25. *Occupational Pension Schemes (Investment) Regulations*, 1996, Regulation 11A.
26. Association of British Insurers (2001). *Disclosure Guidelines on Socially-responsible Investment*.
27. Henderson, David, (2001). *Misguided Virtue*, London: Institute of Economic Affairs, 15.
28. Ibid., 22.
29. Wilson, Ian (2001). *The New Rules of Corporate Conduct*, Westport CT: Quorum Books, 205.
30. Monks, Robert A. G. (2001). *The New Global Investors*, Oxford: Capstone, 153–6.
31. Benjamin, Alan, *Prototype Plc, an imaginary Annual Report*, Centre for Tomorrow's Company.
32. Novo A/S (2001). *Novo Values in a Global Context*, Denmark.
33. Institute of Chartered Accountants (1999). *Internal Control: Guidance for Directors on the Combined Code*, September.
34. Ibid., 5.
35. Institute of Chartered Accountants (1999). *Implementing Turnbull*, Centre for Business Performance, September.
36. Ibid., 4.
37. Monks, Robert A. G. (2001). *The New Global Investors*, Oxford: Capstone, 70.
38. *Corporate Governance* (2000). Blackwell, October, 387.
39. Monks, Robert A. G. (2001). *The New Global Investors*, Oxford: Capstone, 72.
40. *The Economist*, 25 August 2001, 25.
41. Knight, James A. (2001). 'Is Intellectual Capital Rewriting the Rules?', *Journal of Cost Management*.
42. Lorsch, Zelleke and Pick (2001). 'Unbalanced Boards', *Harvard Business Review*, February.
43. I am indebted to Stuart Lyons, author of the *Fleeting Years*, a verse translation of the Odes of Horace, for identifying and translating for me this classic passage from Cicero.
44. Department of Trade and Industry (2001). Company Law Review Steering Group, *Modern Company Law: Final Report*, Vol. 1, 341.
45. Centre for European Policy Studies (1995). *Corporate Governance in Europe*, June, ii.
46. OECD (1999). *OECD Principles of Corporate Governance*, Paris, (ISBN 92-64-17126-6).
47. Demb, Ada and Neubauer, F.-Friedrich (1992). *The Corporate Board*, Oxford: Oxford University Press.
48. Albert, Michel (1993). *Capitalism vs. Capitalism*, New York: Four Walls Eight Windows.
49. Hermes Investment Management (1998). *Statement on Corporate Governance and Voting Policy*, July, 1.
50. Neubauer, Stegler and Rädler (2000). 'The Daimler/Chrysler Merger', *Corporate Governance*, October.

13

Summing-up

In this final chapter, I would like to draw the two threads of the book together, beginning with corporate governance. What remains astonishing is the rapidity with which corporate governance has moved from an arcane technical term to figuring on the agenda of the G8 Summit. What has been its impact and what has driven it to prominence? The development of the concepts of corporate governance has mainly had its impact on boards of directors and shareholders, with a knock-on effect on the supporting professions of accountancy and law. The book's focus is on boards and shareholders and on the ways in which corporate governance doctrines have changed their world and will continue to do so.

What has driven the changes that have taken place? Key is the concentration of share ownership, from individuals to institutions; it is this which has provided the engine for change. With it goes a change in investor attitudes, leading to a more interventionist approach. Other drivers have been the need to attract international investment and the need by companies to tap world capital markets. The latter two drivers are bringing about a degree of convergence of corporate governance standards internationally. Then there has been a move worldwide towards privatization, shifting assets, and the control of those assets from the state sector to the market economy. Finally, there are the changing expectations which society has of companies and their purpose, and of investors. This is a force the potency of which must not be underestimated.

All these forces have their impact against the background of a world being revolutionized by globalization and advances in communications technology, which act as accelerators of change. To a significant extent, the changes which have taken place, and will continue to do so, reflect shifts in the balance of power between the key players. Codes of governance practice are, in the main, expressions of these forces rather than causes of them. Nevertheless, in a period of less than ten years, the corporate scene has been transformed, which is why it would be helpful if the pace of change were now to steady, in order to allow time for the advances which have undoubtedly been made to be consolidated.

In the process, boards around the world have changed to meet pressures from investors and from competition. They have on average become smaller and now include a higher proportion of outside directors, more of whom are independent. These outside directors are, in turn, being selected more purposefully for the value which they can add to the board team. Board committees are proving their worth and they are strengthening the position of the outside directors in the governance structure into the bargain. Boards, in general, have taken greater control over their enterprises, and risk management has become an accepted board function, although there is still unfinished business in relation to accounting and auditing standards. In sum, the role of directors is seen as being both more responsible and more demanding than it once was. Boards needed to change to the degree that they did, in order that their businesses could compete effectively in the global marketplace.

The shareholding picture has changed in parallel with changes in the boardroom. Institutional share ownership has grown rapidly and, at the same time, has become more international in its spread. In 1997, the assets of institutional investors in the US, UK, Germany, France, and Japan totalled $23,000 billion. Not only had their funds under management grown, but they had become concentrated in fewer hands. Two-thirds of the $400 billion of international equities held by US institutions are managed by twenty-five pension funds. It is precisely those funds which take corporate governance seriously, because they see it as an aid to performance. With power comes responsibility. There are a range of reasons why society, in a broad sense, now expects the investing institutions to play a greater role than they have done in the past, socially as well as economically.

One is a consequence of the decline of the state sector worldwide and the corresponding growth of the market sector. The state as a shareholder was seen as able and willing to be a guardian of social and community interests. The expectations which society had of state enterprises have, to an extent, been transferred to their private sector successors. Companies are perceived as a powerful force in society and because global corporations do not fall under any single national jurisdiction, investors are cast as a countervailing force balancing their power. Citizens look to today's major investors to take account of the interests of society, on behalf of those whose funds they are investing, in the way the state sector might have been thought to do in the past.

The stakeholder debate reflected the view that companies should accept that their responsibilities extended beyond creating wealth for their shareholders and, equally, that shareholders had a part to play in ensuring that they did. Again, the manner in which the concept of the social role of companies has developed has been remarkably rapid. Individual shareholders are raising social and environmental issues at AGMs and are supported in this by some of the investing institutions. Shareholders are beginning to show their teeth. In December 2001, a UK company had to withdraw its share option scheme proposals, because over 50 per cent of the proxy votes opposed them.[1]

In July 2001, trustees of UK occupational pension schemes were required to disclose their policies on socially responsible investment. The majority of funds, which responded to a survey on the subject, had already adopted socially responsible investment principles and wanted their fund managers to take them into account. This was no doubt in line with the views of their members. The more general issues of the accountability of investors to those on whose behalf they are investing, and their willingness to intervene more actively with companies, will be future items on the governance agenda.

In summary, patterns of corporate governance and of corporate investing have changed fundamentally over the last ten years. The speed and degree to which corporate governance principles have been accepted by companies and by international institutions might lead to the conclusion that the value of good governance was self-evident. That could be to take too much for granted and would assume that reformation could never be followed by counter-reformation. Boards and their chairmen still have to assess how far corporate governance matters in terms of board effectiveness and performance.

Governance and performance

Ever since corporate governance became a live issue, it has spawned a whole new field for research. Much of this research has been directed at the relationship between governance and performance. Clearly, the factors governing the results of a company over time are complex, and early attempts to correlate board structures—balance between executive and outside directors, whether the top posts were split, and so on—and performance were of little operational value. In the first place, they tended to cover too short a period, when what counts is consistently good performance. Second, the researchers concentrated on the composition of boards, rather than on the quality of the members of those boards, which is the point at issue. Of course structure is important and the corporate casualty rate is sure to be higher where governance structures are inadequate or faulty. Given that none of the headline UK company failures over the last few years complied with best corporate governance practice, there is a sound argument for good governance offering a degree of protection against failure and fraud. That, however, would be insufficient justification for chairmen and boards to give matters of governance the attention they demand and deserve.

The most important factors in the ability of companies to deliver consistently good results are the calibre of board members and how well they work together as a team, which in turn reflects the competence of their chairmen. That is why the most convincing research study of the link between governance and performance is the one published by Ira Millstein and Paul MacAvoy. They classified boards by what they did, rather than by how they were structured. Their conclusion was 'Although the results do not prove causation, corporations with active and independent boards appear to have performed much better in the 1990's than those with passive non-independent boards'.[2]

It is not possible to prove in any mathematical sense that good governance results in good performance. It could be that, because boards are competent and well-chaired, they are in a position to follow sound governance practices. The same argument applies to the observed link between companies which score high both on social responsibility and on performance. This could be because boards, which consistently deliver good results to shareholders, have the capacity to take account of the interests of the community as well. However, as the authors of the study conclude,

Even without proof of causation, the substantial and significant relationship between activist board governance and corporate economic performance cannot be dismissed. It might be inferred that managers willing to assume the risks associated with a professional board are better able to generate higher returns to shareholders. On the other hand, why do so? It seems to us less than likely that good corporate governance is a luxury of firms that are performing extraordinarily well.[3]

In addition, the adoption of sound corporate governance practices has been strongly advocated by such international institutions as the World Bank, the OECD, and the governments of Commonwealth countries. They have given corporate governance a high priority, because they are convinced that it has a key part to play in promoting economic growth, and in improving both the international allocation of resources and the uses to which those resources are put.

To return, however, to the company level, the most persuasive argument for believing that there is a positive link between corporate governance and corporate results is that this is the conclusion of the market. McKinsey & Company conducted a survey to establish the value which investors put on corporate governance in a variety of countries.[4] The results were published in June 2000 and two-thirds of institutional investors responded that they would pay more for a well-governed company. The premium, which they said they were prepared to pay, varied from 18 per cent in the UK to 27 per cent in Indonesia. While the answers to a survey are no more than that, they provide some measure of how much could be added to the value of a company through a reputation for good governance. As McKinsey pointed out, to achieve the same improvement in share price through financial performance alone would demand not only an equivalent increase in earnings, but one that was maintained in perpetuity. They contrasted the effort required to make operational gains of that magnitude with what might prove to be relatively modest changes in board composition and purpose, in order for investors to regard a company as well-governed. A similar recognition of the value of good governance was recorded in a recent UK survey. It found that close to two-thirds of the analysts and fund managers taking part said that they considered governance standards important when making investment decisions.

Compliance with codes of corporate governance depended on both boards and investors accepting that compliance would lead to improved performance. That link is now established and belief in the economic value of high standards of corporate governance is no longer primarily a matter of faith. It is, however, the combination of the soundness of a governance structure, and the integrity and competence of those responsible for it, which counts. When an established company is brought down through the actions of an individual, the immediate reaction is to label it a failure of governance. The control system was by definition inadequate and, therefore, the knee-jerk response is to tighten the control screw. Of course a soundly based and effectively maintained control system is essential in any organization. There is a limit, however, to what controls can sensibly achieve and no system can provide more than reasonable protection against fraud and incompetence. The safeguards against this kind of disaster may lie as much in the field of the selection, training, and support of those whom companies place in positions of trust, as in controls. From the company side, trust cannot be bought, it has to be earned. It is earned through the way in which companies are seen to value those who make them up. This takes us back to the importance of a company's character and values, and to Jack Welch's advice, referred to earlier, on those in whom companies should put their trust. 'Those who live the values, but don't make the numbers are given chances to improve. Those who make the numbers and don't live the values are the worst . . . Unless you get these people out you get your values wrong.'

The best assurance of consistent performance is that companies should have both good governance and strong values, with their system of rewards and promotion based firmly on adherence to those values. Lynn McGregor begins her book, *The Human Face of Governance*,[5] with a quotation from the Hampel Committee's report. I will repeat it to end this part of the chapter, because it puts the contribution of governance to performance into context. 'Business prosperity cannot be commanded. People, teamwork, leadership, enterprise, experience, and skills are what really produce prosperity. There is no single formula to weld these together, and it is dangerous to encourage the belief that rules and regulations about structure will deliver success.'[6]

I would simply add the word 'alone', before the last two words of the final sentence.

Reflections on chairmanship

Turning now to chairmanship, there is no call to summarize the practical points about the chairman's role, which have been covered in preceding chapters. I hope that they will help to promote discussion about the responsibilities of chairmen and the ways in which these responsibilities can best be carried out. Given the variety of chairmen and of companies, chairmen have to work out their own individual roles for themselves in conjunction with their chief executives and boards.

What I have not attempted to do is to list the qualities which might be required of chairmen. This is partly because they have to be much the same as those needed for success in any other field of human endeavour, and partly because I am not sure how useful job criteria of that kind are. It is undoubtedly helpful for chairmen to have a sense of humour, but senses of humour are matters of opinion and it is not clear what those who are told they do not possess one, should do about it. I have not, therefore, dealt in such classical virtues as integrity and judgement, which are perhaps more inherent than acquired. But there are other chairmanly attributes which are easier to define and to cultivate.

One is not to talk too much from the chair. As time goes by, it becomes more difficult to resist the temptation to reminisce, or to bring the discussion at the board on to familiar ground in order to be able to take a full part in it. The chairman's job is to listen and not to chatter. Chairmen are there to orchestrate the discussion, so that it comes to a fruitful conclusion. The test is straightforward: how much of a board's discussion time is taken up by its chairman?

A second chairmanly attribute is the ability to integrate, to pull together the different threads of a complex issue, so that it acquires coherence. The skills of management are becoming increasingly specialized and so the fields of experience of directors are tending to become narrower. As a result, their approach to issues is likely to be determined in fair measure by their particular expertise. Chairmen, however, have to see the business as a whole, in the context of its environment, and need to integrate the skills and perceptions of all those seated round the board table.

The principles to which I believe chairmen and their boards should work have come up regularly, but in different forms, throughout the book. Openness is one of them—the need to be open to ideas and open in explaining the company's actions and intentions. Openness is particularly important in dealing with people. Balance is another of them—the duty to weigh up the consequences of decisions on all those who will be affected by them, and to hold the scales between the demands of today and the needs of tomorrow.

A third principle is the well-established one that rights and responsibilities go together. Chairmen, therefore, have responsibilities towards their boards, as do boards towards their chairmen. Companies have responsibilities towards society, but so does society to companies. Boards have their obligations to their shareholders and shareholders have them to their boards. Boards and their companies have to establish where they stand in an ever-changing network of duties, owed and owing.

The chairman's place in all this does perhaps come nearest to that of the conductor of an orchestra; thus it is appropriate to close with Sir Ralph Vaughan Williams' words: 'All their art and all their skill are valueless without that corporate imagination which distinguishes the orchestra from a fortuitous collection of players.'

It is for chairmen to capture that corporate imagination.

Notes

1. *PIRC Intelligence*, December 2001/January 2002, 2.
2. Millstein, Ira and MacAvoy, Paul (1998). 'The Active Board of Directors and Improved Performance of the Large Publicly Traded Corporation', *Columbia Law Review*, June, Vol. 98/5, 1283.
3. Ibid., 1318.
4. Monks, Robert A. G. (2001). *The New Global Investors*, Oxford: Capstone, 106-7.
5. McGregor, Lynn (2000). *The Human Face of Corporate Governance*, Basingstoke: Palgrave.
6. Gee Publishing Ltd (1998). *Final Report: Committee on Corporate Governance*, January, (ISBN 1 86089 034 2), 7.

Appendix

The Character of the Company

Cadbury Schweppes earns its living in a competitive world. It needs to do so successfully to meet its obligations to all those with a stake in the enterprise and to make the Company one to which people are proud to belong.

We are in business to meet the needs of consumers internationally for products and services of good value and consistent quality. Our success in doing so is measured by the profitable growth of Cadbury Schweppes and by the advancement of its reputation.

The basis of our business is the goodwill of our customers, since we depend on literally millions of repeat purchases daily. The Company's main commercial assets are its brands and it is our responsibility to develop the markets for them. Cadbury Schweppes' brands are a guarantee to consumers of quality and value and we must invest consistently in building their reputation.

In setting out what the Company needs to become, I find no conflict between the values and characteristics we have inherited from the past and the actions we have to take to ensure a successful and independent future for Cadbury Schweppes. We cannot, however, depend on our history to carry us forward. The realities of the market-place are tough and demanding and the Company has to be able to respond rapidly to them. We need to build on the Company's undoubted strengths and to apply them in ways which are appropriate to overcoming the challenges ahead. The characteristics which I believe we must cultivate to succeed are the following:

Competitive ability

Cadbury Schweppes must be competitive in the market-place. To succeed, our products and services must maintain their identity and their edge against the competition. We compete on quality, value, and service and so we must make the most of all the assets of the business. This means innovating and taking risks, while using research and analysis to increase the success rate, not to put decisions off. We are competing in the markets of the world, so we need to combine local initiative with dedication to the long-term interests of the Company as a whole. We are competing in today's markets and in tomorrow's, so profit now must be matched with consistent and imaginative investment in the future.

Clear objectives

Effective competition demands clarity of purpose. Objectives must be attainable, but require us to stretch our abilities, not work within them. Objectives need to be built from the bottom up, but set from the top down. When unit or individual objectives have been fixed, the debate is over and the focus is on their single-minded achievement. All objectives end with individuals, who are accountable for results, and therefore, must know precisely for what they are to be held accountable. But since the success of the Company depends on the sum of these individual efforts, what counts is the way they are coordinated. Everyone in the Company should understand what their individual and team objectives are and how they fit into the wider purpose of the business.

Taking advantage of change

Change is constant—in markets, in ideas, in people, and in technology. In an uncertain and changing world, we therefore need decisive leadership and trading units which are quick on their feet. We have to look ahead to the opportunities which change presents and to use the past only as a staging-post on the way forward. We must accept the risks which attend new ventures; above all we need people with enquiring minds, restlessly searching for new and better ways of advancing the Company. Meeting the challenge of change requires us to adapt to new patterns of work, new jobs and new careers, and to seek the training which will make the best of these changes, in our own and the Company's interests. The aim is to encourage openness to new ideas and a readiness to adapt to changing needs.

Simple organization

We must concentrate on the core tasks of the business and justify every support activity and every level of authority on the value which they add to the goods and services we sell. The basic building-blocks of the organization are the business units, managed by integrated teams in direct touch with their markets. All decisions should be taken as near their point of impact as possible. This freedom of operating action carries with it the responsibility to use the strengths and resources of the Cadbury Schweppes Group where appropriate and to keep the aims of the units in line with those of the Company as a whole. The more straightforward the organization and the way in which it arrives at decisions, the speedier its response, the more readily it can be adapted, the more satisfying it is to work in and the lower the cost it imposes on those it is there to serve. Building up informal links avoids organizational arthritis.

Committed people

The Company is made up of individuals and its success turns on their collective commitment to its aims. That commitment can only be won through our ability to bring about a convergence of individual, team, and company goals. People should know what is expected of them and be given every help to meet those expectations. Our standards should be demanding, and demanding standards require appropriate rewards. Belief in the ability of people to grow means planning to promote from within, except when an outside infusion is needed. Equally, it means that where we fail with people, the situation must be faced up to openly and promptly and resolved with the least loss of individual self-respect, because the failure is shared. In the same way the responsibility for the development of people is shared; the drive must come from the individual and the training resources from the Company. Everyone in the Company should be encouraged to make the most of their abilities.

Openness

The principle of openness should apply in all our dealings inside and outside the Company. It follows that we should keep everyone in the business as well informed as possible within the legal limits of confidentiality. It also implies a readiness to listen. I believe in an open style of management and in involving people in the decisions which affect them, because it is right to do so and because it helps to bring individual and Company aims closer together. The responsibility for decisions rests on those appointed to take them, but if they are arrived at openly, the decisions are likely to be better and the commitment to them greater. Openness and trust are the basis of good working relationships on which the effectiveness of the organisation depends. They imply an acceptance of the mutual balance of rights and duties between individuals and the Company.

Responsibility

The Company recognizes its obligations to all who have a stake in its success—shareholders, employees, customers, suppliers, governments, and society—and seeks to keep its responsibilities to them in balance. We aim to act as good corporate citizens throughout the world and believe that international companies which follow that approach benefit their host countries. We believe in open competition and in doing business wherever there are suitable markets open to our trade. We seek to maintain the Company's reputation for meeting society's legitimate expectations of the business and for contributing to the life of the communities of which we are a part. We support worthwhile causes related to the Company's place in society and we encourage members of the Company to play their part in trade and public affairs.

Quality

The key characteristic we aim for in every aspect of the Company's activities is quality. Our products sell on their quality and their reputation is in the hands of each individual and unit throughout the Cadbury Schweppes business. An early Cadbury statement of aims reads:

Our policy for the future as in the past will be: first, the best possible quality—nothing is too good for the public.

We must always be searching to improve quality and to add measurable value to the goods and services we market. But quality applies to people and to relationships, as well as to our working lives. We should set high standards and expect to be judged by them. The quality we aim for in all our dealings is that of integrity; the word 'integrity' means straight dealing but it also means completeness. Both meanings are relevant in this context, because the quality standard cannot be applied in part; it must be consistently applied to everything which bears the Company's name.

Conclusion

Cadbury Schweppes' concern for the values I have described will not be judged by this statement, but by our actions. The character of the Company is collectively in our hands. We have inherited its reputation and standing and it is for us to advance them. Pride in what we do is important to every one of us in the business and encourages us to give of our best; it is the hallmark of a successful company. Let us earn that pride by the way we put the beliefs set out here into action.

Bibliography

Books

Albert, Michel (1993). *Capitalism vs. Capitalism*. New York: Four Walls Eight Windows.

Beevor, J. G. (1975). *The Effective Board, A Chairman's View*. BIM Paper, OPN 15.

Benn, Ernest (publisher) (1928). *Britain's Industrial Future*. London.

Berle and Means (1932). *The Modern Corporation and Private Property*. New York: Macmillan.

Bingham, Kit (2001). *The Professional Board*. London: Gee Publishing Ltd.

Bosch, Henry (1998). *Conversations with a New Director*. Sydney: Australian Institute of Company Directors.

—— (1999). *Conversations Between Chairmen*. Sydney: Australian Institute of Company Directors.

Bowen, William C. (1994). *Inside the Boardroom*. New York: John Wiley & Sons.

Brancato, Carolyn Kay (1997). *Institutional Investors and Corporate Governance*. Irwin.

Brandeis, Louis D. (1914). *Other People's Money and How the Bankers Use It*. London: Bedford Books, St Martin's Press.

Brittan, Samuel (1995). *Capitalism with a Human Face*. Aldershot: Edward Elgar.

Brodie, M. B. (1963). *The Committee Concept and Business*. Henley Administrative Staff College.

CACG (1999). *Principles for Corporate Governance in the Commonwealth*. New Zealand: November.

Carver, Dr John (2002). *On Board Leadership*. San Francisco: Jossey-Bass.

Charkham, Jonathan (1994). *Keeping Good Company*. Oxford: Oxford University Press.

—— and Simpson, Anne (1999). *Fair Shares*. Oxford: Oxford University Press.

CISCO (1994). *Guidance for Smaller Companies*.

Clurman, Richard M. (1993). *Who's in Charge?* New York: Chief Executive Press.

Clutterbuck, David and Waine, Peter (1994). *The Independent Board Director*. London: McGraw-Hill.

Demb, Ada and Neubauer, F.-Friedrich (1992). *The Corporate Board*. Oxford: Oxford University Press.

Department of Trade and Industry: Company Law Review Steering Group (2001). *Modern Company Law: Final Report*.

Dunne, Patrick (1997). *Running Board Meetings*. London: Kogan Page.

—— (2000). *Directors' Dilemmas*. London: Kogan Page.

Friedman, Milton (1982). *Capitalism and Freedom*. Chicago: University of Chicago Press.

Gee Publishing Ltd (1992). *Report of the Committee on the Financial Aspects of Corporate Governance*. ISBN 0 85258 915 8.

—— (1995). *Compliance with the Code of Best Practice*. ISBN 1 86089 006 7.

—— (1995). *Directors' Remuneration*. ISBN 1 86089 036 9.

—— (1998). *Final Report: Committee on Corporate Governance*. ISBN 1 86089 034 2.

—— (1998). *The Combined Code*. ISBN 1 86089 036 9.

Goold, Michael and Campbell, Andrew (1989). *Strategies and Styles*. Oxford: Basil Blackwell.

Gugler, Klaus (ed.) (2001). *Corporate Governance and Economic Performance*. Oxford: Oxford University Press.

Harper, John (2000). *Chairing the Board*. London: Kogan Page.

Harvey-Jones, John (1988). *Making It Happen*. London: Collins.

Heidrick and Struggles International (1987). *The Role of the Chairman*.

Henderson, David (2001). *Misguided Virtue*. London: Institute of Economic Affairs.

Jay, Antony (1972). *Corporation Man*. London: Jonathan Cape.

Keay, John (1993). *The Honourable Company*. London: Harper Collins.

Keegan, E. Mary et al. (2001). *The Value Reporting Revolution*. New York: Wiley.

Kendall, Nigel and Kendall, Arthur (1998). *Real-World Corporate Governance*. London: Pitman Publishing.

Koontz, Harold (1967). *The Board of Directors and Effective Management*. New York: McGraw-Hill.

Kurtzman, Joel and Rifkin, Glenn (2001). *Radical E*. New York: Wiley.

Lindon-Travers, Ken (1990). *Non-Executive Directors: Their Role, Responsibilities and Appointment*. London: Director Books.

McGregor, Lynn (2000). *The Human Face of Corporate Governance*. Basingstoke: Palgrave.

McKinsey and Co. (1971). *Effective Boardroom Management*. BIM Publications.

Mills, Geoffrey (1988). *Controlling Companies*. London: Unwin.

Monks, Robert A. G. (2001). *The New Global Investors*. Oxford: Capstone.

—— and Minow, Nell (1991). *Power and Accountability*. New York: HarperBusiness.

——, —— (1995). *Corporate Governance*. Oxford: Basil Blackwell.

Moodie, Ann Maree (2001). *The Twenty-First Century Board*. Sydney: Australian Institute of Corporate Directors.

Myners, Paul (2001). *Institutional Investment in the UK: A Review*, HM Treasury.

OECD (1998). *Corporate Governance*. Paris. ISBN 92-64-16056-6.

—— (1999). *OECD Principles of Corporate Governance*. Paris. ISBN 92-64-17126-6.

Parker, Hugh (1990). *Letters to a New Chairman*. London: Director Publications.

Parkinson, Prof. Northcote C. (1958). *Parkinson's Law*. London: John Murray.

Pastin, Mark (1986). *Hard Problems of Management*. San Francisco: Jossey Bass.

Peters' Committee (1997). *Corporate Governance in the Netherlands*.

PricewaterhouseCoopers (2000). *Corporate Governance and the Board*.

Puckey, Sir Walter (1969). *The Board Room*. London: Hutchinson.

Rappaport, Alfred (1986). *Creating Shareholder Value*. New York: The Free Press.

Schoenberg, Robert J. (1985). *Geneen*. W.W. Norton.

Sloan, Alfred P. (1965). *My Years with General Motors*. London: Sidgwick and Jackson.

Smith, Adam (1838). *The Wealth of Nations*. London: Ward Lock.

Stiles, Philip and Taylor, Bernard (2001). *Boards at Work*. Oxford: Oxford University Press.

Tricker, R. I. (1984). *Corporate Governance*. Aldershot: Gower.

Watson Jr., Thomas J. (1963). *A Business and its Beliefs*. New York: McGraw-Hill.

Wendt, Henry (1993). *Global Embrace*. New York: HarperBusiness.

Wilson, Ian (2000). *The New Rules of Corporate Conduct*. Westport, CT: Quorum Books.

World Bank Group (1999). *Corporate Governance: A Framework for Implementation*.

Booklets, articles, and speeches

Allen, William T. (1992). Chancellor Delaware Court of Chancery, *Re-defining the Role of Outside Directors*, April.

Association of British Insurers (2001). *Disclosure Guidelines on Socially-responsible Investment.*

Baladi, André (1994). 'Internationale Lobby für Institutioneller Anleger', *HandelsZeitung*, May.

Bank of England Quarterly Bulletin (1988). May.

Barker, Richard G. (1996). *Financial Reporting and Share Prices*, Price Waterhouse.

Barnette, Curtis H. (1999). 'Realistic Expectations for Audit Committees', *Directors & Boards*, Winter.

BDO Binder Hamlyn (1994). *Non-executive Directors—Watchdogs or Advisers?*

Beesley, M. E. and Evans, T. C. (1973). *The Meaning of Social Responsibility*. London Business School, December.

Benjamin, Alan, *Prototype Plc, an imaginary Annual Report*, Centre for Tomorrow's Company.

Bose, Mihir (1989). 'Pearson's formula for growth', *Director*, September.

Business Roundtable (1990). *Corporate Governance and American Competitiveness*, March.

Cabot, Louis W. (1976). 'On an effective board', *Harvard Business Review*, Sept./Oct.

CalPERS (1998). *US Corporate Governance Core Principles and Guidelines.*

Centre for European Policy Studies (1995). *Corporate Governance in Europe*, June.

Confederation of British Industry (1973). *The Responsibilities of the British Public Company.*

Davis, Evan and Kay, John (1990). 'Corporate governance, takeovers and the role of the non-executive director', *Business Strategy Review*, Autumn.

Davis, Keith (1975). 'Five propositions for social responsibility', *Business Horizons.*

Davison, Ian Hay (2001). 'Is Better Corporate Governance Working?' *P D Leake Lecture*, October.

Dayton, K. N. (1984). 'Corporate governance: the other side of the coin', *Harvard Business Review*, Jan./Feb.

Dixon, Stanley (1975/76). 'The art of chairing a meeting', *Accountants Digest*, Winter.

Drucker, Peter (1976). 'The Bored Board', *The Wharton Magazine*, Vol. 1/1.

—— 'The futures that have already happened', *The Economist*, 21 October 1989.

Egon Zehnder International (1993). *Corporate Governance: The Role of the Non-executive Director.*

—— (1999). *What a Non-executive Director Needs to Know.*

European Commission (2001). *Promoting a European Framework for Corporate Social Responsibility*, July.

Frankfurter Allgemeine Zeitung (1994). *Aufsicht und Kontrolle*, February.

Grand Metropolitan plc (1990). *Annual Report.*

Guinness plc, *Powers of Non-executive Committee*, Articles of Association.

Hermes Investment Management (1998). *Statement on Corporate Governance and Voting Policy*, July.

Hopt, Klaus J., Vandenhoek, and Rupprecht (1979). *The Functions of the Supervisory Board.*

Institute of Chartered Accountants (1997). *Audit Committees.*

—— (1997). *Audit Committees, A Framework for Assessment.*

—— (1999). *Implementing Turnbull*, Centre for Business Performance, September.

Institute of Chartered Accountants (1999). *Internal Control: Guidance for Directors on the Combined Code*, September.

—— (2001). *The Effective Audit Committee: a challenging role*, March.

Institute of Chartered Secretaries and Administrators (1998). *The Appointment and Induction of Directors*, April.

—— (1998). *Terms of Reference: Audit Committee*, October.

—— (1998). *Terms of Reference: Nomination Committee*, October.

—— (1998). *Terms of Reference: Remuneration Committee*, October.

Institutional Shareholders' Committee (1991). *The Role and Duties of Directors*, April.

—— (1991). *The Responsibilities of Institutional Shareholders in the UK*, December.

Kaback, Hoffer (1998). 'Two Modest Proposals', *Directors & Boards*, Winter.

Knight, James, A. (2001). 'Is Intellectual Capital Rewriting the Rules?', *Journal of Cost Management*.

KPMG Peat Marwick (1994). *Survey of Non-executive Directors*.

Labour Party (1994). *Winning for Britain—Labour's Strategy for Success*.

Lipton, Martin and Lorsch, Jay W. (1992). 'A Modest Proposal for Improved Corporate Governance', *Business Lawyer*, November, Vol. 48.

Lorsch, Zelleke and Pick (2001). 'Unbalanced Boards', *Harvard Business Review*, February.

Millstein, Ira (1998). *The Evolution of Corporate Governance in the United States*, World Economic Forum.

—— and MacAvoy, Paul (1998). 'The Active Board of Directors and Improved Performance of the Large Publicly Traded Corporation', *Columbia Law Review*, June, Vol. 98/5.

National Association of Corporate Directors (1994). *Performance Evaluation of Chief Executive Officers, Boards and Directors*.

Neubauer, Stegler and Rädler (2000). 'The Daimler/Chrysler Merger', *Corporate Governance*, October.

Nicholson and Cannon (1997). *The Chief Financial Officer in Top UK Companies*, Egon Zehnder International.

Novo A/S (2001). *Novo Values in a Global Context*, Denmark.

Owen, Sir Geoffrey (1995). *The Future of Britain's Boards of Directors—Two-Tiers or One?* Centre For Economic Performance.

Parker, Hugh (1990). 'The Chairman of the Board', *Directors' Manual*.

—— (1994). 'What can American Boards Learn from the British?' *Directors & Boards*, Spring.

—— (1994). 'The Chairman/CEO Separation', *Directors & Boards*, Spring.

Pensions Investment Research Consultants (1994). *Shareholder Voting Guidelines*, March.

Pickard, Jane (2001). 'Electric General', *People Management*, 22 November.

Porter, Michael E. (1987). 'From Competitive Advantage to Corporate Strategy', *Harvard Business Review*, May–June.

PricewaterhouseCoopers (1999). *Audit Committees, Good Practice for Meeting Market Expectations*, May.

PRO NED (1991). *9th Annual Review*, September.

Rainer, Jenny (2001). *Risky Business*, Institute of Business Ethics, June.

Rees-Mogg, Lord, 'The Value of an Outside Voice in the Drama of a Takeover Bid', *The Independent*, 12 September 1989.

Ringshaw, Grant, 'Interview with Mervyn Davies', *Sunday Telegraph*, 2 December 2001.

Roberts, John (2000). *On Becoming Company Chairman: building the complementary board*, Saxton Bampfylde Hever, July.

—— and Stiles, Philip (1999). 'The Relationship Between Chairmen and Chief Executives: Competitive or Complementary Roles?', *Long Range Planning*, Vol. 32/1.

Russell Reynolds Associates (2002). *Effective Boards*.

Schneider-Lenné, Dr Ellen (1992). 'The Governance of Good Business', *Stockton Lecture*.

—— (1995). 'Die Rolle der institutionellen Anleger in Aufsichtsräten', *Aufsicht und Rat*, February.

Shell International (1998). *Profits and Principles—Does there Have to be a Choice?*.

Skapinker, M., 'Free lunches and privileged information', *Financial Times 1*, June (1987).

3i plc, *The Role and Contribution of an Independent Director*, Associate Directors Resources.

TIAA-CREF (1997). *Policy Statement on Corporate Governance*, October.

Tropman, John E. (1980). 'The Effective Committee Chair, a Primer', *Directors & Boards*, Summer.

Short and Another v. Treasury Commissioners (1947). Court of Appeal.

UK Shareholders' Association (1994). *Bulletin*, Summer.

van Sinderen, A. W. (1985). 'The Board Looks at Itself', *Directors & Boards*, Winter.

Weekly Law Reports, *Byng v. London Life Association*, 28 April 1989.

Woodstock, Stephen (1990). *Corporate Governance in the Single European Market*, Royal Institute of International Affairs.

Index